Magdalene

Gordon Thomas grew up in Palestine. After graduating with honours in Scripture in England he returned to the Middle East as a foreign correspondent. Four years in Egypt, Israel and Syria afforded him a rare opportunity to study the historical background of the Bible. He has written or co-written more than thirty-five books, including *Trial* and *Trespass into Temptation*, both recently re-issued by Lion, as well as several screenplays. He lives near Dublin, Ireland.

Magdalene

The scenario is delightfully vivid... one can almost smell the cattle in the market-place, taste the simple and unappetizing food, sense the power of ignorance and bigotry. Inside all this is Mary. Thomas sees her as a strong, vivacious character, stretching herself dangerously beyond the tradition that her society allowed a woman of her time. As a historical document, I would sense it to be as accurate as humanly possible. As an entertaining story that transcends the centuries, it is simply astounding.

Manchester Evening News

Gives you an insight into the gossip, the politics and the geography of the world in which Jesus lived... he has the storyteller's way of bringing you into the story... Thomas' conclusions will be controversial to some and common sense to others.

Western Mail

Gordon Thomas brings the real Mary out of the darkness and reveals her as an important person in her own right. Magdalene needed a champ and she has found one in Gordon Thomas.

Northern Echo

One cannot but admire Gordon Thomas who has produced an amazingly detailed novel... [the] completely credible tale is cleverly woven.

Methodist Recorder

Magdalene poses some important challenges to the Christian understanding of the role of women today.

Renewal Magazine

Trial

In his search for the truth, Thomas has brought to bear a twentieth-century microscope on the events that led to Calvary – an extraordinary and compelling story.

Sydney Morning Herald

In a unique blend of fact, legend, theology and faith, Gordon Thomas offers a new controversial assessment of the most important event in our history and answers this crucial question – why did Jesus have to die?

William Massie, *Sunday Express*

A suspenseful drama... a moving soliloquy... The pace is quick and compelling. The Jesus presented is real, painstakingly real. As a result, the magnanimity of the sacrifice – in the view of anyone's faith – is overwhelming.

David Jensen, *Washington Times*

Trespass into Temptation

It is a modern *Pilgrim's Progress*... the strength of Mr Thomas' technique which powerfully analyses the motives and feelings, is that it shows the range of spiritual and physical responses which have given rise to the Catholic Church's crisis over celibacy.

Fergus Pyle, *The Irish Times*

A real-life *Thorn Birds*, which grabs you from the first page to the last. Five lives in torment trapped in a world few of us suspected even existed today... It is also a worthy successor of that classic, *The Nun's Story*.

BBC Radio Ulster, Northern Ireland

The book reads like a novel, rushing from one drama to the next, and has a fly on the wall compulsion... It is sensational in the best sense of the word – not least because the Vatican wants to hound out of office those who shared their intimate lives.

Edinburgh Evening News, Scotland

Readable, thought-provoking... exposes all and shrinks from nothing.

Washington Post

Sensitive, intellectual, spiritually moving.

Ian Wilson, author of *Jesus: The Evidence*

For

Edith
Who, long ago, walked the land of the Cross
and believed then, as now, that faith can
overcome everything.

Copyright © 1998 Gordon Thomas

The author asserts the moral right
to be identified as the author of this work

Published by
Lion Publishing plc
Sandy Lane West, Oxford, England
ISBN 0 7459 3810 8

First published in hardback 1998
Paperback edition 1999
10 9 8 7 6 5 4 3 2 1 0

A catalogue record for this book is available
from the British Library

Typeset in 12/14 Caslon 224

Printed and bound in Great Britain by
Caledonian International Book Manufacturing, Glasgow

Magdalene

GORDON THOMAS

Author of <u>Trial</u> and
<u>Trespass into Temptation</u>

A LION BOOK

Special Thanks

S.G.F. Brandon, Zwie Worblowsky, Hubert Richards
Each, in their own way, urged me to go the proverbial
extra mile when the way forward seemed obscured.

Michael Costello
To the very end he remained convinced that anything
was possible.

Sally Brinn
Her insights into another life proved invaluable.

Clive Manning
He saw the need and remained a constant source of
encouragement.

Anne O'Dwyer
A true sister of mercy; whose compassion and
understanding helped to make this book all that more
possible. I owe her more than even she realizes.

Maurice Lyon
An editor in the real sense of the word.

Brian Keogh
The epitome of the healing physician with insights far
beyond clinical matters.

Carolyn Dempsey
The safest pair of hands in my business.

Contents

Understandings

One

No accurate image exists of Mary Magdalene's face. There is no true-life painting, stone carving, wood etching, or even the crudest drawing which can be consulted to show the colour of her hair, eyes and skin. Was she tall, short, thin, or running to fat, as women in her part of the world still often do as the bloom of youth fades? Her parents, whether she had brothers or sisters and, if so how many, are also all lost forever through the trapdoor of time.

Her devotees insist she was a beauty of great passion, imbued with an undeniable presence and a sense of high drama which no other woman subsequently in biblical history has ever possessed. Certainly no other woman could replicate her role in the story of Christianity. That is undoubtedly why she remains a figure of speculation and mystery.

Despite an absence of pictorial corroboration, certain deductions can be made. Her given name, Mary, was of Hebrew origin, Miriam. She had been raised in the strict Jewish tradition of her day which, among much else, pronounced her ready for marriage after her first menstruation. Her life expectancy would have been no more than forty years, the average span for her time.

The physical appearance of her lakeshore people around the Sea of Galilee was typically one of dark eyes and an olive skin, and they spoke in a broad accent often mocked by others. Given her professed way of life and her clients – local fishermen, passing caravan merchants and vendors – there could have been an earthiness about her language, a readiness to exchange one robust epithet with another.

Legend depicts her as the richest harlot in Magdala. Assuming that to be true, it is then also safe to suggest she would have been attractive; an ugly whore has little chance of amassing a fortune – therefore Mary Magdalene would also have been relatively young, perhaps still in her teens when she found her place in history. Prostitution is a profession which ages a person like no other, and an older woman would have been too corrupted, too raddled, to have even begun to show an interest in a life outside the bordello. Only someone young enough to still appreciate that there could be one would have taken the first step to explore a new world.

There is room for further assumptions. With her wealth she could have paid clients to bring her silks from the East, jewellery from Egypt and spices from India. Her hair would have been coloured with the finest of henna and her arms and fingers covered with bracelets and rings. These were the standard trappings of a wealthy wanton in her world. With her servants and finery, it would have been a life like any other successful, bejewelled and painted whore in the land of Judaea until that night it changed irrevocably for her.

Mary Magdalene gives flesh to the words of Paul who launched Christianity into a pagan world with the unchallengeable declaration: 'If Christ has not been raised, then our preaching is useless, and your believing it is useless.'

By her very presence at the moment Jesus was risen, Mary Magdalene makes those words the centrepoint of belief for every Christian. She ensures that no amount of critical reassessment – demythologization, if you will – can diminish the core truth of Paul's words.

In her own words after her encounter with the risen Christ – 'I have seen the Lord', she clearly shows no difficulty in accepting the Messiah had to die in order to save his people.

For Mary Magdalene, Jesus' death was the ultimate reconciliation with God that he had preached about and which he foretold would end in his own self-sacrifice. She understood that, in Jesus' own death, he was reminding her of what he had said so many times: all human life is no more than an awareness of earthly limitations with its succession of anxieties and anguish: what made it bearable was the glorious truth of a better life beyond death. In her case this was manifested in Jesus choosing her to witness his resurrection.

Ultimately, it does not matter at what time on that first Easter Sunday Mary Magdalene witnessed the event. (In the

Gospel of John it is still dark; in Matthew and Luke dawn is breaking; in Mark the sun is up); whether she actually was there at the moment the stone was rolled back (Matthew), or that had already happened (Mark, Luke and John); or if she saw one angel (Matthew, Mark) or two (Luke and John); none of these issues are of importance.

Mary Magdalene *saw* what she *saw*. Her timeless words, reported by John, 'I have seen the Lord', gives the resurrection a framework which is both tangible and measurable – confirming the event was a real one, not a figment of the imagination; that it took place in an objective world, not merely in her mind. Her words are an expression of *faith*. And faith, as it has been from that first moment outside the empty tomb, has been based *always* on a personal encounter with the risen Christ.

The evidence for that faith is there in every representation of her face. It reflects the supreme initiate into Christ's mysteries; the harlot reformed through her love of Jesus, the woman who believed even before his own mother in the totality of what he had come to do. That belief is there in every depiction of her and is formally celebrated on her feast day, 22 July.

Like all great icons of faith, Mary Magdalene has been a figure to which artists have been drawn down the centuries. They have inevitably portrayed her in the likeness of women they knew; the real woman of Magdala has escaped accurate depiction.

Yet, to write about her in any meaningful form does require both imagination and an act of faith. In these closing moments of the twentieth century, it is also important to place her in perspective for her own sex. For many women she remains an undimmed beacon for modern feminism. Both within and outside religious life, Mary Magdalene represents a commitment for *change*; with that goes a desire to remove injustice and introduce reforms.

She was a woman given parity with Jesus at a time when oppressive masculinity dominated the world. Yet, to present her purely as someone who exemplifies the demands of women for equality with men is too simplistic. The biblical scholar, Marina Warner, has succinctly observed:

Men are no longer the benchmark for anything desirable, rather an index of its opposite... and equality with their sex simply entails surrender to an intolerable way of life.

More certain, Christian theology for the past two thousand years has instilled the attitude that women like Mary Magdalene represent little more than the power of male forgiveness – ignoring that such an act of forgiveness is one of the cornerstones of Christ's teaching.

Angela West in her compelling *A Faith for Feminists* evokes a powerful image:

The Messiah was handed over to the Romans and crucified for political subversion. This was ironic because he really hadn't made a very good job of political subversion. What he had done was to identify himself with the weak and powerless, and he had ended up where all such people end up – as a victim of patriarchy. For what else is patriarchy but the permanent defeat of all those who are materially identified with the powerless – the position of most women throughout history.

Emotive though the words are, they do not get to the root of what this book is all about: *who* was Mary Magdalene and *what* is her relevance today?

The status of women and their lifestyles have continued to change over the last century. It is just over a hundred years since married Englishwomen were given the right to control their own money and property; in 1918 they were finally given a vote; a year later the first woman was returned to the Westminster Parliament. Those milestones and those which followed are each in their way related to the unique role of Mary Magdalene. She represents the ultimate change in status: the wanton who became a saint.

Nevertheless, Mary Magdalene cannot be included among that stalwart band of Christian women whose perceived role in the church does not extend far beyond arranging the flowers for a feast day, polishing the altar rails and baking cakes for a church fête. They remain good, decent, God-fearing women who still hold that only a man is suitable to bless and administer the sacrament of Holy Communion; those women do not wish, at least openly, to be part of the feminist rallying call that they too are made in God's image and that there is a powerful case for God to have feminine as well as masculine characteristics beyond those of gender and biological differences. Their more militant sisters say there is a need to strike a balance between the popular image of masculine attributes – controlling, achieving, rationality, ambition and decisiveness – and the qualities popularly associated with femininity; nurturing, comforting and gentleness. Feminists demand that all these attributes should be mingled to describe a God who is both male and female.

Opposition to such a phenomenon can be based on the account in the Book of Genesis in which Eve was formed from one of Adam's ribs. To male die-hards, Eve was created for the prime purpose of procreation. They further point out that it was Eve who first succumbed to the serpent, who bit into the forbidden fruit and finally encouraged Adam to give into temptation. It was only through her actions that both were cast out of the Garden of Eden.

For male traditionalists, the Genesis message is all too clear: a woman must remain subordinate to man, otherwise she can endanger him and herself. The entire Old Testament reflects this attitude; in its books a woman is generally meant to be compliant first to her father, then to her husband. Indeed, at times, a woman's social status appears little more than that of a slave. Women are subject to harsh penalties for any breach of the special laws of purity which apply only to her sex. The Book of Leviticus specifies that during menstruation, 'if any man lies with [a woman], he shall be unclean seven days'. Childbirth must similarly be followed by a period of 'purification': seven days for a male infant, fourteen days for a baby girl, followed by a further thirty-three days when the mother was barred from the synagogue.

Into this world came Mary Magdalene. As one of Jesus' followers she was a direct challenge to the patriarchal society into which Jesus had been born, though as a prostitute she had her appointed place. The mores of that society can explain why none of his chosen twelve apostles was a woman: but Mary Magdalene became as much a disciple as any one of the apostles. Her very presence is a vivid, vibrant reminder of Jesus' own attitude towards women. To him they were persons in their own right, to be treated as equals, to find a place at his side.

It is that which makes Mary Magdalene worthy of study.

In the early Church women, following her example, did play an active role, reflecting the words of the apostle Paul: 'There is neither male nor female, for you are all one in Christ Jesus.'

That equality has steadily been eroded down the centuries. Tertullian, an early Christian theologian, condemned women as 'the devil's gateway'. St Jerome pronounced: 'woman is a temple built over a sewer'.

As a result of such bigotry, Mary Magdalene's early career as a prostitute has all too often been used as a means to exercise control over women: unless they obey the men in their life – father, brother, husband, lover – they are little better than the woman of Magdala.

That kind of rampant sexism ultimately contributed to my need to write this book.

The seeds for doing so had been planted on an autumn day in 1966. Israel, aided and abetted by Britain and France, had won a resounding victory in the Suez–Sinai war against Egypt. Having reported from the Egyptian side, I had then travelled to Israel to write a series of reports from the victor's standpoint. The assignment completed, I had stayed on for a short holiday in a country I knew well, having been to school there.

Driving towards Galilee, I was once again reminded of the psalmist's words: 'The earth is the Lord's.' Though the Promised Land is a narrow tract of stony hills and fertile valleys, a corridor between Asia and Africa, no place on earth has contributed more to human life. On that November morning it was easy for me to see in my mind's eye the dying Moses looking down on the land he had brought his people to but would himself never set foot in; to imagine the first settlements – no more than small towns really – which had later united to become a nation.

Here its people had worked gold from distant Ophir, silver and lead from Asia Minor, copper and iron from the mines of Edom, even tin from far-off Britain. Here too its inhabitants had fought and died to protect their land against the empires of antiquity: Egypt, Assyria, Babylonia, Persia, Greece and the greatest of them all, the imperial empire of Rome.

Heading north, I was struck again how the very names of these parts of Israel's central highlands – Judaea, Samaria and Galilee – conveyed so well the separate and distinctive qualities of each area. *Judaea* conjures an image of the rugged strength of its great mountains and the wilderness; *Samaria* rings of the broad and open plains; *Galilee* flows off the tongue with liquid, rhythmical ease, as pleasant a sound as the endless streams which flow into its own great inland sea.

There is something about Galilee which has drawn me back time and again, not least because in Jesus' day its people were dismissed by the religious leaders in Jerusalem. For the High Priest of the Second Temple, the very idea the Messiah could emerge out of Galilee was unthinkable. 'Is the Christ to come from there?'

The attitude that Galilee has little to offer except as Israel's prime food producer has persisted. Like many a rush to judgment, it is an unjust one. For instance, from Galilee came the system of vowel-pointing used in the consonantal Hebrew text of the Scriptures.

Each time I had previously visited the area was for a specific purpose: to learn more of the geographical background to Jesus' life, the setting for the Gospels. This was essential preparation for what eventually became my book, *Trial*, which deals with the events leading up to Jesus' passion.

On that November day in 1966 my quest was different. I had come in search of the historical Mary Magdalene.

Walking along the west shore of the lake around which Jesus had performed so many of his miraculous feats, I came to the ruinous tower standing a little apart from the Arab village of El Magdal.

Here once had stood Magdala, marked now by partly-excavated ruins and water conduits. In its heyday, Magdala had been one of the largest of ten towns around the lake at the time of Jesus.

Stepping among the ruins, I wondered if Mary Magdalene had walked this way, among these ruined gateways and broken walls. She had always fascinated me, exemplifying the greatest of all true love stories: her love for Jesus. She had helped me to understand the humanity of Jesus, and to discover more of his true divinity. Through her, I had come to know the other women of the Gospel story: Mary, Jesus' mother, Mary, Martha of Bethany, Salome and Joanna. Together, they were the women of the cross, steadfast in their faith, a lesson to us all.

In my mind's eye Mary Magdalene was, without doubt, also a woman of immense passion: wild, fiery and easily moved to temper and tears of joy.

In the sunshine of that November morning in 1966, there was both a beauty and a mysteriousness about Magdala as I tried to imagine what it had been like two millennia ago when a thriving community had lived here. Caravans had passed by on their way to and from Jerusalem and Damascus. There had been gardens, trees and bushes; crops planted in the fields; domed roofs beneath which men and women had loved; a burial place.

Now, only vague shapes of walls and doorways remained. Occasionally a stone staircase rose a few faltering steps, then stopped. Had Mary Magdalene once climbed them?

Buried beneath my feet were the bones of the long dead which could still provide answers as to how the people of Magdala had lived: not just what they ate, but perhaps how they lied and stole, even how they betrayed one to another. Beneath the ground could be the answers to how injustices were righted, wrongdoers punished. Was it my own imagination or was there a dankness in the air of a past that did not wish to be disinterred?

The tantalizing outline of buildings continued to absorb me. Were those stone stumps all that remained of columns marking the entrance to the town forum? And, over there, beyond where another piece of wall rose – had that once been part of the home of the local rabbi? Or a wealthy merchant she had numbered among her clients? Certainly the ground space between the walls suggested this had been a more imposing structure than the exposed foundations. A little further on, I reached yet another truncated staircase. Beneath was an opening, a storage place perhaps? Was this where she would have kept her precious ointment cool from the summer heat?

Picking up a handful of dust, I wondered had it once mingled with blood spilled by the Roman conquerors: they were once fond of doing that. Pontius Pilate, the Procurator, had once said a strong sword led to a quiescent people. Had that been the fate of Mary Magdalene's own parents, casually killed by some centurion, in death anonymous to the last? The dust only felt lifeless between my fingers as I allowed it to dribble back to the ground.

Dusk was scudding across the Sea of Galilee when I finally left Magdala, my questions unanswered about its most famous inhabitant. How had the penitent whore become a prominent and beloved saint? How had she become such a fixed figure in folklore? Was she no more than another example of how legend is woven into the history of a people and its time to help provide a clearer perspective?

In between reporting assignments and writing other books, seeking answers became almost an obsession. No clue was too insignificant to ignore; no place too inaccessible to be persuaded to open its doors. I spent time in the Sacred Archives of the Vatican reading how Pope Gregory the Great (590-604) created for Mary Magdalene her own feast day; how in the Middle Ages she became the ideal of Christian repentance: when the Reformation challenged the doctrine of penance imposed to show contrition, Rome responded by reminding its faithful that Mary Magdalene was the greatest of all saints who had been redeemed through penitence. In the Sacred Archives were a whole shelf of documents devoted to presenting Mary Magdalene as the perfect example of how to reconcile the constant conflicts between body and soul.

And, in between, I returned to Magdala to walk again through its ruins or simply sit on some stump of a column and ponder.

I have always found a personal affirmation in these ruins which I have not found elsewhere in the Holy Land: neither on the Mount of Olives; the commercialization of Bethlehem; by Jacob's Well; in the valley of Nazareth; in all those other places where the lives of Jesus and Mary Magdalene co-mingled.

Gradually it came to me that I must try and write her story. Just as I did with *Trial*, I would approach the task from the point of a believer. Let others cast doubt on her existence, claim that she is an amalgam of unrelated stories from an earlier Judaic tradition: that she fits the classic theme of the faithless wife; that she is a reincarnation of the wicked queen Jezebel; or she is like Rahab, another prostitute who was saved by her faith

The doubters can have their doubts. For me, Mary Magdalene is the woman who witnessed some of Jesus' most memorable revelations such as, 'Whosoever drinketh of the water that I shall give him, shall never thirst.'

That alone for me ensured that Mary Magdalene not only existed, but has continued to exercise an incomparable fascination. I suspect many people who share this fascination do so because they also simply *believe*. There is more than enough of the other kind who pour scorn. Impugning the Gospel story continues to be a growth industry. I wish no part of it. In coming to the story of Mary Magdalene I would write it as a Christian believer to believers and those seeking faith alike.

More than any other woman in the New Testament – where even the Virgin as a *person* is passed over without any real hint of her human personality – Mary Magdalene is a reminder that within the Christian faith women have been subtly denigrated for almost two thousand years.

On the one hand she exemplifies the doctrine that every person is open to God's forgiveness. On the other she serves as a powerful reminder of the male Christian views on the sins of the flesh. She remains an example not only of symbolic penitence and masculine-dominated Christianity's fear and rejection of women. That symbolism was created by the Fathers of the early Church whose descendants continue to use it to reinforce the purity of the Virgin. Their attitude does no justice to either woman, and continues to play a significant role in shaping Christianity's attitude to women in general.

The Catholic Church, by far the largest member of the Christian community, still actively promotes the idea that a working wife does not accord with its ideal of a 'proper marriage'. Successive popes have promulgated the claim that a wife's role is predominantly to rear children and attend to domestic affairs. In the closing years of the 20th century, Rome's priests encourage married women to accept what amounts to domestic drudgery in return for receiving only their keep. Calls for housewives to receive an income for their domestic work and so give them financial independence are resisted by many clerics. Instead they concentrate on the glorification of motherhood – epitomized by Catholicism's veneration of Jesus' mother. In reality such worship cloaks a life of oppression for many women. The stress that creates has led to a breakdown in marriage and a consequent increase in divorce.

Often women have no alternative but to accept reduced financial circumstances to escape from a marriage where anger and violence predominate. Despite all the talk of a 'new deal for a new millennium' for women, the reality is that within what is still a male-dominated Church, they are not accorded fully equal structures – though Jesus chose one of them to reveal himself as the 'resurrection and the life'. She, of course, was Mary Magdalene.

Mary Magdalene has been classified as fitting one of the many different types of mental disturbances: neurosis, anxiety state, hysteria, disassociation, derealization and hypomania. The word schizoid has been used to describe her behaviour. She has been called an obsessive personality, perhaps verging close to one of the manic-depressive psychoses. Almost all those 'diagnoses' have been made by men. The truth is that nothing is known of the emotional development in her early childhood, let alone specific events which shaped her inner and outer world. No records exist to give precision to her upbringing; at best she can only be placed in the general context of her time.

Given that we do not even know her vital signs – her heart and pulse beat, blood pressure – her mental state can only be said to be the product of her culture, shaped by the society in which she lived. Very likely she would have tried to use the resources of her inner world, her personality, to cope with her feelings and give them form. Her previous way of life, together with the three years she spent at the side of Jesus, suggests no less.

Despite the absence of any medical evidence, physically she would almost certainly have been in good shape. There is not a single mention in the Gospels that she was ever taken ill during the long days spent travelling with her Master. She often slept rough and food was never more than plain. Only a fit woman, both in body and spirit, would have survived the demands of the road. How she lived on a day-to-day basis is beyond conjecture.

In the New Testament she appears only twice in any significant form, at her first meeting with Jesus and her encounter with the risen Christ. Both events offer important clues to her personality. At a time when, by tradition, women were regarded as compliant and servile, she was clearly strong-willed and determined and possessed of considerable insight. But above all she had a shining, indomitable faith.

Those attributes would have been the reasons why Jesus ensured that, next to his own mother, Mary Magdalene became the most unforgettable woman of the Gospel story, forever enshrined as the first witness to the resurrection.

Such a distinction is not even claimed for Jesus' mother. Her role was to give God an earthly body, to be the bearer of his gifts to humanity, to provide him with flesh and blood with which to suffer. She was the means for him to reveal the purpose of his coming. She was there at his earthly end.

Mary Magdalene was there for his new beginning, the first of Christ's eleven recorded appearances after his resurrection that would culminate in his return to God – the ascension.

It cannot be an accident she was chosen for such prominence. In her moment of witnessing the very core of Christian belief, his resurrection, Mary Magdalene represented all those Jesus had tried to reach; the wicked and the profane, the damned and the decadent, the denying Peters and the persecuting Pauls of this world. Just as the Son of God was given to a virgin to bear, so it was to a woman who had gone wrong that his resurrection was first revealed. He had chosen her to be present on that unique occasion to provide a permanent reminder that the first sermon

Jesus had preached had been to all who sinned: 'Repent, for the Kingdom of Heaven is upon you.'

In appearing first to her in his resurrected body, Christ was once more telling her – and the world – that repentance was not only a renouncing of sin, but also a turning to God. In taking on a new body he was also reminding her of certain important truths which he had spoken before his death: 'Dwell in me as I in you. I am the vine, you are the branches... There will be one flock, one shepherd... Because I have chosen you out of the world, for that reason the world hates you.'

Who, then was this woman who, above all others was the first witness of the reality of those words?

A closer look at the resurrection account by John reveals a curious moment. He suddenly interrupts the flow of Mary Magdalene's recollections by the insertion of Peter into the story. Peter – 'the disciple Jesus loved' – became the first to enter the empty tomb and so, by implication, the first witness to the risen Christ.

The simple explanation for the interpolation is that, in the culture of the time, a woman could not be allowed as a witness for such a momentous moment. (Within the Catholic Church the tradition has remained: when Pope John Paul I was found dead in his bed in 1978 by his devoted nun housekeeper, the discovery was attributed by the Vatican to his male secretary.)

John, when he returns to Mary Magdalene's narrative, makes the point that she first broke the news of what she had seen to Peter – who at the time was manifestly not present. From then on, the role of Mary Magdalene is subtly downplayed and Peter becomes the rock on which Christianity will be built.

Yet, by all the criteria laid down by Jesus, she was someone who could understand better than any of the apostles who he was and what he represented. Her life serves as a parable of the best of Christian reality. She knew that through love comes the Spirit of Christ, that love exemplifies his very presence. From the time she became part of Jesus' life, she understood that God does not make contact in the abstract, but in flesh and blood.

Yet, in the libraries devoted to the life of Jesus, Mary Magdalene's position is strangely ambiguous – as if her very relationship with Jesus could have been misunderstood. Certainly, in his time, it was almost unheard of for an unmarried woman, let alone a reformed harlot, to be among the entourage of an itinerant rabbi.

Is this why Matthew makes no mention of her until quite late in the Gospel attributed to him? Perhaps the author – or authors – of this most conservative of New Testament accounts decided that Mary Magdalene's undoubtedly close and special friendship with Jesus could have placed them both under suspicion. Luke places Mary Magdalene early on among Jesus' followers when he begins his ministry in Galilee. Luke's Gospel, the most sensitive of the Gospel accounts is filled with the truth that the basis of all forgiveness is love.

Luke also offers important clues to Mary Magdalene's character. He reveals that 'seven demons had gone out of her'. Two possible deductions can be made from this. Mary Magdalene may well have been an epileptic as, at that time, the disease was commonly attributed to possession by evil spirits. But there is no Gospel evidence that Jesus himself cured her, or that she suffered from any illness. Luke's clear-cut claim of those demons having been exorcised could have a more intriguing explanation. A cult which revolved around the pagan worship of Ishtar, the 'Queen of Heaven', still existed among the Romans in Judaea. Pilate is said to have flirted with it during the procuratorship. Had Mary Magdalene been a cult member? Ishtar's ranks were filled with prostitutes.

The cult's initiation ceremony included a seven-stage ritual with a strong undertow of demonism. Could Mary Magdalene, realizing the wretched life she was leading, have decided, even *before* meeting Jesus, to leave the cult? It is not unthinkable that conducting an act of self-exorcism could have been her first step to wholeness.

It can surely only be deliberate that Luke places the casting-out revelation immediately before his equally powerful account of her anointing the feet of Jesus during a meal at the home of Simon the Pharisee. That the Gospel account does not specifically name her is again of no real importance; tradition testifies as to who Luke is talking about. No one else but the woman of Magdala fits the bill.

The story is Luke at his dramatic best as he compares the passion of penitence with the coldness of logic. His account stamps Mary Magdalene forever in our minds as someone for all Christians to accept as the model penitent.

Luke sets the scene with an admirable economy of words. Jesus has been invited to a meal at the home of a leading Pharisee, Simon. Strongly orthodox in belief, the Pharisees had contributed much Judaism, not least the beautiful liturgy which formed the core of the Jewish Daily Prayer Book (it still does, and was a critical influence in the formation of the Christian liturgy).

The Pharisees regarded themselves as Judaism's true religious Establishment, but neither sought or received recognition from the hated Roman occupiers. The militant Jewish reaction came from the Zealots, a guerrilla force pledged to remove the yoke of foreign rule by whatever force was at their disposal. Galilee, where Jesus had begun his ministry shortly after accepting Simon's invitation to dine, was the centre of Zealot resistance. The Zealots were not cowed by the huge difference between their military strength and that of the Romans. They believed God would come to their aid, just as he had done for Samson, Gideon and Joshua. All had fought and triumphed against seemingly hopeless odds. On the other hand, the Zealots did not believe that God would assist the Jews if they merely waited passively for deliverance. He would only help those who showed they were ready to help themselves.

Jesus, then, had chosen to launch his heavenly Kingdom against a background of growing earthly conflict, for the moment confined to Galilee, but which could spill over to Samaria and Judaea. It is not fanciful to suppose that during the meal the subject of the Jewish Resistance would have come up.

There would have also been another matter close to any Pharisee's heart: the deep-seated religious differences over the Oral Law with the other main Jewish religious group, the Sadducees. Central to Pharisee belief was the unshakeable tenet that as well as the revealed God in Scripture there existed a verbal tradition – interpretations – which both supplemented and developed the Written Word. The Sadducees believed the Word required no further interpretation or, if it did, only they could provide it. Other issues which might have been discussed over the meal could have been the future of the High Priesthood, long in the gift of the Sadducees, and the Temple which they controlled. This was an abiding subject of intense debate.

Finally, the position of Jesus himself could have come up. He was a rabbi (Master), travelling from place to place to dispense knowledge and offer advice based on Scripture. There may have been as many as forty other itinerant rabbis out in the hills of Galilee on that evening Jesus sat down at Simon the Pharisee's table.

That Jesus was Simon's guest was probably deliberate. Unlike many of the other travelling preachers, Jesus was making a name for himself. The crowds he attracted were larger. He was a spell-binding orator, making effective use of yet another Pharisee creation – the parable. Jesus was able to tie them in to the exegesis of a biblical text. Simon and his fellow Pharisees would understandably want to know all they could about Jesus. He was someone who had burst upon the scene from the humblest of backgrounds – the son of a carpenter – yet immediately had displayed an assurance and certainty in all he said that was truly breath-taking.

Simon's interest in Jesus could well have also been sparked by resentment of his claim to the right to discuss the Torah, to teach in public. Among the Pharisees, only the most learned were granted this after long and demanding years of study. Yet Jesus had not gone through any formal process of religious education. Only when it came to teaching did he follow the style of other rabbis: using imaginative illustrations, rhetorical questions and explaining abstract concepts in dramatic terms.

Like the other guests, Jesus would have reclined on a low couch, feet turned out towards the spectators standing outside the circle of diners. It was the custom for onlookers to be allowed to listen-in so that they could impart to others the received wisdom being offered over the meal.

Into this convivial setting came a women 'notorious for her

evil life'. Luke brings Mary Magdalene on stage slowly, first positioning her among the listeners standing behind Jesus who, not for the first time, has taken command of the conversation.

The scene was not hard to envisage: the night sky bright with stars, the Galilean chill kept at bay by cedarwood-burning braziers and reed torches casting their glow while servants poured and served. Only the presence of a handful of strangers – Jesus, the apostles and Mary Magdalene – gave an edge to an occasion otherwise familiar to the other guests and onlookers. Their interest would have been focused on Jesus in his tasselled rabbinical robe. He could only have been an impressive figure as he displayed the aspects of his personality that would forever identify him as human; one moment gentle and tender, the next firm and steel-sharp. A man capable of anger and scorn but often gripped by some inner sorrow. All combined to reveal his magnificent soul and showed he was all too aware of why he was there as Simon's guest.

What would Jesus have made of Mary Magdalene and she of him?

For Jesus, the presence of this 'fallen woman' was the very opening he needed to reaffirm one of the cornerstones of his ministry: forgiveness through repentance. For her there was the growing realization that, through Jesus, she could change her life.

Who can doubt the frisson of excitement Mary Magdalene felt at the profound effect his words, let alone his presence had on her. Here was the stainless purity of a holy and youthful leader – and here was she, a stained woman, notorious for her own lifestyle.

Simon and his guests, with their ostentation and sheer lovelessness, coupled to an inability to forgive all those who did not follow their ways, were the very antithesis of what Jesus had come to proclaim. And Mary Magdalene, quicker than anyone else, must have sensed she had been chosen to play her part.

No wonder then that, at some point, she moved to stand before Jesus and, as Luke reports, to 'wet his feet with her tears and wipe them with the hair of her head and kiss his feet and anoint them with ointment.'

The ointment may have been spikenard, a sweet-smelling gel which Mary Magdalene used for clients who could afford the extra money to have her massage their bodies. Simon and his other guests were shocked by her actions. They waited for Jesus to show his own revulsion and order her away. Instead, he turned to his host. The exchanges, chronicled by Luke, retain down the centuries the power of timeless theatre.

'Simon, I have something to say to you.'

'What is it, Master?'

'A certain creditor had two debtors. One owed five hundred denarii, the other forty. When neither could pay back the money, he forgave them both. Now, which one of them loved him the most?'

'The one, I suppose, to whom he forgave the most, Master.'

'You have judged right, Simon.'

Then – the sterner for its very gentleness and forbearance – Jesus delivered the moral, couching it in the rhythmic contrasts of antithetical parallelism which he often used in his teaching.

'Simon! Do you see this woman? I entered your house and you gave me no water for my feet. But yet she has wet them with her tears and wiped them dry with her hair. You gave me no kiss of welcome but she has not ceased to kiss my feet. You did not anoint my head with oil but she has anointed my feet with ointment. Therefore, I tell you, her sins which are many are forgiven. But remember also that he to whom there is but little forgiveness also loves little.'

Jesus turned to Mary Magdalene and said 'your sins are forgiven. Your faith has spared you. Go in peace.'

In that scene lies the centre of Jesus' revelation that forgiveness is the ultimate loving.

Who can doubt the stunned reaction from Simon and the others? Then their furious, silent question. 'Who is this man who forgives sins? Only God can do that.'

In the continuing silence Mary Magdalene walked away, unaware that her name would pass into the language as a synonym for penitence and pardon for sin. From then on she would be his constant companion, a witness to all Jesus said and did.

Her next major appearance places Mary Magdalene in a central role following the crucifixion.

It began with the electrifying moment when she discovered the empty tomb. She fetched Peter and John. They confirmed the sepulchre was indeed empty. Whether they were puzzled, surprised, fearful, we will never know.

We do know that when the huge boulder had been rolled in place to seal off the entrance to the sepulchre, not only was Jesus buried but so were all the hopes of his disciples. None of them at that moment believed he could have risen from the dead. The resurrection was something beyond their expectation, their comprehension. They had neither the imagination or faith to believe otherwise. In that moment they were indeed men of little faith. They left Mary Magdalene alone and weeping at the mouth of the tomb.

What happens then is recounted by John.

'She turned round and saw Jesus standing there but did not know it was him. Jesus said to her, 'Woman, why are you weeping? Whom do you seek?' Supposing him to be the gardener, she said to him, 'Sir, if you have carried him away, tell me where you have laid him and I will take him away.' Jesus said to her, 'Mary'. She said to him, 'Rabboni'. Jesus said to her, 'Do not hold me for I have not yet ascended to my Father and your Father. Go back to my brethren and say to them I am ascending to my Father and your Father, to my God and your God.'

In that moment Mary Magdalene moved from the depths of despair at the loss of her beloved Master to the height of ecstasy that Jesus lived. After hours of blinding hopelessness had come dazzling hope, after the loss, the finding. She had been among the closest to the Cross on what became known as the first Good Friday; she was the first witness to the first Easter Monday. She had always been at his feet: first anointing them in Simon's house, then for burial. She had stood at the Cross watching Jesus breathe his last after one of the centurions had pierced his side.

It was only natural outside the tomb she should want to throw herself at his feet to soothe his terrible wounds. Jesus gently stopped her: 'Do not cling to me for I have not yet ascended to the Father.'

The risen Christ was reminding the repentant sinner that he was not only the Son of Man, but the Son of God. Jesus told her: 'Go to my brothers and tell them I am now ascending to my Father and your Father, my God and your God.'

Mary Magdalene had been chosen to tell the world of the significance of the empty tomb as the ultimate victory of God's love over sin and evil.

In a voice which can only have been ringing with a certainty that has remained undimmed down the ages, she exclaimed: 'I have seen the Lord.'

But who *was* this woman who said that?

There is a sustainable argument that her presence with Jesus from the moment in Simon's house to the resurrection makes the example of Mary Magdalene a powerful encouragement for women today to have a fully active role in ministry. In choosing her as his personal messenger, Jesus was not only giving full recognition to her sex – but plainly stating the role women must have in sharing his ministry.

There remained the question of how to tell her story. There would, inevitably, have to be speculation. The Gospel accounts are sketchy, ambiguous and often contradicting one another; they read like biography and we may try to approach them as such. One story is joined to the other with key words like 'then', 'next', 'afterwards', a further encouragement to accept the text as a literal moment-by-moment description of events.

The Gospels are *not* biographies. They were written by believing Christians for believing Christians and they were written *after* the most important event they contain: the resurrection.

The early Christian Church was primarily concerned with spreading the Gospel through the story of Jesus' Passion: his death and resurrection. The recounting was meant to be simple and straightforward – an account of his ministry, a collection of his sayings and a practical guide how to live a life like his by accepting his resurrection.

But there were those who had also been part of Jesus' inner circles – the apostles James, Thomas, Andrew, Philip, Thaddeus and Bartholomew – who equally wanted their version of events set down. From them came portraits of Jesus as a boy, his schooldays, growing up in Nazareth working for his earthly father, his relationship with his mother.

Others who had been drawn into the life of Jesus once he began his ministry – notably Nicodemus, the judge who played a crucial role in the final week of Jesus' life on earth – also set down their recollections. Further accounts, among them the Epistles of Ignatius and the writings of Barnabas, followed. Collectively, this considerable body of literature became the nearest we have to a 'life' or biography of the time of Jesus.

In these writings Mary Magdalene is no longer a shadowy figure. Instead she becomes a strong, vital person and, next to Mary, Jesus' mother, the closest woman to him. It is her life in those three years when she was a constant companion to Jesus that comes into focus in this collection of writings. She was present at almost every major event in his ministry.

The early church did not have the confidence to give credit to these other writings. They were discarded and labelled as 'Apocrypha', hidden or secret things. They are sometimes called the Lost Books of the New Testament. In all, thirty-one accounts, beginning with the Gospel of the Birth of Mary, form the collection. It contains a wealth of material which provides a much clearer picture of Jesus' life on earth and his relationships with those who were close to him. What comes through these books is a very real sense of the dissension, personal jealousies, rivalries, intolerance, persecution and bigotry in which Jesus conducted his ministry.

The Apocrypha also reinforce the authority upon which the Canonical Gospels rests. A former Archbishop of Canterbury, Thomas Wake, who translated the books into English, said they represented 'a full and perfect collection of all the genuine writings that remain to us... and I hope that such writings would find a more general and unprejudiced acceptance.' The Apocrypha are part of the Christian heritage. There is warmth, intimacy and humanity in their telling – a description that could very well fit the life of Jesus himself.

I was directed to this Baedeker of information by arguably two of the great Scripturologists of this century, the late S.G. Brandon, Professor of Comparative Religion at the University of Manchester, England, and Professor Zwie Worblowsky, who then held a comparable post at the Hebrew University, Jerusalem. Reading the discarded literature, I entered a world that included material not only radically different in content, but also sometimes older than the Canonical Gospels. Both Brandon and Worblowsky assured me that the earlier writings could claim a validity equal to that of those Gospels. Indeed, Brandon even went further, saying that they had a unique veracity all of their own – because they had escaped the censorship and revisionism of the early Church.

By the second century most churches accepted a canon comprising the present four Gospels, the Books of Acts, the thirteen letters of Paul, the first letters of Peter and John. But there was still fierce disagreement about the inclusion of the books of James, Hebrews, 2 John, 2 Peter, Jude and Revelation. The debate continued well into the fourth century until Eusebius, the Bishop of Caesarea and the accepted 'Father of Church History', classified Christian writings into two categories: acceptable or rejected.

In the year AD 327, agreement was reached that the twenty-seven books listed by Athanasius, Bishop of Alexandria, would form the New Testament. Formal approval was given at the Synod of Carthage in the year AD 395. At the Council of Nicea in AD 325, the divergent forms of Christianity were compelled to reconcile their differences – and Rome became the core of Christian orthodoxy. It became an article of faith that any deviation from Rome was a heresy, no longer an honestly-held difference of opinion or interpretation.

At Nicea, the divinity of Jesus was promulgated and Mary, his mother, became the Virgin who represented motherhood in all its fullness and perfection.

Mary Magdalene – the repentant whore – was carefully presented so that together she and the Virgin formed a diptych of the Early Fathers' ideas of womanhood – the consecrated purity of the Virgin and the reformed sexuality of Mary Magdalene.

But was that the whole truth? I put the same questions to my distinguished guides, Professors Brandon and Worblowsky. Each gave the same resounding answer: no. The full truth, the human truth, lay in that other discarded collection of writings. Not all of what was written there was true, by any means. But there was sufficient truth to be found to provide a rounded portrait of the woman of Magdala which the Canonical Gospels had been unable to retain.

And so it proved. There is one passage in particular which I came across early on and which has remained with me. It is from the Gospel of Mary when Peter speaks these words to Mary Magdalene: 'Sister, we know that the Saviour loved you more than the rest of women. Tell us the words of the Saviour you remember – which you know but we do not.'

It seemed a good leitmotif for my book.

In finally writing it, I have chosen to do so in the same way I told the story of Jesus in *Trial* – by once more recounting events as they probably occurred in the time they happened.

Macauley wrote that 'the perfect historian must possess an imagination sufficiently powerful to make his narrative affecting and picturesque. Yet he must control it so absolutely as to content himself with the materials he finds.' That I have tried to do. But there is also a need for informed conjecture to be ready to deal in the middle range of probability. I hope my writing about Mary Magdalene will encourage people that they need not live their faith in blinkers. My own experience has been that, far from weakening my faith, it has been strengthened by such an approach. I have clothed Mary Magdalene, so to speak, not only in the dress of the day – a verifiable piece of research – but in the customs of her daily life: what she ate, where she went with Jesus, what those places were like at the time, whom they would have met, the dangers they ran from the Roman occupiers, the

Jewish Resistance and, of course, the High Priesthood in the Temple.

Through her eyes – and the authors of the Christian Apocrypha – it is possible to see more clearly the personalities of many of those only glimpsed in the New Testament: Pontius Pilate, the authority of Rome; Joseph Caiaphas, the High Priest; and Annas, his father-in-law. All come and go through her own story, adding to our understanding of them – and of Mary Magdalene.

In recreating her life, I faced the same question as I did over *Trial*. Where was the absolute proof that this or that happened the way I say it could have?

Hubert Richards, in his admirable *The First Easter*, deals with the matter succinctly:

> To call something a myth is not to dismiss it as a legend. There is nothing more real, or more true, than a myth. Myths are, in fact, what we live by. They are the symbols in which we express our deepest insights about ourselves and our universe. They are the poetry in which we express what we are and what we hold most dearly. The truths we live by, the values on which we base our lives – these can only be expressed inadequately, and in an indirect and symbolic way. What the myth speaks of will always need to be fleshed out in one form or another. The truths we live by should be expressed in a myth which is meaningful to us.

The Christian of today lives in an increasingly secularized world which seems to be determined to relegate the Biblical stories to something which has little to do with everyday life. But does there need to be this dichotomy between faith and belief?

Surely the question is what kind of reality are we dealing with? What do we commit ourselves to when, for instance, we say we believe absolutely that on the third day Jesus rose from the dead – and Mary Magdalene was the first witness? We must remain committed to believing the truth handed down to us.

✻　　✻　　✻

The answer is perfectly illustrated in the story of the Nativity. Here Matthew gives us a masterpiece of concise narration and flawless characterization, yet allows us to conjecture beyond the two acts of a superb drama.

The first act opens on a bleak Judaean landscape where shepherds huddle against the night cold, keeping watch over their flocks. Then through the faint moonlight comes the beating of innumerable wings sweeping invisibly over the startled shepherds. For a moment they are startled until they hear an angel's voice telling them not to be afraid because, of all the people in Israel, they have been chosen to be the first to know the good news. At this time they have a new king. As they go to pay homage, there is just a hint that this charming story will change into something very different.

Act two is one of unmitigated horror: of wealth and power, of treachery and betrayal, and finally of murder. Of a star and Wise Men following it. Of the slaughter of the new-born innocents and the flight of the Messiah.

There are those who say it never happened, could not have happened. To them I say: why not?

We know in his dying year utter madness had consumed Herod's reason. All his life had been punctuated by insensate brutality, aggravated by the contempt in which his subjects held him. Appointed by Rome, he understood well that any threat to him was one to Rome. And any threat to Rome would see him swiftly removed from office. News that a King had been born who would surely usurp him would have been more than enough for Herod to murder the infants of Bethlehem. In his long life he had slaughtered so many men, women and children.

Neither can the Magi be dismissed as figments of the imagination. Their history can be traced back to the sacred caste of the Medes. After Cyrus had consolidated the empires of Media and Persia, the Magi performed all the religious functions in the new kingdom. But they were not magicians, since their religious beliefs condemned sorcery. They were, in the best sense of the world they lived in, Wise Men.

Though the Magi was a pagan cult, there was much about it that was almost identical to Hebrew belief and ritual: the mode of sacrifice; beasts were clean or unclean; the priestly caste resembled the Jewish groupings of High Priest, Priest and Levites; the Magi were supported by tithes; they worshipped one God, Creator and Sustainer of all; they believed in the immortality of the soul, the resurrection of the dead and the eternity of happiness or misery. Their most sacred book, the *Zend-Huesta*, was somewhat similar to the Old Testament, with matching accounts of the Creation, of Abraham and Joseph, and the Psalms.

Most crucially, the Magi believed in a star being the sign to foretell the virgin birth of a King who would be the precursor of a new age of peace and justice for all people on earth. The Magi themselves were trained to attach special significance to any new star.

None of this ultimately matters. The Magi followed their star into history.

We either believe that happened, or become side-tracked by such perfectly charming but irrelevant claims as that the Magi were actually the representatives of the three races to the ancient world: the white, the yellow and the black. More certain is that between them they represented theology which recognizes revelation, knowledge which abases itself before innocence, riches prostrating themselves at the feet of poverty.

Those who have spent their lives trying to defeat the harmonists – exegetes who have no problem with reconciling the accounts of the canonical Gospels and refute that any of the four might have fallen into inaccuracy – make great play with the fact that Matthew places the slaughter of the innocents and the flight into Egypt just prior to the arrival of the Magi – while Luke says not a word about any of this. Disbelievers further point out that Luke instead reports that Jesus was taken to the Temple forty days after his birth and that immediately afterwards Joseph, Mary and the child went back to Nazareth. So, say the sceptics, if there had been any danger to the child Jesus, his parents would never have dared to take him to the Temple.

Luke's Gospel was one of the last to be written and set down at a time when Christianity was beginning to spread throughout the Mediterranean world. Filling at least one-quarter of the New

Testament, with his Gospel and its sequel, the Acts of the apostles, Luke is primarily concerned with the message of universal salvation. Never one of the twelve apostles, Luke may have been an early convert to Christianity and almost certainly never met Jesus. What little we know of Luke suggests he was a slave in some Greco-Roman household in the city of Antioch who was set free and qualified as a doctor before becoming the close companion of the apostle Paul. Though only mentioned twice by name within the New Testament, Luke has been fully accepted as the author of both the Third Gospel and the Acts of the apostles. In Acts Luke describes the early development of Christianity while his own Gospel focuses on the teachings of Jesus, laying no undue emphasis on his birth or how he had come to fulfil Old Testament prophecy.

Luke is primarily concerned with setting down the rules for Christian living: compassion, kindness, forgiveness and, of course, love. All this is illustrated through a succession of parables: the Good Samaritan, the Healing of the Ten Lepers, the Rich Man and Lazarus, the Pharisee and the Tax-Collector. Luke's Gospel also lays great stress – which the others do not – on Jesus' sensitivity towards women and children.

He is the most powerful of the Evangelists in advocating prayer life. Luke not only tells us how Jesus prayed, but how he taught others to do so. Luke uses great literary skill to present a Jewish story in a global setting; the central figure is not simply the Jewish Messiah, but the Saviour of the world. Luke is also the first to identify Mary Magdalene.

The events around Jesus' birth described in Matthew's Gospel may well have been inserted into Matthew's Gospel from material supplied by the author of the Gospel of Mark. That, of course, does not negate its validity. Further, the account of the Magi following the star fits very well with Old Testament prophecies. There is also a persuasive argument that the First Gospel is so positioned to show that Christianity is the fulfilment of Judaism and that Matthew is primarily concerned to prove that Jesus' mission was originally only to the Jews. When Judaism refused to accept him as their Messiah, the new way Jesus proclaimed was extended to the Gentiles.

✳   ✳   ✳

From the outset of my research, I have always taken the position that the Gospels should not be taken as a point of departure – rather as the first stage of arrival. In trying to separate these various strata, the overwhelming impression is of centuries of zealous work to interpret, adapt and correct the message of Jesus.

Faced with that unchallengeable truth, it is overwhelmingly difficult for me to accept the claims of the New Revisionists who continue to spring up, that the Gospels – and of course the Apocrypha – are an invention in which prosaic events have been given supernatural importance, either through the ingenuous credibility of the original writers or, more seriously, a calculated attempt to deceive.

I prefer to believe that the authors of the Gospels, as well as those of the body of supportive writings, wrote in the mode of expression suitable to their time. They believed what they originally put down. So should we.

Proof of the kind lawyers demand – the sworn affidavit, the deposition duly witnessed – is not part of this story. That kind of 'proof' is ultimately of small consequence. There is little that can be 'proven' in today's understanding of the world of Jesus in the Canonical Gospels. What is available is that large body of discarded work which time and again points to other possibilities, often highly plausible.

Brandon articulated reality when he told me:

You must survey all the available evidence and examine it most carefully. Your conclusions must always be based on one premise: is something more likely to have happened the way you perceive it than not? Answering that question honestly is the key to your success. All else flows from that. An honestly held belief is sufficient justification to set it down on paper to distinguish between what could have happened, what did happen and why it should have happened. Your conclusions may be disputed. You may be disparaged and attacked. Accept it all as a tribute. You are making people think. There is no greater achievement for any writer.

In his powerful book, *Can We Trust the New Testament?*, Bishop John Robinson argues that, in the confusion of voices on what is acceptable in the New Testament, there are four definite positions. There is the cynicism of the foolish, the fundamentalism of the fearful, the scepticism of the wise and the conservatism of the committed.

I belong firmly in the last camp. In the close to a quarter of a century I have been involved in Biblical research for various quests, I have detected that, despite all the upheavals, a deep mass of water has steadfastly refused to be shifted by what was happening on the surface. This body is not, as many revisionists insist, primarily composed of what are now labelled Christian fundamentalists. rather, it is a rational body which simply does not accept what the revisionists claim. They come and go, kicking up their passing storms, but to the committed our anchors are sufficient to ride them out. We simply bend before the gales of cynicism and rejection and, when they have passed, remain secure in our belief.

This is not to say that, so often like 'the fundamentalism of the fearful', as Bishop Robinson labels it, we have a suspicion of all scholarship. Far from it. Those of us who are genuinely committed to Christ as 'the truth' are prepared to take the risk Jesus himself took when he committed himself to history. We know very well that it is fatal to equate orthodoxy with ignorance. That is the road to defeat.

As John Robinson writes:

The truth of the Gospel stories involves a more complex inter-relationship of fact and interpretation, for Jesus, unlike Adam, was a historical individual. So, the way we can 'trust' the New Testament is less simple than the way in which we can 'trust' the Old Testament. For the 'mix' in the Christ-event is richer. It calls for a full alliance of conviction and criticism.

It is precisely the absence of that alliance which makes the 'cynicism of the foolish' fail to see the story of Jesus is faith in the Word made flesh. Whatever the differences in their accounts, we can be very sure, from the Gospels and the 'lost books' of the Bible, that those first Christian chroniclers had a reverence for what had happened to and around Jesus which would have stopped them from simply promulgating their own account. And, whenever we check against non-Christian sources, the Gospel accounts and the Apocrypha stand up.

The 'fundamentalism of the fearful' is based upon faith that is blinkered and consequently insecure. That kind of truth depends on the infallibility of blind doctrine. The fear of letting go of such dogma can be removed by truly understanding the greatest gift Jesus gave the world – how to love.

The 'scepticism of the wise' has several attractions. There is no doubting the faithfulness and genuine devotion to Christ of those who belong in the grouping. But in the end scepticism prevails: belief is replaced by degrees of probability.

And so we come back to the 'conservatism of the committed'. For those of us who claim membership of this group we know, as Christians, we have 'to fear from the truth'. Those of us who know this have no guarantee where it will take us, or how many times along the way we will be tempted to give up. Time and again I myself have been led to conclusions I did not expect, both negative and positive, in my own biblical research. But then there can be nothing fixed or final; expanding knowledge ensures that. Yet, in the end, my own trust in those primary documents of the Christian faith – the Gospels and the Apocrypha – remains unshaken. It is not my years of research that ensures that. It is faith.

In preparing this book I decided that I would not burden or bore readers with footnotes or source notes throughout the main text. My sources are the Canonical Gospels and those discarded by the early church and Jewish literature; it is the only way to understand the geographical and historical background.

But most of all, from the beginning I had hoped to create a

highly personal – yes, intimate – portrait of a very remarkable woman. As well as the great assistance of those I have already mentioned, there are still others whose editorial help has been invaluable. To be sure, some of those at first were concerned that to focus on Mary Magdalene could somehow take away from the central role of Jesus. Others pointed out that Mary Magdalene is a notable biblical figure in her own right and deserved book-length attention.

Dr Robert Fleming, then in charge of the Tantur Ecumenical Institute nestling on the road between Jerusalem and Bethlehem, provided important insights into how a woman like Mary Magdalene would have fitted into the social structure of her time. He brought her alive in a way few others could do, speaking candidly of her morals and sexuality, and the part they could have played in her own relationship with Jesus. Fleming, an American Bible scholar and social scientist, ran a centre that offered students theology, history and active ministry. He accepted that what he said made him a controversial figure – not least that Judas was not merely motivated by base motives, but may altogether have been a more complex and disturbed personality.

Haim Cohen was an example of the fact that my quest for Mary Magdalene sometimes constituted a race with death. The former Justice of the Supreme Court of Israel and long a renowned biblical scholar, with the mentality of a lawyer's lawyer, he was already dying when we met. Over dinner in the King David's Hotel in Jerusalem he cheerfully told me he was willing to 'go over everything that will help you understand the motivation and relationship of this truly remarkable woman with your Lord'.

He proved as good as his word. From his substantial private library emerged a wealth of detail right up until shortly before his untimely death. He will be sorely missed, not only by me but by future scholars.

Zev Vilney, Lecturer in Military History and Cartography at the Military Academy of Israel, who has made what will surely remain as an unsurpassed study of the land Mary Magdalene would have known, made it possible to place her in a geographical context. Zev Fack, Professor of Family Law at the Hebrew University of Jerusalem, waited patiently while I referred to my notebooks and answered my questions, pertinent and impertinent.

Last but by no means least, I was encouraged by Clive Manning of the Bible Society. He has a passion for his work that is inspiring, matched with an insatiable curiosity. No detail, however small, was not open to debate. Shrewd and clever, at first he had an understandable concern the book might not fully reflect what must stand as one of the greatest love stories of all time. Once satisfied, he plunged energetically into helping me. Ny debt to him, as to all the others, is beyond computing.

When people ask me why I should enter into such a controversial area as the life of Mary Magdalene, I can only echo the words of G.K. Chesterton: 'I believe in getting into hot water. I think it keeps you clean.'

In the end, what I have written must come down to a matter of interpretation. I say in all humility it must be mine. If nothing else, I hope that what follows will justify that. This is the story of the repentant sinner, the first to witness the fulfilment of the promise of the resurrection. Her faith enabled Mary Magdalene to see Jesus. In that moment her unshakeable love of God received its greatest confirmation. In death and beyond Jesus loved her.

Her loving relationship with her Saviour can properly be said to have begun in the time the world would come to know as the Year of Our Lord, *Anno Domini* or AD 26.

Two

Magdala was a small town on the west shore of the Sea of Galilee. The great lake was the second basin through which the Jordan flowed. Larger than Lake Huleh, it was however smaller than the Sea of Salt which, because of its appalling desolation, is now called the Dead Sea.

By contrast, the Sea of Galilee remained a vast tract of fresh water which controlled the lives of the people along its shores, who either lived off the abundant fish and their by-products, or worked the fields. The area had long been famed as the market-garden of All-Judaea. Protected by mountains and plains to the west and the Rift Valley to the east, it was a land of heavy night-time dews which helped to sustain the streams which still flowed into the lake during the long, rainless summers. The earth was fertile, creating verdant pastures, bountiful crops and wooded hills that rose on all sides of the water.

The lake was known locally as *Gennesaret*, the water of the flowers, because of the wide variety of blooms which grew on its banks. It was also rich in mineral deposits, some of which were used for medicinal purposes by those who lived on its shores. People swore they had witnessed miraculous cures of those who drank the lake's waters or daubed its dark brown mud on their bodies. Others, usually sophisticated Jerusalemites, said such claims were only further evidence of the gullibility of Galileans.

Such taunts had little impact on the people of the lakeshore. Self-sufficient and secure in their faith, they despised the airs and graces of the rich Jews who passed through on their way to and from Jerusalem. To strangers, the lake people were clannish, introspective, obdurate and unyielding: their stubbornness, like their bargaining, was legendary: they would rather see a catch of fish rot than sell it below price. To their own, they were supportive to a degree rarely found elsewhere in time of joy or tribulation; a marriage or a death was the occasion for a whole town to celebrate or mourn. God-fearing, the Torah or five books of Moses was the lexicon which ruled their life. The synagogue had pride of place, rising stark and proud above all other buildings. So it was in Magdala.

In summer, the tracks through the town were baked hard; in the short winter the mud was often knee-deep. Yet, to its population, Magdala was a prosperous town, its people staunch nationalists. It was a matter of pride to every Magdalean that Galilee remained the most troublesome province in All-Judaea and its people's resentment for the Romans as fiercely burnished as it had been against all previous occupiers of their land.

This was the world in which Mary Magdalene had been raised, an atmosphere which would have nourished her own strong belief in independence. From early on she would have learned that out of Galilee had come almost all the revolutionaries. Most recently Zadok, the founder of the Zealots, had raised his battle-banner near Magdala. And, before him, the mighty Simon Maccabeus had enlisted every man and boy in the town to help free Jerusalem from the Syrians.

Like every Magdalean she would have been taught to believe absolutely that one day would come the Deliverer prophesied by the prophet Malachi. But in Magdala, as elsewhere in Galilee, there was disagreement on who he would be and in what form he would appear.

Some thought he would come from the family of Joseph, the oldest and most revered family in the land. Others were convinced their saviour would be a descendant of Aaron, the brother of Moses. Equally popular was the notion he would come from the House of David. Some even believed that God would send an angel called the Son of God – or that God himself would even descend from heaven and free his people from bondage.

Whichever form deliverance assumed, it was generally accepted that the man who would bring it would be known as the Messiah, and also rejoice in the title of the King of the Jews. Under him they would live for all time as a free people. For centuries people had been born, lived their lives and died waiting for that freedom. It is not difficult to imagine Mary Magdalene as a growing child scanning the starlit skies for a sign that the Messiah was about to come and then, as dawn broke, looking towards the distant mountains to see if he was physically visible. As a caravanserai had plodded into town, she would have hung on every word of the camel drovers and merchants to see if they had news of the Anointed One.

On Sabbath she would have stood with other children and women in their section of the synagogue and listened for the rabbi to make any references to the prophecies of Isaiah, Joel and Zachariah. All had spoken of the forthcoming Messianic Age. But for them the world to come would be here on earth, an earthly paradise not a bodiless heaven. So had every child in Magdala been taught down the years.

In the streets boys vied with each other to portray their two favourite Zealot heroes: Judas of Gamala and Zadok. Twenty-three years before, in AD 6, those Jewish warriors had fought a courageous battle against the Romans; in death they were enshrined as patriots. After school they would race to high ground outside the town and relive the epic conflict.

Hopes were fuelled in a dozen and more other ways. The Zealots had once more begun to attack Roman patrols as well as those of the tetrarch, Herod Antipas. In the synagogue there was a new militaristic tendency in the interpretation of Scripture; passages that favoured subduing the nations hostile to Israel were given pride of place in readings. On lips everywhere could be heard words dedicated to the celebration of liberty and the end of enslavement. There was talk of a coming end to bondage by an act even more momentous than the Exodus from Egypt, the return from Babylon and the expulsion of the Greeks two full centuries before. The taste for freedom was a tangible living thing that every day came that much closer. In the lakeshore taverns and market-places, people were beginning to say aloud that the 'elect one' of the Book of Daniel was soon coming to create a new political system in which God would reign on earth in human form. There was probably not a man, woman or child who could not describe the prophet Enoch's vivid description of this super-human being. 'One like a son of man coming with the clouds of heaven.'

Though the Second Commandment of Moses expressly banned the making of images, it would not have stopped the speculation about what Enoch's inspiration would look like. Would he come in the guise of a great Jewish warrior? Would he be tall and powerful like Samson or short and muscular like David? Or perhaps reflect Isaiah's prediction that he 'hath no comeliness and when we shall see him, there is no beauty that we should desire him.' Would he be gentle like Elisha or would he possess the firmness of a Joel? Would he be wise like Solomon or hard like Malachi? There would surely have been as many questions as there were no certain answers. But no man doubted they would recognize him – if he really *had* come to deliver them.

For a woman in a male-dominated society, there was no place to join in the debate, let alone lead it. A woman could only listen and reflect; to do more would be an act of disobedience. To openly espouse any cause would be scandalous.

Nevertheless there was not a wife, mother or sister who did not yearn for the day when almost a century of cruel Roman occupation would end – lifting the threat of a husband, son or brother being transported to serve as a galley slave on board a Roman ship or sent in chains to some far-flung part of the Empire, never to be seen again. It had happened so often in Magdala and elsewhere. A Roman force would suddenly emerge out of the hills and snatch as many able-bodied men as they could, dragging them off to Caesarea, their port-headquarters. The presence of the Zealots had reduced these forays. But no woman could be certain when she saw her menfolk set off for work if she would see them again.

In a land of ancient settlements, Magdala was among the oldest. There had been fishermen there when the Holy Ark of the Covenant was brought to Jerusalem almost a thousand years previously. By the time Nebuchadnezzar captured the city in 586 BC, destroying the First Temple and the Jews were sent to Babylon, Magdala was a sizeable village.

Among those who returned fifty years later from exile, a number broke their long journey at the lake and, entranced by its beauty, settled in Magdala. By the time the building of the Second Temple had begun and the first Knesset Parliament had opened in Jerusalem in 448 BC, Magdala was a thriving town. Then, once more, the shadow of occupation fell over the land. Like everywhere else in All-Judaea, Magdala came under the control of the Syrians for the next two hundred years until the Jews found leaders in the Maccabeus family. It was Simon Maccabeus who finally drove out the occupiers in 141 BC and created an independent state. To ensure its continuance, he made a treaty of friendship with Rome.

For almost a century, the Promised Land prospered without interference. A queen, Alexandra, ruled. When she died, there was a falling-out over which one of her two brothers should succeed to the throne. Sensing an opportunity to add Judaea to the expanding rump of Rome, Pompey and an army of ten legions, 30,000 well-trained troops, imperiously broke the treaty. To the horror of every Jew, the Romans entered the Temple in Jerusalem and slaughtered all those priests who protested.

Pompey himself went further. He walked into the Temple's Holy of Holies, that most secret sacred place where only the High Priest could enter, and then only on the Day of Atonement. Pompey's curiosity was driven by a conviction that in the inner sanctum dwelled the Invisible God the Jews worshipped. Finding nothing, Pompey went about the business of establishing Rome's hold over the land and its people. But the sacrilege of his act ensured the occupation would foment resistance.

Men who, under previous occupiers, had offered no more than sullen lack of cooperation, pledged themselves to fight to the death the Romans and those Jews appointed to help them govern. Among these was the client-king, Herod the Great. When he died, gripped by madness, his son Herod Antipas became tetrarch of Galilee in 4 BC. His rule had been every bit as violent as that of his father.

Pompey had been followed by a succession of Imperial procurators, brutal men indifferent to Jewish religious practices or beliefs. Sensing this could lead to open revolt and an unnecessary spillage of Imperial blood, the Emperor, Augustus Caesar, decreed that the very symbol of the Jewish religious establishment, the High Priesthood, should be in the gift of Rome. 'Control their Chief Priest and we control the people,' the

Emperor told the Senate. Caesar's successor, Tiberias, continued the policy. In a period of thirty years no fewer than five High Priests were appointed and swiftly removed when they were not sufficiently malleable.

Coinciding with the arrival of Pontius Pilate as the country's fifth procurator in the year AD 26, yet another High Priest had been appointed. His name was Joseph Caiaphas, a lawyer who understood how to work an accommodation with the occupying powers. It suited Pilate perfectly that the relationship between Caiaphas and Herod Antipas was at best fractious. It had always been Imperial policy to rule over a conquered nation by manipulating divisions among its leaders.

But to the people of Magdala, all this was happening in every sense a long way away. Jerusalem was a distant four-day walk. People only went there for high holidays like Passover or for a special pilgrimage to the Temple to give thanks for a first-born son, or seek intercession for a barren wife.

Caesarea, the seat of Pilate and his Roman administration, was over a day's journey. Few Magdaleans had actually been to the fortress city where the galleys arrived from other parts of the Empire bringing fresh legions and embarking those Romans who had served their term of duty in a land they detested because its people refused to conform. No matter how much the Jewish population was threatened and brutalized, the people remained stubbornly wedded to their faith that there was but one God, and those of Rome were idols.

In Galilee, interpretation of the Scriptures was in the hands of ultra-conservative Pharisee lawyers and teachers. For them the minutiae of the holy writ was all-important. Within a closed society like Magdala, this outside pressure would have been less than welcome. The lakeshore people had a deserved reputation for having their own ideas on how to live their religious life. It went with their self-sufficiency.

For the population of Magdala, the world beyond their fields of black basaltic soil, the richest in all Galilee, was a remote, alien place. From time to time its young men went away to seek a bride, thus avoiding the perils of inbreeding. Usually they chose a woman from within the borders of Galilee, from towns with biblical names and traditions like Sepphoris, Jotopata and, on the far side of the lake, Gergesa and Hippos.

The women of Galilee were renowned for the delicate olive of their skin, their raven-black hair which they often highlighted with henna in later years, and figures that did not automatically run to fat after childbirth. Trained to be good housekeepers by their own mothers, they had also been instructed that their husbands would seek sexual satisfaction outside the marriage bed during those days when, as wives, they were scripturally unclean. For their hard-working men to seek temporary relief elsewhere was quite different from the continuing licentious behaviour of Herod and his court, and that of the Romans.

Consequently every town in Galilee had its whores. They worked without hindrance, but mostly remained within their walls. When they died, they were buried in a separate part of the local cemetery. In Magdala the arrangements had satisfactorily existed for centuries.

When news came to Magdala, it travelled slowly. Reports of unrest in Spain and Armenia would have taken a full year to reach the town, arriving with one of the camel caravans which regularly travelled from the far ends of the Empire to bring their wares to Jerusalem. Drovers often made a detour to the lakeside towns to collect fresh produce and fish to sell in the city. A caravan wended its way past crops of wheat, grapes and olives that produced some of the finest corn, wine and oil.

Almost certainly the first the people of Magdala learned there was a new Emperor in Rome was when Herod Antipas, the tetrarch, built an entire city in his honour. He named it Tiberias. At the same time the tetrarch erected a massive fort-palace overlooking the city from where he now ruled over a quarter of a million Galileans. Tiberias was another place Magdaleans rarely visited. To them the town was sacrilegious because it was built on the site of a Jewish graveyard.

Romans themselves rarely ventured into Galilee except on man-hunting raiding parties. Apart from a road linking their port city of Caesarea with Jerusalem, they had built no other major highways in Galilee. Its town and villages were connected by little more than dirt tracks along which people either walked or led donkeys and camels. Away from the lakeshore, the ground was strewn with boulders from prehistoric volcanic eruptions and hills were often only accessible to shepherds and herdsmen. Elsewhere were forests and swampy areas.

It was an area ideal for the Jewish Resistance movement, the Zealots, to wage its renewed guerrilla war against the Roman occupiers and the troops of Herod Antipas. For the Zealots Magdala was a safe haven. The slogan of the Zealots – 'God is our only Ruler and Lord' – was a clarion call to which every Magdalean subscribed. They saw the cry as the forerunner of the long-awaited Messiah who would, among much else, end the draconian taxation which Magdaleans, like everyone else, could not avoid.

One of the first things Pilate had done was to increase the levies. Never before had a Magdalean household faced such demands. There was a land tax, an income tax and a poll tax, a water tax, a tax on every living animal, another for every net of fish, taxes on meat and salt, a road tax, a tax to maintain the town boundaries, a tax for the privilege of holding the weekly market, a tax to maintain the bridges every Magdalean had to cross once he or she had walked out of the town. In addition, every male Magdalean – like every other Jew – once he reached adulthood, paid a voluntary tax for the upkeep of the Temple. All told, the average household in Magdala could expect to part with up to forty per cent of its annual income in taxes.

The Roman authorities made no pretence that these onerous penalties would be used for the benefit of the people. The money, or goods offered in lieu, was sent to Rome, earmarked for the Emperor's personal account, the *fiscus*. There was no appeal against a levy. Any attempt to avoid payment resulted in beatings or imprisonment. The ultimate sanction was to be shipped to Rome as a slave.

As well as the official taxes, Roman officials from Pilate downwards extracted what they could for themselves. The procurator, like his predecessors, was heavily in debt by the time he came to Judaea. Despite the exalted position of his wife, Claudia Procula, the grand-daughter of the Emperor Augustus Caesar, Pilate had still spent considerable sums on entertainment and bribes to work his way up the Imperial ladder. His senior staff had done the same. The quickest way to recoup their expenditure was to exact tribute from the Jews. Consequently, for every service a Jew required, he had to pay a *baksheesh* – literally, a back-hander. This could be anything from an exemption for an order to supply free grain to the army, to having a travel permit stamped. There were scores of pieces of paper a Jew needed ratified before he could set about earning a living – on which he would then pay the highest taxation in the Empire.

Pilate had introduced further refinement, importing from Rome teams of money-lenders. Quite different from those who operated in the Temple, these non-Jews travelled the land, advancing money to those who could not pay their taxes – loans at fifty per cent interest, repayable within a year. Those who could not meet the repayments lost everything – their homes, flocks and herds, the very wheat they had harvested. Even these rapacious marauders hesitated about entering Galilee. Here they could expect to meet the same ruthlessness as they meted out.

Three times a year Pilate, as procurator, made the sixty-mile journey to Jerusalem with his legions to remind pilgrims of Rome's might during each of the great Jewish festivals, of which Passover was the most important. On those occasions, the Galilean air would resound to the tramp of Roman foot soldiers and the clank of harness of its mounted horsemen heading south.

But otherwise Magdaleans could go on hating their occupiers, knowing there was almost no risk of retribution.

Little wonder that when news finally reached Magdala there was a rabbi who had started to preach against such iniquities as over-taxation, it created more than a stir of interest. The prophet's Hebrew name was 'God saves' – Jesus. He was from Nazareth, a hamlet ten miles to the south-west and the son of a carpenter; the latest census figure gave the population of Nazareth as under 500 souls. The village itself overlooked the Plain of Esdraselon, a broad corridor between the Mediterranean and the mountains to the east. Throughout history, the armies of Egypt, Assyria, Babylon, as well as those from Persia and Macedonia, had swept across the plain to do battle. None had stayed as long as the legions of Rome.

Could it possibly be, Magdaleans would have asked the Zealot guerrillas when they came down from the surrounding hills, that this rabbi, Jesus, could be the Messiah they had all been waiting for? But the fighters at least for the moment could well have been more interested in earthly matters. In the hills they led spartan, nomadic lives. But in Magdala they could find relief for their physical needs.

Inside the town's north gate was a small area walled off from the rest of Magdala and entered only through a narrow, arched gate. By day the quarter appeared deserted apart from the comings and going of girl servants with shopping. But when darkness fell there would be a discreet procession of men passing through the gate to visit the houses inside the enclave, whose occupants shared the collective label of Women Beyond Redemption. They were the whores of Magdala.

Among them lived Mary Magdalene.

Whether she was seduced or persuaded into a career of prostitution remains beyond record. She may have learned her skills in one of Jerusalem's bordellos then, having made sufficient money, returned home. If she had city ways and clothes, she would certainly have been a cut above the other harlots of Magdala. Her speech may have contained something of the precise enunciation of the Jerusalem dialect. Some male Magdaleans were so slipshod in their pronunciation that they were never called upon to read the Torah in public when they were away from home.

Given her business her house, like all such places, was altogether more spacious and grand than homes elsewhere in Magdala. As she almost certainly owned her own establishment – for organized brothels were still a rarity in Galilee – then some of those men who slipped through the narrow gate and made their urgent way across the paving stones of her courtyard would have influence, possibly direct links to the Herodian court: wealthy travelling merchants whose contacts extended high into Jerusalem society.

Mary Magdalene then, would have been no pox-marked

woman, but one of definite physical attraction, able to command the highest fees for her skills. She would also have been of an age where men were prepared to pay for her youth coupled with her experience, a powerful and irresistible combination.

Most certainly her house was a place of entertainment where clients came to relax, drink the finest wines and, while waiting for her service, would enjoy such delicacies as stuffed dates and olives and, a delicacy of the area, filleted dormice roasted over a wood fire.

The reception rooms were covered with rich floor coverings and wall hangings. On low tables were gold and silver ornaments given to her by clients instead of cash. But hard currency flowed to her as streams did into the great lake beyond the walled enclave. Women at the top end of her procession were invariably wealthy.

Mary Magdalene's day clothes came from the bazaars of Tiberias. But for her work she wore the finest robes and gowns, either purchased in the souks of Jerusalem or brought to her by caravan-masters from Constantinople, Athens, Naples or even Rome itself. These would be made of silk or cotton and embroidered with gold threads. In summer she would wear only a *stola*, a full-length robe. But in winter she would add a *palla*, or shawl. Beneath her gown she wore brief cotton undergarments.

Winter or summer – the two seasons of Galilee – her servants wore tunics made from wool or linen. However, her personal handmaid who ran the household and its staff, wore her cast-offs and had other privileges. She would be entitled to eat with Mary Magdalene, sleep at the foot of her bed and receive a minute percentage of her mistress' earnings.

The private entrance to the house, through which Mary Magdalene and her servants came and went, faced east, to allow the breeze off the lake to cool the rooms. In winter, when the winds could reach gale force, the arch and window openings were covered with heavy bead curtains or woven drapes.

Clients entered through a courtyard at the front, passing into a small garden. To one side, sheltered by conifers and other evergreens, were the servants' quarters. Next door was the kitchen. Most of the cooking was done in earthenware pots on wood or charcoal stoves and meat and fish were roasted over an open fire. Wine was usually mixed with water before being served in goblets. Galilee, like every province, had its own style of pottery; it broke easily but was cheap to replace.

Opposite the kitchen were several ante-rooms, furnished with couches and low tables. Here a client waited to be escorted by a servant to her presence or, if he was specially important, he would wait in a room of his own. Servants would bring clients water with which to wash their hands and feet, followed by savouries and wine.

Beyond the ante-rooms was the spacious chamber where Mary Magdalene entertained. The bed was the focal point, its frame made of wood to which was attached leather webbing supporting a mattress of straw or sheep's wool. There would be a bedspread and a bolster-pillow.

The room, like others in the house, would be lit by oil-burning lamps, the fuel made either from olives, fish or sesame seeds. Heating was provided by braziers burning charcoal.

Before entering, a client would have settled payment with Mary Magdalene's personal servant and removed his shoes. To violate such protocol was to risk banishment from the house.

Mary Magdalene's private quarters were beyond where she worked. This consisted of her bedroom, a dining-room, and a pool to catch winter rainwater, sufficient to last through the dry, hot, summer months. Leading off her bedroom were alcoves where she kept her clothes. It was not unusual for a women of her position to have a hundred and more gowns and capes. Under her bed would be her most prized possession: a strong iron chest to keep her earnings and her most precious jewels.

Her professional services ended relatively early; her clients were men who often rose before dawn and worked until dusk. Well before the moon was high over the Sea of Galilee, she herself would be in bed. In the morning she would rise late, sit in the courtyard listening to the everyday sounds beyond the walled enclave. She might lunch with one of her neighbours, exchanging gossip gleaned from clients. In the afternoon she would bathe, having her handmaiden rub oil on her body and then scrape it off with a sandalwood stock. Afterwards the servant would massage her body and paint her finger and toe nails. The pampering could take most of the afternoon. By early evening, having eaten, Mary Magdalene, like any other whore in Magdala, would be ready for another night's work.

This had been her life-style ever since she had entered her profession. But now it was about to change.

For she too had heard the reports about Jesus – and that the Nazarene, as he was coming to be known through Galilee, had moved the centre of his preaching to Capernaum.

It was a surprising decision. Capernaum permanently reeked of the dried fish and pungent stocks made from fish heads that were its culinary specialities. The town itself was an unpleasant place in which to live for another reason: the houses were built of basalt which made the interiors gloomy and muggy in summer and cold in winter. It was not a place that immediately came to mind from which to launch a revolution.

Nevertheless, from there had come a remarkable report which had spread not only through the lakeside towns, but beyond. The Nazarene planned to create a kingdom, one which all people could enter, secure in the knowledge that they would be free of Rome's yoke and that of Herod's – free of all the present constraints on their lives.

Despite this, the good tidings had not been well received in his own village synagogue. On the day the Nazarene announced his plans, the observances had followed their customary precise course. First the congregation had stood in the body of the hall – the men divided by a barrier from the women – chanting psalms. Then an elder of the community, wrapped in his *tallith*, or prayer shawl, had read the Mosaic commandments before intoning the *Shema*, the prayer to the One God. Next had come the chanting of the six benedictions. The service had wound its way to an uneventful close with the recitation of the *Bereku*, one of the oldest of all Hebrew prayers.

The *Shammash* had removed from the wooden rack the parchment scrolls of the Pentateuch and the Prophets. Holding them reverently in both hands, he had waited for one of the male congregation to come forward and read from them; women were not entitled to do so. To have read the entire one hundred and seventy-five scrolls would have required over three years, so each reader made his own short selection from passages he would already have learned by rote.

Jesus had stepped forward and taken from the Shammash's hands the scroll containing the Book of Isaiah. The passage he had read was brief. 'The Spirit of the Lord God has been given to me for he has anointed me. He has sent me to bring good news to the poor, to proclaim liberty to the captives and to the blind new sight, to set the downtrodden free, to proclaim the Lord's year of favour.'

There could not have been a man, woman or child in the synagogue who would not have thrilled to the words. They were a reaffirmation that one day freedom would come. It might not be soon, it might not even be in their lifetime. But it would surely come.

Having read, Jesus was required to perform one further act, to interpret what the words meant. Instead, he rolled up the scroll and handed it back to the Shammash.

After a while the whispering started, people asking him to interpret the passage. Finally Jesus spoke these prophetic words: 'This day is the Word fulfilled in your ears.'

What then followed had spread to all parts of Galilee. Even allowing for the natural exaggeration that was another hallmark of Galileans, the shock the words had created was not lost in their re-telling by the time they reached Magdala.

In the Nazareth synagogue, the stunned silence had given way to mounting anger. Worshippers had turned to each other to remind themselves who Jesus was: 'Is this not the carpenter, the son of Mary, the brother of James and Joseph, and of Judas and Simon? And are not his sisters with us?'

They most certainly were. But that had not stopped Jesus from continuing to accuse the congregation of being so blinkered that they could not even recognize him: 'No prophet is accepted in his own country.'

It was a bold response that, if it stirred something in Mary Magdalene's heart, had only provoked fury in the people of Nazareth. They had begun to shout and scream at Jesus for blasphemously claiming to be able to fulfil the deliverance they had all been awaiting for so long.

Sensing their mood, Jesus had fled the synagogue and had barely managed to escape from the clutches of his pursuers and their intention of hurling him to his death in a gorge.

From Nazareth, he had passed through the Valley of the Doves, and walked down the gentle slopes of the hills to Capernaum. There, once more, Jesus had said deliverance was close, if people believed that God had sent his only begotten Son to ensure it. No one in Capernaum understood what exactly that meant. But they agreed the Nazarene behaved 'as one having authority'.

Then in the town's synagogue Jesus had demonstrated his healing powers for the first time.

Coming to the end of once more reading the passage from Isaiah, a man 'possessed by demons' shouted out: 'Have you come to destroy us?'

Jesus had transfixed him. 'Be quiet! Come out of him!'

Falling to the synagogue floor, the man had gone into convulsions before becoming suddenly quiet. After a while he had stood up and pronounced he had been miraculously cured. To the congregation what had happened was further dramatic confirmation of what they anyway firmly believed: nervous diseases – epitomized in the catch-all 'possession by demons' – could be exorcized by those rabbis who had been given the special powers to do so.

In that act of exorcism, Jesus had ensured an acceptance for himself in Capernaum.

Who cannot sense Mary Magdalene's curiosity swiftly giving way to a wonder which just as quickly turned to excitement and heart-warming hope as the reports reached her, perhaps through a client or a servant returning from Magdala's market? No matter the source, what she heard was high drama on a scale equal to any story in the books of Moses. Here was one man single-handedly defying family, friends, everyone, in that most sacred place of all, the synagogue. Then, fleeing before their fury, he not only calmly did so again, but proceeded to demonstrate mystical healing powers.

Perhaps under the shade of a courtyard tree, Mary Magdala would have sat and pondered about this remarkable personality. Clearly the Nazarene had great charisma. How else to explain the winning over of the hearts and minds of the people of Capernaum? That he had so spectacularly failed to do so with his own village people was not surprising: at the best of times the people of Nazareth were renowned for their obduracy.

And perhaps later in the cool of the evening, as servants helped her prepare for another night's work, Mary Magdalene may well have questioned them about what people were saying about Jesus. And she would have heard it was being increasingly whispered that the Nazarene was no ordinary healer, someone who well understood the power of suggestion in curing diseases: there were plenty of rabbis in the hills of Galilee who could do that. The Nazarene was something more. He was the reincarnation of the greatest of all the prophets; the one who had been the most political of them all, the one everyone knew was closely associated with deliverance: Elijah the Prophet.

The very notion must have sent a shiver of excitement through Mary Magdalene. No other prophet, sage or priest had kept so firm a hold on the collective imagination as Elijah – *Elihyahu-ha-Navi* in Hebrew. No one knew where he had come from all those centuries ago to fight as a soldier of the Lord against a multitude of heathen gods. Then, just as mysteriously, he had vanished to wander the earth, unseen, waiting to reappear to usher in the final salvation of mankind. So every Jew was taught from birth.

More than any other prophet, Elijah was their very symbol of hope. At the circumcision of every male infant, a chair was reserved for Elijah, with the entreaty that he would protect the child; at the Passover meal an extra cup of wine was poured for Elijah and a door symbolically opened to allow him to enter.

For all those long centuries of suffering, the ancestors of Mary Magdalene had clung resolutely to the belief that one day Elijah would again appear to them as the precursor of their freedom. For, with him he would bring the Expected One, the Messiah.

Can there be any doubt then that, at some point, she decided to discover more about this son of a carpenter who had proclaimed he could achieve more than any other Jew since Moses led his people out of Egypt? In the long and thrilling history of her people, nothing contained a promise so full of portent as the Nazarene's. Not even Joshua, who had defeated the combined forces of five pagan kings to lead his people into the land of Canaan, or King David who single-handedly slew Goliath in the great War of Attrition, had dared promise what the Nazarene was offering.

His coming had already been foretold by a man known and respected not only through Galilee but in All-Judaea: John the Baptist.

His story was further proof that something remarkable had already happened.

Come, Follow Me

Three

Everyone, in re-telling the story of John, invariably began with John's father being Zachariah, the priest of Ein Karem, 'Gracious Spring', a tiny village within sight of Nazareth and below Mount Orah. This was sheep-raising country and there was not a shepherd in the village who, at some time or another, had not followed one of the tracks into the foothills to that historic place where David had slain Goliath.

Like them, he too had been a shepherd, the youngest of the eight sons of Jesse and destined for an uneventful life until that day the Prophet Samuel anointed David's head with oil, 'and the Spirit of the Lord came mightily upon David from that day forward'. And there a place in history might still have passed him by but for his momentous encounter with the Philistine giant. With his heavy brass armour and wielding a sword most men could not even have lifted, Goliath was a fearful sight as he paraded before the Israelite army of King Saul. Arriving at the scene of the impending battle, the boy David had persuaded the king to let him challenge Goliath in one-to-one combat. Saul, desperate enough to try anything, and visibly moved by David's faith, agreed. Equipped only with his shepherd's stave, a sling and five smooth stones in his pouch, he stepped on to the battlefield. There was not a boy in Ein Karem, indeed in the whole of Israel, who could not describe what happened then: Goliath's astonishment turning to raucous laughter; the giant lumbering forward, the clank of his armour loud and menacing; David circling, all the time staying just out of reach of Goliath's flailing sword; Goliath's fury growing with each blow that missed. Then: standing as calm as if he was driving off a dog harassing his sheep, David loaded a stone in the sling and, with unerring accuracy, hit Goliath squarely on the small area of exposed forehead where his helmet ended and the top of his nose armour began. Goliath dropped to the ground, stunned. David raced forward, grabbed the giant's sword with both hands and, with one blow, severed

Goliath's head. The Philistines had turned and run. David's name became synonymous with the Hebrew for hero.

His subsequent years were every bit as dramatic as the killing of Goliath. He fell out with Saul shortly after marrying one of the king's daughters, Michal. His bride helped him escape the King's execution squad and David began the life of a fugitive, hiding in the hills, never sleeping in the same cave twice. Gradually he gathered a growing band of fugitives from Saul's wrath and turned them into a lethal guerrilla force, the first of its kind. David's marauders fought and won battle after battle against Saul's superior forces.

Saul retaliated by marrying off Michal to another man. In turn, David took another wife, then a second. But there had been little time for domestic repose. David found himself caught up in the civil war which ensued following the death of Saul. The land was split between Judah in the south and Israel in the north. David set about reuniting the country, a task which would take him many years. Central to his plan was to turn Jerusalem into a capital acceptable to all Jews. Until then it had remained a pagan enclave in Jewish territory – a virtually impregnable stronghold built on a ridge surrounded by steep valleys on three sides. David took the city in a brilliantly executed night attack, his first and greatest success as newly-crowned king of his reunited people.

He then decided to turn Jerusalem into the religious centre of the nation by installing the sacred Ark of the Covenant within its walls. He then began to expand the borders of his Kingdom so that they stretched north beyond Damascus, in the east to the edge of the Arabian desert, to the south as far as the warm waters of the Gulf of Aqaba, and in the west to the shores of the Mediterranean.

In that momentous time, almost 1,000 years before Ein Karem would also find its place in legend. David had become the most powerful king his people had ever crowned, commanding an army unsurpassed in numbers and skills. But a lifetime of attaining what had seemed impossible had left their mark: David began to display signs of the melancholia which had once gripped Saul. David decided the time had come to abdicate in favour of Solomon. The new king would recall how David had reminded him to 'follow the Lord's commandments and walk before him in truth, and to be strong and show yourself a man.'

Down the centuries had come many a man and woman imbued with David's characteristics: his physical toughness, his shrewdness at negotiating, his passion and compassion, his love of family, poetry and music, his courage equalled by his faith and humility.

In the tiny hamlet of Ein Karem, there were many who saw some of those qualities in Zachariah's wife, Elizabeth. She was the only one among their community who could claim a lineage all the way back to the Royal House of David. Further, her own father's genealogy could be traced back to one of the twenty-four families of the sons of Aaron who were responsible in rotation for the services in the Temple. That would have earned her further respect. Her own name in Hebrew meant, 'God is my oath', and at no time in her long life would she need to live up to that more than during the event which was about to place her centre stage.

Zachariah – in Hebrew, 'whom God remembers' – had an equally respectable pedigree. He came from a long line of the *abijah* section of the priesthood, among the most devout and scrupulous in their observance of the Law. From time to time Zachariah took his turn to travel to Jerusalem and serve in the Temple. Elizabeth invariably travelled with him.

She had been married to Zachariah long enough to accept they would end their days childless, despite the repeated entreaties they had made in their visits to the Temple. At each Passover they had gone to the Courtyard of the Altar and handed over their sacrificial dove to one of the priest-sacrificers. After watching the bird consumed in the great open furnace, they had come home and once more prayed that their home beside the synagogue would be blessed with a child.

During the latter stages of those long years of barrenness, Elizabeth had begun to share her disappointment with her young relative, Mary, the wife of Nazareth's carpenter, Joseph.

Mary was in her teens and herself the child of elderly parents, Joachim and Anna. Nothing is known of him or his antecedents. Anna came from a priestly family with connections to the Temple. Mary herself may have been in Sepphoris in Galilee before, at an early age, she had travelled to Galilee to be close to her future husband, Joseph. By popular consensus he was a kindly, understanding, humble and deeply-religious man. His age, like much else about him was indeterminable, save that he was 'elderly'. That a man of advanced years would take a young wife was not exceptional but it may account why Mary was also without child.

In their meetings, both women could well have agreed that Elizabeth should continue to ask for intercession, a custom most barren women followed, by continuing to offer animal sacrifice at the Temple.

Then, in the year it was once more Zachariah's turn to serve at the Great Altar, an event occurred which would forever change their lives.

Zachariah was by then well into his seventies and very likely stiff-legged from rheumatism, a common complaint in the climatic extremes of Judaea. More certain, he had never lost his reverence for the religious ceremonies: the rubric of the sacrifice, the utterance of the ancient prayers, the swinging of his own censer holding the burning, pungent spices whose smoke cast its own spell over those who handed him their sacrificial birds and animals.

Time and again he would have climbed the walkways around the Great Altar, a forty-foot square slab of polished rock rising above the walls of the Temple courtyards, so that its flames could be seen from all over Jerusalem.

A thriving centre for commerce when Rome was a village, Jerusalem remained a city of great wealth and nothing could rob it of its unique importance to every religious Jew throughout the Diaspora. Each male Jew annually paid a half-shekel tax to maintain the city and the Temple which every Jew had to visit at least once in his or her lifetime to give thanks to the Lord.

In this well-ordered world, the priests were a powerful, hereditary group, the descendants of Aaron, the brother of Moses. Effectively they ran the Temple, providing the music, carrying water for ablutions and conducting the services, but they had no teaching role or authority to pronounce on matters of religious doctrine or practice. That belonged to the rabbis, the religious teachers: it had been so since Moses had given the priestly function to Aaron. Aaron had shared with Moses the receipt of later commands from God, the authentication of miracles, and leadership over the people of Israel. Though he may have lacked the spiritual grandeur of Moses, he was the ideal person to protect the traditions of Jewish faith. His two sons, Eleazar and Ithamar, founded the two priestly orders which became the most powerful in the Temple. One of them, the Zadokites, claimed Zachariah as a member.

In his ceremonial robes Zachariah was a revered figure, performing sacred duties as an anointed servant of the living Lord. The sacrifices at the Great Altar were very different from those offered in the nearby Antonia Fortress, the massive edifice of the Roman garrison. Sacrifices inside its walls were to pagan gods. Those offered up at the Great Altar were in thanks to the True God.

Zachariah had been coming to the end of his long day, the atmosphere redolent of swift, methodical action, the business of slaughtering and despatching, when an event occurred which produced a spate of stories which eventually made their way to Magdala.

Mary Magdalene could not fail to have been riveted by them; they were unassailable confirmation that God did indeed move in mysterious ways.

These accounts had started with a description of how Zachariah had gone down the steps beneath the Temple and stumbled past the bakers preparing the votive cakes from wheat and barley and the holy shew-bread for the priests, past the perfume-makers at their vats, the dye-makers and weavers, and the gold- and silversmiths. An invisible and all-powerful force had drawn him on through the vast underground complex where hundreds of men worked in an atmosphere of shadows, noise and bustle. Some, no doubt, would have made obeisance as the old priest in his flapping robes had staggered on past them. And then, at some point, Zachariah had a momentous encounter, one that had left him literally speechless. Retracing his steps, his mouth had worked, but no sound came.

Emerging into the Courtyard of the Altar, the flames of its furnace smouldering against the gathering night, Zachariah had struggled out of his robes and staggered from the sacrificial area. He badly needed to share the news of what had happened with the one person above all he trusted – his loving and faithful Elizabeth.

But when they met, words still would not come. Almost desperate, Zachariah had snatched a wax tablet and stylus, writing implements. He had used them to write a sentence which would ensure them both a place in history. 'An angel has spoken to me.'

No doubt fearful now for her husband's sanity, even safety, for to make such a claim, even for a priest in the sanctified walls of the Temple, was blasphemy indeed, Elizabeth had quickly led Zachariah to where their donkeys awaited and had begun the long journey back to Ein Karem.

During three long days and nights they journeyed back to Galilee, always a dangerous and difficult journey, for the hills were alive with marauding money-lenders, tax-collectors and Zealots waiting to ambush Herod's troops. Led by their commander, Molath, the tetrarch's soldiers had no compunction about robbing their own people, even killing those who resisted.

But Zachariah and Elizabeth reached the safety of their home, he still not having spoken a word, she clutching the wax tablet on which was written that extraordinary claim: an angel of the Lord had spoken to her husband.

The story would have been remarkable enough, but now it took on elements that verged on the truly mystical.

Hardly had they crossed the courtyard of their home than Zachariah had once more reached for his own writing materials and set down the rest of what the messenger from God had told him in the Temple.

For centuries the people of Israel had believed they were guided and protected by angels. To Jews all angels were the agents and instruments of God's will: they carried out his orders and delivered his messages. The second greatest of them all was Gabriel, one of the seven archangels, and the messenger of divine comfort. Gabriel was only superseded by Michael, whose very name in Hebrew translated as 'who is like God.' Michael was the appointed guardian of Israel. He had earned his pre-eminent position after challenging Satan who had accused Moses of murder and being unworthy of burial. There was not a Jewish child who couldn't recount the thrilling story of how Michael and his angels had taken on the Devil and his hordes and driven them out of Heaven.

Zachariah showed Elizabeth what he had written.

'Do not be afraid, Zachariah, your prayer has been heard. Your wife Elizabeth is to bear you a son and you must name him John. He will be your joy and delight and many will rejoice at his birth, for he will be great in the sight of the Lord; he must drink no wine, no strong drink. Even from his mother's womb he will be filled with the Holy Spirit.'

Elizabeth's reaction gave a human dimension to a story she had been unable to keep to herself. She told friends how she had first laughed in hysterical disbelief, and then wept. And her neighbours recounted how she had asked Zachariah, her disparaging tone all too clear, whether the angel had given his name.

Zachariah had scratched on his wax tablet: Gabriel.

That was the moment, Elizabeth had said, when she realized that here was veritable proof of the Scriptural truth that angels did speak to humans. No one, not even her husband, would have dared invent such a name for his heavenly visitor.

Gabriel was the angel who normally interpreted visions. But now, according to what may have been Zachariah's understandably shaking hand as he continued to write, Gabriel had foretold that John would 'bring back many of the sons of Israel to the Lord their God. With the spirit and power of Elijah, he will go before him to turn the hearts of fathers towards their children and the disobedient back to the wisdom that the virtuous have, preparing for the Lord a people fit for him.'

The encounter between the archangel had ended with a rebuke from Gabriel:

'Listen! Since you have not believed my words, which will come true at their appointed time, you will be silenced and have no power of speech until this has happened.'

The people of Ein Karem were stunned and then perplexed by

all this. How could Elizabeth, already well into the foothills of old age, possibly produce a child? And though she was undoubtedly filled with the grace of God, why had Gabriel chosen her? There were other women in the village who were also barren but of more realistic child-bearing years.

But, week by week, visible proof that Elizabeth was indeed pregnant became manifestly true. And her neighbours' perplexity turned to bewilderment and then joy. A new life was always to be welcomed. Villagers began to adjust, to accept when, in the sixth month of Elizabeth's pregnancy Mary, the wife of Joseph the carpenter in Nazareth, arrived.

Even in an area noted for its religious fervour, Mary was renowned for her simple and uncomplicated faith. For as long as her neighbours had known the daughter of the widowed Anna, they had remarked upon her steadfast claim that one day she would be chosen to serve the Lord in a special way. In keeping with her straightforward manner, Mary admitted she had no inkling what that role would be, only she was certain it would happen in the lifetime of her husband, Joseph. Beyond that she would not be drawn.

But now, in the shadow of the synagogue and Ein Karem, she stunned villagers with the news that she, too, was pregnant as a result of a visit from Gabriel who had told her: 'For with God nothing will be impossible.'

Because of Joseph's advanced years, she had come to stay with Elizabeth to avoid the prying eyes and malicious tongues in Nazareth who whispered the child could not be Joseph's and that Mary was guilty of the greatest sin a wife could commit – unfaithfulness.

In Ein Karem she had found a more understanding community; having come to accept how Elizabeth had conceived, its villagers saw no reason to doubt Mary when she made an equally stunning announcement:

'My soul magnifies the Lord! And my spirit rejoices in God, my Saviour. For behold, all generations shall call me blessed. For he that is mighty has done great things for me; and holy is his name.'

*　*　*

With those words, a young girl, hitherto unknown to the world, had reserved for herself a place forever in the redemption of humanity – God's act of liberation from sin. She became the exemplar of the person ready to accept the word of God. For her nothing else mattered. She had not stopped and wondered why she had been chosen. Any fear she had felt – perhaps incredulity would be a better word – had been removed by Gabriel's promise she had 'found favour with God'. Her premonition had finally come true.

Three months later, Elizabeth gave birth to a lusty, screaming son. Zachariah helped to bathe his son and rub his body with salt to harden the skin. On the eighth day, he had the boy circumcised and wrote down the infant's name on a tablet: John.

At that moment Zachariah regained his speech.

A few months later, Mary gave birth to her son. She called him Jesus.

Mary fulfilled the duty of every Jewish mother, to purify herself again after giving birth. Only then could she and Joseph take their baby to Jerusalem to present him to the Lord by offering a sacrifice of a pair of turtle doves. The custom was to 'redeem' or buy back every first-born male child from God to whom his life was owed (whence came the idea of 'redemption').

Once more the Temple would serve as a background to a momentous encounter. Simeon, a devout old Jew singled out Mary and Joseph and said he had waited all his life for this moment – the precursor to the deliverance of Israel.

Taking the child, Jesus, in his arms, Simeon prayed: 'My eyes have seen the salvation which you have prepared for all the nations to see, a light to enlighten the pagans and the glory of your people Israel.'

Handing the infant back to his mother Simeon, after blessing both parents, added a prophecy that thirty years later had made Mary Magdalene ponder among much else whether the Messiah had indeed come to Capernaum. 'Behold, this child is set for the fall and rising of many in Israel.'

* * *

Through the words of that old man – nothing else is known about Simeon except his advanced years – comes the eternal prehistory of Jesus. His birth is the final coming together of the many messianic currents in the Old Testament: the prediction in the first translation of the Hebrew Bible into Greek, the Septuagint, that the Messiah would be born of a virgin; the words of Isaiah that the Servant of the Lord would come to give his own life as a guilt-offering for the failings of all others. And not only his own people, but the pagans expected him. The Roman historian, Tacitus, predicted that 'from Judaea was to come the master and ruler of the world'. The Fourth Ecologue of Virgil recounted that 'a chaste women will smile on her infant boy with whom the Iron Age would pass away.' But it had been left to the otherwise unknown Simeon to articulate Jesus' impact from birth onwards.

The world would never be the same again. It had been divided into two parts: the one before his birth; the other that would follow it. And, in that separation, Jesus showed from the very beginning he is different from all the other great prophets. They were born to live. He came into the world to die. Death, for Jesus, was to be from the outset the overwhelming reason he was born – to die that others could be saved: 'Mine eyes have seen the salvation which you have prepared.'

No mere mortal man could have dared to promise that. But Jesus even in his mother's arms, was inviting, the world to make a choice: either to reject or to accept him as True God. There could be no half measure. With acceptance would come the guarantee he would crush sin, remove the fear of death – and offer eternal redemption from sin.

Simeon had been the first to see the choice being offered. Jesus had been born as a human being, though without sin. And, through that sinlessness, he could remove all other sin. That was the glorious promise in the brief encounter between an old man coming to the end of his earthly days and a new-born infant in swaddling clothes. In their meeting was the timeless truth that God writes his name on the soul of every man, women and child from the moment of birth.

Remarkable though the circumstances surrounding both the pregnancies of Elizabeth and Mary were, they were by no means unique. The Greeks were convinced that Perseus owned his power because he was the son of the virgin, Danae, whom Zeus made pregnant. And the same great god had fathered another son, this time with a mortal woman, Acame, after assuming the form of her own husband. The child was Hercules. Aeneas was the son of the goddess Aphrodite and an earthly man. Achilles was the son of a Nereid married to a mortal. And when Rhea Silvia had taken Mars as her lover, their offspring had been Romulus and Remus. More recently, Plato, Aristotle, and even Alexander the Great – who had passed near Magdala on his way to Damascus – were all believed to be of divine origin.

All these events can indeed be accepted only through faith. Who can doubt that Mary Magdalene, when she finally heard the story of the births of John and Jesus, could only regard the accounts as further evidence God wished them to remain incomprehensible in order that the faith of those who accepted them should be that much stronger?

By the time he was close to his thirtieth birthday, John had been living a hermit's life, clothed in a camel's hide, surviving mostly on wild honey and locust beans since he had left Ein Karem and travelled east to the banks of the river Jordan. After the death of both his parents, he had become a man who had no interest in earthly comforts. At the Jordan he began to preach.

In the year John started his ministry, the new Roman procurator, Pontius Pilate, arrived and John began to speak of divine anger that God's people should still be in bondage. He also began to warn of the imminence of the Day of Judgment. All those who failed to repent would perish. Repentance could only come through being baptized in the Jordan.

Baptism as such was not new. In India, Brahmins believed evil, like disease, could be washed away by immersion in the waters of the holy river Ganges. In Judaism too, the use of water was common to purifactory ritual.

But John's baptisms were very different. They symbolized the total separation from the profane world and an admission to one of new purity. His baptisms were a prerequisite for entry to the Kingdom of Heaven.

For a while John preached and baptized at a caravan staging post on the way to Jerusalem, a collection of hovels around the five wells of Aenon, known as the 'place of the spring'. Later he moved a little further south, to a place called Bethabara where a ferry crossed back and forth between the provinces of Judaea and Perea. This was not an ideal place to carry out immersion because in the rainy season the Jordan was flooded. John moved about a mile downstream where he found what he was looking for: smooth, clean water.

It was there he started to give voice to the coming of the Messiah, standing in the waters of the Jordan, raising his massive bronzed arms heavenward he uttered through his tangled beard words which had become a mantra of hope for all Jews who wished to be free of their oppressors.

'He that comes after me whose sandals I am not worthy to untie is mightier than I. He shall baptize you with the Holy Spirit and with fire.'

To those he attracted, John resembled a heroic figure: Elijah. Those who left the river bank with his uncompromising message ringing in their ears – repent! – would have found a description of John in their Scripture: 'Here is my herald, whom I send on ahead of you, and he will prepare your way. A voice crying aloud in the wilderness: prepare a way for the Lord; clear a path for him.'

John, eager not to have expectations wrongly raised, began to insist: 'I am a voice crying aloud in the wilderness', and 'After me comes one who is mightier than I.'

Then, in a brave effort to make clear that the one who was coming would not bring political solutions, John continued to remind them that the Expected One would first and foremost look to people to liberate their own hearts and minds by repentance.

That the underlying message was truly heroic there can be no doubt; that it was just as easily misunderstood is equally certain. For those increasing numbers who came to stand on the bank of the muddy Jordan to patiently await their turn to be baptized, all they heard was John's promise that the Messiah was coming.

While John's promise of what baptism offered was new to Jews, his linking it with the coming of the Messiah was not. Every king of Israel had been anointed with oil at his inauguration and proclaimed to be the Messiah – the Anointed One (in Greek, *Christos*). David had been the most famous to hold the title and through his actions had given it a powerful aura of romance and glamour. Down the centuries, the Anointed One had come to symbolize the Deliverer who would rescue the Jews from the cruel tyranny of occupation. While the Davidic dynasty had briefly fulfilled that promise, subsequent dynasties had not. Indeed the most recent, the Herodian, was the most hated because the Herods were no more than creatures of Rome. In the Scripture John articulated, there was the recurring theme that the line of David would once more come forward to save Israel. That one of his king's descendants would be the new Messiah.

A year before Jesus had walked from Nazareth to the bank of the Jordan where John continued to baptize. Many witnessed what followed when the two met and stood face to face.

The crowd fell suddenly silent, as if they too recognized the momentous importance of the occasion. There had been a quiet deference about the request from Jesus to be baptized. John's response contained a ringing certainty: it was *he* who should be baptized by Jesus.

Jesus' answer was filled with implications: 'Leave it like this for the time being; it is fitting that we should, in this way, do all that righteousness demands.'

John then baptized his cousin.

Jesus was fulfilling another part of the promise that had begun with his birth. He was identifying himself with the sins of all humanity, allowing himself to be included in Isaiah's prediction that the Messiah would be 'numbered with the transgressors'.

While Jesus had no sin to repent and be washed away, he was showing that to be able to truly call himself the 'Son of Man', he had to embrace the guilty. By being immersed in the murky waters of the Jordan, he was revealing the purity of the salvation he was offering. The act of baptism was his promise to be at one with the victims of sin – because that was the only way he could free them from it. His baptism marked the end of his private life and the onset of his public ministry. He had entered the world as a human being. But Jesus was also revealed as God come to earth in that moment John baptized him.

As the pair emerged from the water, the onlookers were convinced they saw a pure white dove descend and hover for a moment. Folding its wings, the bird settled on the shoulder of Jesus. Then, as it flew away, the hushed crowd would insist they heard an unseen voice cry out. 'This is my beloved Son in whom I am well pleased.'

In the same respectful silence, the crowd followed as Jesus went with John into his cave. The onlookers crowded close to the entrance trying to catch the exchanges between the two men, no doubt hoping for an explanation for the extraordinary events they had just witnessed.

Among them were the brothers, Andrew and Simon (soon to be called Peter), with James and John, the sons of Zebedee, as well as the youthful Philip. They were all fishermen from Capernaum and knew each other well – and in fact all worked for Zebedee, a man of some substance who could afford to employ men to fish for him. For some years Zebedee had been contracted to supply fish to the High Priest's palace in Jerusalem.

They had much in common, not least their Galilean accents which were a matter of endless mockery to snobbish Jerusalemites who ridiculed the way their country brethren spoke. Galileans had a propensity to drop their alephs which made them sound as if they were confusing a donkey (hamar) with wine (hamar), or even a lamb (immar). Names too could be confusing – Lazarus in Galilean patois was 'Lazar' or even 'Laze'.

Inside the cave, almost lost in the gloom, John and Jesus squatted opposite each.

* * *

While the actual words between them have escaped record, this may have been the moment Jesus revealed the true purpose of the baptism: it had been to identify himself with the guilt of all humanity; to recognize that was the only way he could begin his mission of salvation. To do so he would live among the sinful and offer God's forgiveness to them. Through his baptism he would carry the great bundle of all their collective guilt.

That voice the crowd had heard was announcing him as the everlasting link between heaven and earth, symbolized by the dove. Historically the bird had always been the humblest form of sacrifice open to the poorest; when Jesus' own mother had given thanks at the Temple, her offering had been a dove. While the act of baptism had forever united him with all people, the presence of the dove confirmed his readiness to be sacrificed in their name. In addition, since God's Holy Spirit had first hovered over the waters of chaos in the creation story of Genesis, the dove had been taken as a symbol of the Spirit.

In that cave, facing Jesus, John may have been the first to hear first hand how Jesus intended to implement his earthly reign. The sheer breath-taking scale of what the Baptist learned would later make him pronounce he was unworthy to untie the shoes of Jesus. All those years of being 'a voice crying aloud in the wilderness' had been worthwhile. John had indeed been the herald which the ancient prophets had said would one day foretell the coming of the Messiah. It was a role John was both grateful and humbled to have been given.

When Jesus emerged from the cave, he walked up to the men from Capernaum, searching each face in turn. Then he told them to wait there until he returned.

Jesus began to walk south, away from the river delta into the arid wastes of the greatest of all Judean deserts. The wilderness was enervating, inchoate; a place of deep ravines, beds of treacherous shale, miles of blistering sand and temperatures high enough almost to boil blood during the day and, at night, icy cold to freeze a man's breath on his lips. It was a place of prowling leopards and dangerous wild boars who could rip out a man's entrails with one jab of their tusks.

Caravan traders who were forced to negotiate the wilderness on their way to and from Egypt spoke of being enveloped in its total and deafening silence. Not so much as a blade of grass softened the earth beneath which God himself had once engulfed the immoral souls of the people of Sodom and Gomorrah. At night the silent desolation was broken only by jackals howling in the mountains that seemed to stretch forever beyond the Sea of Salt or the sudden unnerving sound of a slab of asphalt breaking free from the lake bed and shooting to the surface.

From remembered times prophets had gone to the wilderness to purify their bodies.

It was there that Moses and Elijah had gone, to prepare themselves, to receive the strength which only great trial and testing can produce. So it was for Jesus. He had gone there to steel himself to become the sacrificial victim for sin. In the vastness of the wilderness he had done battle with the ultimate force of evil – the devil. He had done so for forty days and nights, living off the berries and the brackish water found in caves.

The way tradition retold the story, it is not hard to imagine them circling one another like two fighters, Satan dancing and weaving, using his dark supernatural powers to conjure up images and all the time offering blandishments to seek an opening. And Jesus, watchful and resolute, ready to counter the first deadly moves that would destroy him and all he stood for. It was a battle of the minds, in the mind, and one like no other.

Suddenly, the story goes, the devil pointed to stones that resembled the flat loaves of the region. 'If you are the Son of God, make those stones become bread.'

It was a shrewdly delivered temptation, designed to examine the human reality of the starving Jesus, to show that, perhaps at the flick of a finger, he would stop behaving like a man – subjecting himself to the ardours of the wilderness – and show he was God.

But Jesus would not be drawn into proving himself to Satan.

Instead he answered with the words Moses had used when manna had fallen from the sky at the time his people had been starving in the desert after fleeing from Egypt. 'Man cannot live on bread alone; he lives on every word that God utters.'

Jesus was saying he would never use miraculous powers for his own benefit – but only to save others. Neither had he come to earth to fill people's stomachs. He was here to claim their souls. Bread was important as long as people never forgot that the power to assuage the greatest hunger of all, spiritual hunger, came from God. Without that no amount of earthly satisfaction could remove their inner emptiness.

Rebuffed but far from defeated, Satan moved to another tack. He took Jesus to the highest peak in the wilderness. For a moment they stood, side by side, staring down at the rock piles far below. Then, almost casually, the devil said, 'Throw yourself down.'

Then he quoted Scripture back at Jesus. 'God will put his angels in charge of you and they will support you in their arms, for fear you should strike your foot against a stone.'

The taunt in the challenge was all too clear. Why should Jesus go through all the pain and torment he had chosen as a way to convince people, when all he needed to do was jump and, just before he hit the ground, save himself? That would surely get people's attention! And he would be showing the power of God to protect. Then people would surely follow him.

Jesus' answer was short and to the point. 'Scripture says again, you are not to put the Lord your God to the test.'

Jesus would refuse to display his omnipotence by trickery. The way to true faith was by sacrifice, not manipulations; not with sorcery, but with the reasoning of free will – the only way to the world he was announcing.

If Satan was disappointed, he did not show it. Instead he delivered his third temptation with all the aplomb of a master conjurer. The devil showed Jesus in a flash all the kingdoms of the world. 'All this dominion will I give to you,' he said, 'and the glory that goes with it; for it has been put in my hands and I can give it to anyone I choose. You have only to do homage to me and it shall be yours.'

Satan was offering a deal: he and Jesus could co-exist if they *could not actually work together, at least live side by side. In other words, the status quo would remain as it was.*

But Jesus would have none of it. 'Begone, Satan! Scripture says, you shall do homage to the Lord your God and worship him alone.'

Such a stark rejection would have stunned Satan. All his blandishments meant nothing – because they were not his to give. All the devil could offer was the old sinful ways of the world. Jesus was promising a new peace of mind – one that would rid people of their past. One that would see come true the injunction: 'Begone, Satan!'

And there, in the wilderness, Satan had indeed gone from Jesus – for the moment defeated.

For Jesus, overcoming temptation was as important as baptism had been. He did so because the reward was manifestly so great: 'Happy the man who remains steadfast under trial, for having passed the test he will receive for his prize the gift of life promised to those who love God.'

In confronting the devil, Jesus had deliberately exposed his human defences to their ultimate test. What was at stake was not only the temptation of earthly sin, but the far greater temptation for Jesus to give up his divine mission. In not doing so, he had 'himself passed through the test of suffering'. That was the only way he could help all those who would believe in him. Through his own experiences in the wilderness, Jesus was showing that salvation had a cost, though it was freely offered.

Afterwards, so tradition tells, Jesus made his way past the eerie mists of the Dead Sea and the Herodian fortress of Masada, back to the place on the bank of the Jordan where he had left the fishermen from Capernaum. They had been patiently waiting. From there they had all trekked the long way up into Galilee.

Again, what passed between them on that journey has escaped record. But they would have questioned Jesus – how could they not? – about what had happened in the wilderness. And he would

77

have taken the opportunity to impart the true meaning of his time there: that for each of them, as indeed with all humanity, understanding and coping with temptation was a prerequisite for the life he had come to offer. Overcoming temptation would strengthen the soul and character of each one of them. Temptation would always be there, invisible, beguiling and often offering short-term rewards. It would emerge in all kinds of guises: lust, greed, power; it would remain with them until the grave. The only way to resist temptation was to confront it. And to believe in Jesus' power to overcome it. Whether the disciples could begin to understand what he was saying is problematic. Would they not see Jesus as the son of Mary: a human being, however compelling?

Very probably trying to answer that question was what made Mary Magdalene decide to travel to Capernaum and see for herself what kind of man the Nazarene was.

She herself may well have come to a crossroads in her own life. She was still young and also intelligent. She could see there was no real future for her; she would die, old before her years, almost certainly raddled with the diseases of her profession.

Like everyone else in Magdala, she had heard the reports about what Jesus had done in Nazareth and then Capernaum. Many of her neighbours had dismissed those actions as the outlandish behaviour of another of the Galilean itinerant preachers. History was full of men who claimed they had been sent by God; each one had proven to be cruelly mistaken.

Yet something about the Nazarene *was* different. He spoke differently from all the other rabbis who roamed the hills beyond Magdala. He seemed to be saying if people could prove him wrong then he was the greatest liar who had ever lived. Yet those who had seen and heard him speak did not seem to be saying that – far from it. They said he was different.

That may have been the exciting thought that decided Mary Magdalene to begin her momentous journey. The one certainty is that as she set out from Magdala she could have no inkling how it would end.

Four

Mary Magdalene made the journey on foot, walking north along the shore of the Sea of Galilee. Like any other woman, she would have worn a cloak for modesty's sake, its hood covering her head. The only visible sign of her wealth would be her sandals. Only the highborn or rich wore them; most women went barefoot.

In the mind's eye of legend, Mary Magdalene had the economical stride of her people; they were used to walking considerable distances. Leaving Magdala, she may have begun to sing; women often did as they set off on an exciting journey and certainly few could have equalled the sense of purpose Mary Magdalene must have felt. If curiosity had been her original motive, every stride would surely have reinforced her expectations. What otherwise could have persuaded her to rise at an hour when the other harlots of Magdala would be still asleep and begin the long walk to Capernaum?

Minutes after leaving Magdala she found herself walking between vineyards and olive groves. Beyond were fields of wheat and root crops. Away to her right was the great lake, at this early hour dotted with fishing boats returning to their harbours with a night's catch. The flap of their sails catching the wind of sunrise was a comforting reminder of the timelessness of life along the shore. For centuries it had been like this, as well defined as the track beaten out by the plodding hooves of laden asses and camels.

Their drovers would likely have given Mary Magdalene no more than a cursory glance as they passed. A woman out alone was a common sight, going about some domestic chore: perhaps to collect firewood or gather fruits and vegetables from the family smallholding.

Clear of the fields she encountered the first of the streams tumbling down from the hills and often bridged with no more than fir-tree trunks. The sound of rushing water would be a constant one for the greater part of her journey.

The dwellings she passed were altogether more modest than those in Magdala. Squat and square, with walls made from stones and mud covered with a thick white plaster, the houses were without windows and their flat roofs were formed by reeds plucked from the lake and laid on tree branches. The whole was coated with a mixture of mud and stone and allowed to harden in the sun. The roof provided a terrace reached by an external staircase. People slept there on all but the coldest of nights with the strongest member of the family positioned closest to the top of the stairs, ready to repel intruders. The houses were grouped together in twos and threes, sharing a common courtyard with its clay oven for making bread from the small grain-grinding mill.

Directly ahead of Mary Magdalene rose the peaks of Upper Galilee. Few people of the lakeshore ventured up among those crags and precipices. Lower Galilee, with its milder climate and lower hills, was an altogether friendlier place where men could fish, raise herds and flocks and cultivate orchards of pomegranates and olives.

Capernaum acted as a natural geological divide between Upper and Lower Galilee, marked by the fault break in the ground. When the earth had been still young, the ground almost immediately beyond Capernaum had been forced up several thousand feet by volcanic activity.

Lower Galilee remained in many ways a powerful reminder of the history of Mary Magdalene's people. The broad sweep of the great Plain of Esdraelon had been the scene of Barak's and Gideon's glorious victories, and also the place where Saul and Josiah had met bitter defeats. Not more than an hour from where she walked was where Judas Maccabeus had assembled his forces to march upon Jerusalem. Even closer was where Jezebel, the most notorious of female Biblical characters, a name which had long become symbolic of human depravity, met her terrible death, fulfilling the prophet Elijah's prediction that wild dogs would eat her.

And, across the lake, lay the forbidden valley of the Jordan; like Upper Galilee, it was a place not to be visited unless absolutely necessary, an untamed area of wild animals where only holy men or the half-mad lived. So people believed.

Wherever Mary Magdalene looked was a reminder of some event which had produced the historical writings, legends and folk-tales, prophecies and proverbs which ensured her people's life had been woven into a sacred anthology. At its centre was their covenant with a universal God. Everything else depended on accepting that totality. When her ancestors had been pillaged by pagan armies, when this very ground she walked upon had been blighted by plague and poor harvests, when the fish had risen to float, dead, in their millions on the lake's surface: when all this and much more had happened, it was because the Lord had been angry with her people for failing to honour that covenant.

That was why her people consistently refused to create demigods out of their heroes. Even the kings of Israel were not above God's law and were treated as such. David, the hero who had destroyed Goliath, was also remembered as the man who later behaved shamefully, seducing Bathsheba, the young wife of one of his officers. Having made her pregnant, David sent her husband on a mission, knowing he would be killed. And there had been Jacob, another national hero, who had tricked his old, blind father Isaac into giving him the position of head of the family upon Isaac's death, when it should rightfully have gone to his elder brother, Esau. There was a memory at every twist and turn in the path she trod.

Early though the hour, many others had also started their own journeys to avoid the enervating heat of the day. At noon it could be hot enough to dip a fish in olive oil and bake it on a rock. After their meal, people sought the nearest shelter until the sun lost some of its power.

The literate among them read the books of Moses. Since the emergence of first John and then Jesus, they had done so with renewed eagerness to see if what they had heard corresponded to the predictions in Scripture. Some of the lakeshore people had been among the crowd who had asked John the Baptist a repeated question: was he the Expected One? Instead John had reached far back into his people's history to find a suitable symbol. He had said, 'the Lamb of God is the one who takes away the sins of our world.'

John had first spoken those words after baptizing Jesus.

The symbolism of the image would not have been lost on his listeners. The lamb had always been close to the Jewish faith. Abel had used one as a sacrifice to expiate sin. The suggestion of a lamb had been there when God had asked Abraham to sacrifice his own son, Isaac. From Genesis onwards the lamb had been used as an offering and, most notably, the Passover Lamb had come to represent Israel's deliverance from out of Egypt.

But John was now saying something very different when he spoke of the Lamb of God. He was revealing that Jesus had not merely come to lift the yoke of physical enslavement epitomized by the Roman occupation; he had come to sacrifice himself so that all others, for all time, could be free from sin.

Would those who pondered the predictions also understand that the forgiveness of sin was not merely through animal sacrifice, as Abel had tried to achieve? Only through redemptive suffering would true spiritual freedom come.

That same concept lay at the heart of Mary Magdalene's own journey to faith along the Galilee shores.

Capernaum was about six miles from Magdala. In between were several small clusters of houses where fishermen and their families lived. Their women eked out a living by offering travellers water and food. At these lakeshore dwellings, Mary Magdalene would surely have heard further reports about Jesus. His defeat of Satan in the wilderness had placed him, in the eyes of these simple, devout people, on a par with Samson whom legend claimed had gone there and single-handedly slain ten thousand of Israel's enemies with the jawbone of an ass.

To these people Jesus was now cast in a similar mould. There was no greater opponent than Satan; his very name was still spoken of in a hushed whisper. The great prophet, Job, had not named the Devil when he had acted as his public prosecutor before God; even King David himself had been tempted by Satan. Time and again the Evil One had shown himself to be more powerful and malevolent than all the combined demons of the pagan world. They were visible, cast in stone and wood, to be seen and avoided. But Satan could make himself invisible as he pleased, only to manifest himself in human form, weaving his temptations, bewitching at one moment with his seductive skills, and the next terrifying with his most obscene guises.

Originally, so every Israelite believed, Satan's function had been to point out their failings to God. But he had been cast out from the Almighty's presence after trying to usurp the authority of God himself. Since then he had roamed the earth, a veritable prince of darkness. For every child he was the ultimate fear, whose very breath could strike them dead. For adults too, he was no less threatening. Satan was the god of excrement, the bringer of plagues, the curse upon the land. Even the Pharisees, who had an answer for everything, had no prayer capable of defeating *Ba'al Zebub*, the Lord of the Flies.

Yet the Nazarene had single-handedly confronted Satan in the wilderness, his home. He called him 'the evil one', 'the father of lies', 'a murderer from the beginning with nothing to do with the truth because there is no truth in him.'

In the telling, the story of Jesus' temptations had grown: how Satan had used every trick to try and seduce the Nazarene from his beliefs and how, each time, Jesus had thwarted him. No one had ever succeeded in doing that. So how had the Nazarene achieved such a stunning victory over the Evil One? Was Jesus imbued with extraordinary powers?

The people of the lake could not answer the questions for Mary Magdalene. But they would have told her what they knew of Jesus' background.

Joseph, his putative father, had died in the earthly poverty which had dogged his whole life. The most frequent words used to describe Joseph were humble, kindly, generous, hard-working and a loving husband and father. He had never missed a synagogue service in Nazareth and may well have been present when Jesus made his now celebrated intervention. Whatever Joseph had felt about that, he had shared with no one up until the time of his own death. The exact moment and circumstances of his passing had escaped record. Joseph's other siblings had grown up and married and lived similarly modest lives either in Nazareth or one of the towns surrounding it. One was said to be settled on the slope of the hill of Moreh, another in Chorazin. Apart from James and Joseph, little is known about Jesus' four brothers and nothing of his sisters: some said there were three of these, others only two. The one certainty is they were all younger.

During their father's lifetime the boys had all worked in Joseph's carpenter shop, fashioning ploughs and yokes for the oxen teams. The girls would have helped their mother, fetching water from the village well, laying out clothes to dry in the sun, preparing the evening meal. Like all villagers, the family spoke two languages, Aramaic for daily use, and the liturgical language of Hebrew. Their intellectual development had depended on an understanding of the Scripture. Obedience would have been a cornerstone of their daily life: obedience to their parents, to their elders and, above all, to God. From early on they were taught that was the only way they could grow in grace and wisdom. It was the same in every household in Nazareth.

Like most travelling rabbis, at the onset of his Ministry Jesus had moved away from the family, though he still had a close and loving relationship with his mother and brother James; everyone who had seen the brothers together agreed that James openly adored his elder sibling.

Jesus had followed a well-trodden path for preachers, first speaking on the slopes of Mount Gilboa and Mount Tabor, and in the village of Nain nestling between. Later, he had visited Chorazin and the towns out on the Plain of Esdraelon: Megiddo, Taanach, Jezreel and Bethshan. There was not a rabbi who had not included these places in his itinerary. They came, gathered who they could, and spoke long and passionately about those parts of Scripture which fitted their themes, drawn from two sources. The Pentateuch had for some 400 years been a sacred text. It consisted of the Five Books of Moses: Genesis, Exodus, Leviticus, Numbers and Deuteronomy. The Former and Latter Prophets had been assembled some two hundred years later, starting with Joshua and Samuel, followed by the books of Isaiah, Jeremiah and Ezekiel, and concluding with twelve minor prophets including Hosea, Amos, Jonah and Malachi. The Writings, including the books of Psalms and Proverbs, were of a more philosophical and poetic nature. In all, twenty-four books formed the Hebrew Bible and combined a legal code with an intensely powerful human-interest chronicle. Galilee had long been the traditional home for recounting the most apocalyptic passages of Scripture – those which spoke of the end of the world.

The ministry of Jesus could not easily be confined within Judaic language and thought. It was filled with his personal interpretation of faith. And he continued to speak of a time, not too far away, when the Kingdom of God would be at hand. It would be one of the Spirit of God himself.

And where Nazareth had seen his humiliation, in Capernaum and elsewhere in the small Galilean towns he found the first of his followers: old men, women and children, the defenceless and the dispossessed. He spoke to them in their own language; he taught in a way they could understand. He used homely analogies to explain his message, speaking about how a hen gathers her brood under her wings and how to revive a barren fig tree; he was well-informed on the quality of yeast needed to leaven dough and interpreted a red sky at night as promising good weather for the following day.

And always he led them back to his profound knowledge of Scripture and the Law. The predictions of the Books of Moses began to live as never before as he told them that redemption had been uppermost in God's thoughts when the world was created. But to be redeemed they had to enter the Kingdom he had come to launch. Those who heard remembered that the prophet Daniel had foretold that one day would come: 'a Son of Man descending from beyond the sky to establish God's authority over all the people on earth.'

On an increasing number of lips the question Mary Magdalene had asked was repeated: Could the Nazarene possibly be that person?

And there was something else which had aroused comment. Jesus had drawn to himself a permanent band of twelve men, each of whom had immediately dropped whatever commitments they had in response to his command: 'Come, follow me.'

No other travelling preacher had created a similar circle around himself. Some were surprising to find in a rabbi's company, they were active nationalists, openly sympathetic to every aspect of the Jewish Resistance. For men like Simon, whom their Master had renamed Peter, and his younger brother, Andrew, overthrowing the Romans and Herod Antipas was a constant preoccupation. The other Simon in the group was called the Zealot, a reminder he had once served in the ranks of the guerrillas.

And there was that other object of curiosity, the group's treasurer, Judas Iscariot. Unlike the others he was not from Galilee but from far to the south, from Kerioth, a town of renowned violence close to those twin cities of wickedness, Sodom and Gomorrah. In Galilee people from that region were naturally looked upon with suspicion and anyone with a modicum of schooling knew that *Iscariot* was Aramaic for 'dagger man'.

People said he was the most militant of them all, endlessly echoing his Master's claim that the Kingdom *was* at hand. But Judas had added that the coming kingdom was of *this* world.

Among the twelve was an inner coterie: John, his brother James, and Peter. They walked beside Jesus on the treks from one preaching mission to another and stood nearest to him when he spoke. They were fishermen, strong-boned men whose sinews and hands were toughened from years of pulling in full nets. By the very nature of their work – long nights spent out on the lake – they were used to their own company. Men of few words, with little formal education, they had fished from the time they could handle an oar and cast a net.

The people of the lakeshore knew them well – and their surprise would have been genuine that these same three men had abandoned a life of guaranteed income and modest comforts to wander over the hills of Galilee in the wake of a rabbi who depended on the skills of his bagman for money.

No one knew how Judas had been drawn into the Nazarene's coterie. One day there had been eleven, then twelve. But there he was, darker-skinned than the others, squat and muscled as so many men from Kerioth were, his accent markedly different from the broad vowelly tones of the others. Galileans would not easily have understood him; Judas would not have always understood them. It would have made for an essentially lonely and misunderstood life. But there would be no doubting Judas' passionate nationalism and commitment to Jesus.

Had it been reinforced by an event which was already passing into the anecdotal claims about the Nazarene – what had happened at the marriage feast at Cana?

Cana was a considerable distance from the lakeshore and to reach it needed the best part of a long day's walk. Jesus was accompanied by his mother and his disciples to the wedding.

The ceremony was held in the early evening when the men, having returned from the fields, accompanied the bridegroom's procession to fetch the bride from her home. Dressed in his finest robe, the groom wore a crown as Solomon had done at his nuptials. The bride's hair had been freshly washed and hennaed, her face hidden behind a veil. Both were carried through the streets on a litter, the guests singing songs dating back to King David's time.

At the wedding the rabbi offered traditional blessings, each invocation repeated in turn by the guests and the bridal couple sat under a canopy, the *huppah*, surrounded by a bevy of bridesmaids. Tradition demanded there should be ten.

After the ceremony the celebrations began with the guests squatting around low tables stacked with wooden platters of boiled meats and vegetables. The wine was from local vineyards. The vintages of Galilee were justifiably famed throughout the land, and Galileans were equally renowned for their capacity to drink them. Nathaniel, the caterer, and his staff moved from table to table with pitchers and jugs of fruit juices for the children.

As a sign of his growing importance, Jesus and his mother sat at the table of the bride's father. The other disciples were seated among the other guests. From the time he had emerged in public, Jesus had made it clear he had no need for alcohol. That, too, had made him different from other travelling preachers. Many had been known to drink themselves into a stupor between their preaching.

As the evening wore on, the guests became increasingly rumbustious under the heady influence of the alcohol. Suddenly Nathaniel was at his host's elbow whispering that for once he had misjudged the amount of wine that would be consumed. These were farmers and their wives; the night was warm and the food had been salty and spicy. More wine was needed to slake their thirst. But to bring vats from the caterer's store would take time.

Mary understood all too well the man's plight. There was no greater social gaffe than to invite guests, then be unable to feed and wine them properly. And already some of her fellow guests were starting to make good-natured but insistent demands to have their goblets refilled. John, one of the trio closest to Jesus, could see what was happening and caught an aside which were the opening words in a momentous saga.

Mary had turned to Jesus and said: 'They have no wine.'

And Jesus, in John's words, had responded: 'Woman, what have I to do with thee? Mine hour is not yet come.'

Was Jesus saying that, as a guest, she need not take on the responsibility for catering? Was he also insisting this was not the way he wanted to begin to show his miraculous power? But, given his close and loving relationship with his mother, Jesus would equally have wished not to disappoint her.

According to John, Mary stood up and motioned for Jesus to join her where Nathaniel and his men were draining the last of the wine into pitchers and, no doubt, wondering how best to handle a very embarrassing situation. Events took on momentum. Mary had a whispered conversation with Jesus. What passed between them would remain forever private. But an event was about to occur which would remain beyond normal human understanding.

Jesus turned to the caterer. John, who had still remained within earshot, recalled that after pointing to her son, Mary told Nathaniel: 'Do whatever he tells you.'

Her public speech went unrecorded from that time on. It was as if Mary recognized that Jesus was about to reveal the full power of his divinity and that she accepted her own role was over save for the climactic moment of the journey upon which he was already embarked.

On Jesus' instruction, the waiters filled the wine vats to the brim with water. He turned to Nathaniel and asked him to draw a ladle from one of the containers. The liquid was the colour of a mature claret. The caterer tasted it and pronounced it to be the finest wine he had ever sipped.

The already tipsy guests had drunk their fill and, no doubt, gone home happily to bed. But Nathaniel and his staff, having seen what had happened, could hardly contain themselves. Within hours, the story had spread of how Jesus had chosen the transmutation of water into wine as the first public evidence of his power.

By his very action, Jesus was also sounding a warning note, 'Mine hour is not yet come.' He was reminding everyone of his true purpose on earth. In turning water into wine, he was signalling his readiness to begin his own journey to an earthly death, secure in knowing what would follow. His decision to use the wedding to demonstrate his power was surely deliberate. Jesus was showing he was ready to announce his Messiahship – that the antiphon of his life was there for others to see. Everyone else was born to live; he had come into the world to die.

As Mary Magdalene continued to make her way along the pathway that ran the fifteen-mile length of the Sea of Galilee, she could only have pondered about all she was hearing about the man she was hoping to meet, and who continued to proclaim a message that was both repetitive, yet compelling: the Kingdom of Heaven was coming, and that to enter it, people needed to repent and believe in the good news.

The word – repent – would have struck a chord deep within Mary Magdalene. To do so meant she could begin a new life. The prospect must have sent a shiver of excitement through her. She was still young enough to appreciate what her future could be: no more empty, loveless coupling; no more growing old before her time; no more the stigma of being branded a whore; no more living outside society. The attraction of that new life was too compelling to be ignored.

Until now, Moses had been the greatest of all her people's leaders. Throughout the land he was simply known as *Moshe Rabbenu* – Moses our Teacher, our law-giver. No one else until now had the same close contact with God: 'The Lord used to speak to Moses face to face as a man speaks to his friend.'

Now, thirteen hundred years later, Jesus claimed the same relationship to reaffirm that the dark inner forces which ravage the souls of every man and woman could be exorcised by faith.

What would have appealed to Mary Magdalene, to any woman, was that Jesus spoke a great deal about the power of love. Not just the love between a man and a woman, but the love that meant being forgiving, helping others without seeking reward. That was certainly new. The harsh reality of her world was that people grabbed what they could by exploiting and manipulating. The prostitute was at the very bottom of the social scale, a necessity to be used but never remotely accepted. On that, the Sadducees and Pharisees were both agreed.

It was hard to decide which grouping she disliked the most.

The Sadducees were a politico-religious party holding the highest offices in the land. Their seat of influence was Jerusalem and the Temple. Wealthy and endowed with great earthly powers, they had so far shown themselves to be indifferent to any hopes of being delivered from their occupiers. They were the party of the Jewish Èlite.

The Pharisees were the party of the people, the descendants of the 'Holy Ones', who had fought for their religious freedom during the Greek occupation three centuries earlier. Unlike the Sadducees, they believed in angels as intermediaries between God and people, in resurrection and in judgment in the world to come. They fasted twice a week, a reminder of the days Moses went up and descended from Mount Sinai with the Ten Commandments. Observing God's laws was all that mattered to them.

How, Mary Magdalene would not have been the first to wonder, did they regard the Nazarene's bold concepts, which went so radically further than all others?

Her intention would have been to reach Capernaum before the full heat of the midday sun.

The lake was at its deepest point at Capernaum, some seven hundred feet below sea level, and the heat shimmered above its surface, in which was mirrored the snow-capped Mount Hebron, some fifty miles to the north.

The town was slightly smaller than Magdala, with a census population of 1,700 residents. But most days it was increased by camel and donkey caravans coming down through Upper Galilee from Damascus and points beyond, and by fishermen from further down the lake. They brought their catches to Capernaum to be dried in its smoke houses. The stench permeated the city and its environs.

There were a number of inns to cope with the passing trade and Mary Magdalene would have eaten in one of them. The fare was fish or lamb and the conversation normally revolved around current market prices, how safe was the route to Jerusalem and, of course, the latest iniquities of the Romans.

But there was a fresh topic – the extraordinary happenings that continued to centre on Jesus.

On a previous Sabbath he had gone to the town's synagogue, arriving just as the congregation finished reciting the Benedictions. Jesus and his followers had stood at the back of the synagogue listening as the Rabbi Yehuda finished reading from the Law and said it was time for the lesson from the Prophets. Once more Jesus had gone forward and chosen the scroll containing the words of Isaiah: 'The Spirit of the Lord is upon me, because he has anointed me to bring good news to the poor. He has sent me to announce to the prisoners that they will be liberated, and to the blind they will see again; to send away in freedom those who have been broken in life; to announce the year when the favour of God has come.'

There was a timeless certainty about the words that no one could object to. But suddenly Jesus galvanized his listeners – just as he had done in the Nazareth synagogue. He told the Capernaum congregation. 'Today this passage in Scripture has come true as you listened.'

Then he had calmly walked out of the synagogue. In Nazareth they had threatened him. But in Capernaum people stared, curious and uncertain. As the evening shadows gathered, Jesus had stood in the town square and preached on a subject no one had ever challenged before: the accepted concept of the Sabbath. Jesus made it clear he did not object to it being a day of rest; indeed it was a necessary pause for everyone to remember God was the Creator of all things. But what once more set his listeners agog was when Jesus began to denounce the Sabbath as it presently stood.

What was the sense in the Law saying it was permissible for a person to walk, for example, the length of the lake, but not a yard further? Where was the logic that someone could write one, but not two letters on the Sabbath? What religious basis could there be for allowing a housewife to fasten a rope to her bucket but not actually to walk to the well to draw water on that day? Why was it possible for a musician to mend a broken string but not replace it with a new one? For food to be eaten but not prepared? For vinegar to be used to relieve a headache but not spat out? Where, Jesus demanded, was any of this written in the Word? How could doing any of those things possibly offend the Lord their God? In a sentence which, days later, was still being endlessly debated, Jesus had told the people of Capernaum: 'The Sabbath is made for man, not man for the Sabbath.'

He concluded with a familiar peroration. 'I bring you the good news for which you have all awaited. God today fulfils the promise he made to our people. Whoever believes this will be free for all time from the captivity of sin. Mark this day as the day of forgiveness.'

Men who had asked questions at the time – for it was always men who did the questioning – repeated them now as Mary Magdalene sat in the cool of a Capernaum inn. What had the Nazarene meant about fulfilling a promise God had made? And this good news – how could he guarantee that? Or free them from captivity? The Nazarene had only a handful of men. How could they take on the Romans, the tetrarch's troops – anyone?

The questions were still being debated when, from outside the inn, came a commotion.

Mary Magdalene joined the others who rushed outside. A man was shouting that, a few hours ago on the road to Nain, a miracle had happened. The Nazarene had rid his son of demons which had possessed the youth from birth. As the crowd gathered, the man continued to tell his story. As much as he loved him, his son was a raving lunatic, strong beyond his years with the strength of a wild animal. They had been travelling back from Nain when they had come upon the Nazarene and his followers resting by the wayside. Immediately his son had started to crouch as if he was about to attack. Some of the Nazarene's men had picked up their staves and formed a protective circle around their Master. Waving them away and ignoring the youth for a moment, the Nazarene had asked the father in a calm and quiet voice if he believed in the coming of the Kingdom. The father had admitted he didn't understand the question, but if this kingdom could calm his son, then yes, he believed.

By now the boy was writhing and foaming at the mouth. But, when several of the Nazarene's men tried to drive him away, their Master rebuked them. Once more turning to the boy's father, Jesus had spoken. 'Everything is possible to him who believes.'

In the streets of Capernaum men looked at each other in astonishment. Here was another of the perplexing sayings of the Nazarene. 'Your son,' one of the onlookers prompted the father, 'what happened to him?' The man, no doubt savouring the moment, explained how Jesus knelt and placed one hand on the youth's head. Then, in a sharp, imperious voice the Nazarene had said: 'Be gone, Satan. Leave the pit of hell you have placed inside this boy. Leave him – now!'

The boy had immediately gone into terrible convulsions before, after a final paroxysm, falling asleep. After for a short while, Jesus told the youth to awaken. When he opened his eyes, the madness was no longer in the boy's eyes.

In the crowd in Capernaum, an old man spoke for many when he pronounced that, while restoring the boy to normality was commendable, there was a danger in what had happened. Tampering with Satan could well lead the devil to commit further excesses.

Angry at this turn of events, the father turned to the crowd. 'The Nazarene anticipated you would think that! So he said to me that it was impossible for Satan to cast out Satan. But that if a kingdom is divided against itself, then it is bound to collapse. No: it is through the Kingdom of God that he had cast out demons. And he did so that you might know that the Kingdom of God is upon you.'

Once more the onlookers looked at each other, mystified. There were those words again – the Kingdom of God is upon you. But where was it? Question him as they did, the boy's father could provide no answer other than Jesus' dogged insistence everything was possible if you believed.

Could that explain what had happened shortly before Jesus left Capernaum? The story itself was every bit as remarkable as the account of the boy's father.

Peter had asked if he could help his mother-in-law. She was elderly and had spent all her life next to one of the fish-curing factories which, with its pungent fumes, may well have been the cause of her sickness. Over the years, doctors in Capernaum had prescribed every known remedy. Potions had been made from the crushed brain of an owl, fish heads, and the legs of a lake frog. But nothing, not even massaging the urine of unweaned calves on her body, had eased the debilitating stomach cramps and the swelling in her legs. One by one her body functions had failed.

Jesus had gone to her bedside and held her hand. For a moment, like the youth on the road to Nain, she had stared with hostility at him. Suddenly the old woman's face had cleared and she had smiled. Her pain had gone, and for the first time in years, she rose from her bed. Neighbours were astounded.

They supported the father's story, inviting anyone who doubted it to visit Peter's mother-in-law.

Those first miracles, like all those which followed, were firmly anchored in a belief in redemption. Those who believed would not only be physically cured, but also receive spiritual relief. In time, Jesus helped so many that: 'If it were all to be recorded in detail, the whole world could not hold the book that would be written.'

Yet no matter how many miracles he performed, there would still be those who would refuse to accept him. They would fail to understand that no miracle was possible without its accompanying belief in him.

Surely that realization was the overwhelming reason for Mary Magdalene to leave Capernaum and take the track up into the hills towards the town of Nain? That evening Jesus had been invited to sit down at the table of the most important man in Nain, Simon the Pharisee. Beyond Capernaum the track forked. The one to the south led to Jerusalem. On an ass rode a man who had listened to the accounts of the exorcism by the boy's father and the curing of Peter's mother-in-law. That man was an agent of the Temple.

Five

At noon, as it did every day, the mournful sound of a horn drifted out across the Second Temple in Jerusalem. The first Temple had been destroyed by Nebuchadnezzar in 586 BC. Built by Herod the Great, the Second Temple was an enormous structure, designed on three irregular levels, each becoming progressively higher and smaller, its golden dome dominating Jerusalem. Standing on a plateau in the east of the city, the structure was deliberately intended to intimidate and impress. To pilgrims it was the very symbol of their faith.

As the black-robed priest continued to play a melody which dug deep into the turbulent history of his people – the sound had first been heard as Moses led his people out of Egypt – Temple guards, under the watchful eye of their commander, Jonathan, emerged from the Inner Temple and positioned a podium in front of the Nicanor Gate. The massive gateway divided the sacrosanct Court of the Priests from all those courtyards of the Outer Temple.

There, commerce ruled. Scores of moneychangers operated in their own pillared courtyard where pilgrims exchanged pagan Roman denars into the Jewish shekel, the only coinage allowed within the Temple. At its thirteen gates, herbalists had booths where they sold a range of potions and ointments to the afflicted. In the Temple courtyards were dozens of scholars and rabbis who, for a fee, interpreted Scripture for the untutored.

These wise men were most in demand in the Courtyard of the Women, a cruciform space surrounded by four chambers where a wife could consult a scholar in semi-privacy for the appropriate words of divine intervention for her to conceive, or a widow find succour in her bereavement from verses a rabbi would select.

A broad stairway led down from the Women's Court to a vast trapezoidal courtyard, open to everyone, even the heathens. This was the Court of the Gentiles. The largest of all the courtyards, it was bounded on one side by one hundred and sixty-two pillars of white marble, each as thick as a ram's body, with capitals formed in the Corinthian style. This was the only part of the Temple with a visible foreign influence in its architecture. Here pagans co-mingled with the faithful in an impious atmosphere where almost anything that could be bought or sold, was. This secular area provided the Temple proper with a significant portion of its income through the tax collected on each sale.

No woman could pass beyond her courtyard into other areas of the complex. If she had a sacrifice to make, she bought it from the vendors licensed to sell in the women's courtyard, and then handed it to one of the priests waiting at the steps which led up into the Courtyard of the Altar. The other courtyards in the Temple also had arched openings leading into the sacrificial area.

The Great Altar, a massive slab of polished stone, had ramps and walkways leading to the roaring sacrificial open furnace at the top. To the left was the immense bronze basin in which priests purified their hands and feet and drew water for other ritual purposes. The water was replenished from huge cisterns beneath the Temple, themselves connected to a system of aqueducts leading to underground springs in the surrounding hills.

To the right of the altar worked the sacrificial butchers, slaughtering and preparing animals for the flames. Boys constantly swept away the blood and offal into the drainage system beneath the Temple. On an average day there could be up to ten thousand pilgrims coming and going through the outer courtyards to make sacrifices. On festivals, their number trebled.

No one could have failed to glance towards the brooding edifice which overlooked the courtyards. Only the patrolling centurions on its ramparts gave a clue that this was the Antonia Fortress, the bastion of the occupying power in the city. Within its keep was a permanent garrison of some five hundred troops. Since early morning the fortress courtyard had echoed with their sounds.

But, at the first sound of the horn, silence had also fallen over the Antonia. Even the sentries had turned their backs on the Temple.

The gesture was a small but significant indication of the

current relationship between the occupiers and the occupied – part of the live-and-let-live accommodation between a self-serving Pontius Pilate and the High Priest of the Temple, Joseph Caiaphas. Both men were well versed in political realities. Neither, not for a moment, could have suspected that the consequences of their pact would soon sweep away their world forever – and that the precursor for that happening was already underway in Galilee.

Within the Temple complex, the sound of the horn, followed by the positioning of the podium provoked an immediate response.

Through the Water Gate, through which the flagon of holy liquid was brought for the libation at the Feast of Tabernacles; the Mourner's Gate, restricted for the recently bereaved to come and worship; the Bridegroom's Gate, used only by newly-weds; the Eastern Gate, through which the Ark had first come into the Temple: through every one of the outer gates, pilgrims came to stand before the most sacred gate of all – the Nicanor.

This was the gate which protected the most divine place in Judaism – a sanctuary of which it was said, 'whenever it is written in the Bible, "before God", it is here.'

Proportioned in perfect symmetry, a full fifty feet in height, the twin doors of the gates were cast from bronze and decorated with a filigree of vine leaves. Each door was a foot thick, sufficient to resist the most powerful of battering-rams. Every morning and evening it needed a dozen Temple guards to open and shut them. The top of the wall into which the Nicanor Gate was set was out of reach of any scaling ladder.

Those protective measures were designed so that, in the event of an enemy threatening the Temple, the High Priest and his priests would have sufficient time to remove the Temple's precious artefacts and make good their escape through an underground passage which eventually led up into the hills. The escape route had been created so that, by a pull of a lever, it would cave in after the last priest reached safety.

As with almost everything else which happened beyond the

Nicanor Gate, those assembling before it had no knowledge of the escape route.

At the first sound of the horn, vendors covered with sacking the cages containing sacrifices. On and around the Great Altar all activity stopped. Pilgrims who had been haggling with herbalists at the Gate of Singing, the Kindling Gate and the Firstlings' Gate hurried to stand before the Nicanor Gate. They were joined by the scribes and judges from the various religious law courts. Every man and boy who was of age stopped what he was doing, donned his prayer shawl and held in his hand the small black box containing passages of Scripture. It had been so since the Second Temple had been rededicated and pronounced free of all heathen contamination.

Visible beyond the Nicanor Gate was the very core of the Temple. Approached by twelve steps, each representing one of the original tribes of Israel, the towering structure was supported by four massive pillars. This was the outer façade of the Holy of Holies.

There was not a man waiting before the Nicanor Gate who would not have dreamed of having sufficient wealth to be able to pay for a gold leaf or a solid gold cluster of grapes to be added to the golden trellis which hid the Holy of Holies from view.

Only the High Priest could make the offering of incense in this sanctified place, tend to the seven-branded candlestick and set out shewbread on its special table. And even he could not pull aside the double curtain hiding the innermost sanctuary from view. Inviolable, invisible to all, this was where the True God resided on earth.

From the Temple roof the lament continued to play, slow and sonorous, a reminder that at this moment time itself did not matter in an earthly sense – only for the Lord.

As the silence settled, Jonathan himself stood still and watchful. He bore a proud name – in Hebrew it meant 'Given by God' – and, since the Second Temple was built, there had been a Jonathan who had commanded the Temple guards. The first Jonathan had been Saul's son and a daring and successful young officer in his army. His many distinguished feats in battle against the Philistines ensured his name would be forever commemorated by being given to that of the Temple guard commander upon his appointment.

Dressed in the imposing regalia of a Jewish warrior, Jonathan waited until complete silence had fallen over the crowd tightly packed before the podium. Only then did he turn and lead his guards back into the Inner Temple. Moments later he reappeared, accompanied by a magnificently-robed figure.

This was Joseph Caiaphas, as High Priest, the single most important figure for all Jews everywhere. His authority extended to the furthest corner of the Empire. It was Caiaphas, not Tiberius in Rome, who was the spiritual leader of ten million Jews within the Diaspora.

Within the Temple, he exercised total authority over more than twenty thousand men. There were one hundred chief priests, each with equal status to the three Treasurers who administered the Temple finances. Next came seven thousand two hundred consecrated priests. Ranking below them were twelve thousand Levites who assisted with the sacrifices, collected Temple dues from the vendors, supervised the daily rate set for the moneychangers and overall, had general custody of the Temple. They were assisted by five hundred clerks and ushers to the religious courts.

Jonathan had a force of seven hundred guards. Their responsibilities extended to protecting more than a thousand singers and musicians, as well as the bakers and the other artisans who toiled beneath the Temple in their kitchens and workshops. These numbered some five hundred. Finally came the cleaners, the fetchers-and-carriers. This lowest rung in the Temple hierarchy ran close to another thousand persons.

There was a separate group, some six hundred in number, who also worked within the Temple. They were the judges of religious courts and the scribes, each one a specialist in explaining how the Law must be interpreted. Their authority was founded in the Book of Nehemiah when Ezra had appointed himself as the first scribe.

Joseph Caiaphas had enjoyed a brief but promising career as a scribe until he chose the priesthood to further his legal career. His day of ordination had begun with a ritual bath in perfumed water. Dressed in a new white linen robe, he made three animal sacrifices: a bullock and two rams. After slitting their throats, he placed his hands upon the carcasses and asked God to accept them.

The High Priest of the Temple had taken blood from each animal, mixed it with holy oil and anointed Caiaphas, receiving him into religious life with prayers which Moses first spoke. Ram's fat, unleavened bread and a cake baked from flour and olive oil had been ceremoniously placed on Caiaphas' open palms and exposed thighs. Afterwards these offerings were consumed in the fire of the Great Altar.

When Caiaphas had himself become High Priest, the ceremonies were even more elaborate. The three Treasurers had anointed him with the Temple's most precious perfume, a drop of which cost more than the yearly levy a Jew could expect to pay in tax. The ritual sacrifices were spread over six days to commemorate the time God had needed to create the earth.

On the last day, standing before the entire assembled staff at the Nicanor Gate, Joseph Caiaphas had solemnly promised he would never eat meat or drink wine before any service and to protect the Temple by every means at his command.

No one could doubt he did so.

As usual, his appearance at the noon hour would have been the first sight the waiting crowd would have seen of him. Already an intimidating figure through the office he held, Caiaphas was more so because he was clearly a man used to his world revolving around him. His ceremonial robe, with its gold tassels at its fringes, enhanced the power he exuded.

Caiaphas was now in his middle years. He could trace his family history back to the ruling families who traced their lineage from the original Twelve Tribes of Israel who had settled in Canaan. Those families had controlled the lives of the exiles in Babylon, keeping their faith alive. Joseph Caiaphas was rooted in history and precedent. Because of who he was and the background he came from, his choice of wife had been restricted. Tradition demanded he could only marry the daughter of a priest of the Temple and, given his exalted background, preferably one from within the family of the ruling High Priest.

Twenty years ago, when he had been appointed as a judge to the Little Sanhedrin, the Temple's lower court, Caiaphas had married Rachel, the youngest daughter of Annas, whose family had held the high priesthood for almost half a century. There had been two children from the union, a son, Matthias, and a daughter, Rebekah. Matthias had followed his father into Temple service and was a scribe.

Approaching the podium, Caiaphas would have seen his son among the other scribes who had their own special enclave for the brief ceremony which was about to begin. In another roped-off area among the judges would have been Annas. No longer High Priest, he still wielded considerable influence inside the Temple. Beyond its walls, Rome had dealt less kindly with the family. Annas' own six sons and himself had all been dismissed from the office of High Priest. Each time the charge had been a refusal to bend to the Imperial will.

Among the other black-robed judges were two Caiaphas would have viewed with mixed feelings. One was Gamaliel, from the Hebrew 'Reward of God'. He was the pupil and grandson of the legendary scholar and doctor of the Law, Hillel. Following his mentor's teaching, Gamaliel was the recognized liberal of the Great Sanhedrin, usually erring on the side of mercy when it came to justice. He was one of the seven judges honoured with the supreme title of Rabban. In terms of jurisprudence it gave the same status as Caiaphas.

The second judge was Nicodemus whose name was derived from the Greek, 'Victor over the people'. He had also established a name for being merciful. Older than Gamaliel and Caiaphas, his reputation as a thinker was reflected over many years by his judgments. Like Gamaliel his verdicts had often contradicted the conservative views of Caiaphas.

Gamaliel and Nicodemus were Pharisees, the minority group in the Great Sanhedrin. But both judges had little in common with their kinfolk in Galilee who were rigid in their religious outlook. In many ways, the Pharisees of Galilee echoed the conservatism of Caiaphas, the Sadducee.

Joseph Caiaphas had been appointed High Priest by Pontius Pilate's predecessor, Valerius Gratus, an unusually brutal Procurator even by Imperial standards. After the Temple sent a delegation to Rome to protest against the last increase in taxation, Gratus publicly crucified a hundred priests in Jerusalem.

It was the first time such cruelty had been used against the Jewish religious establishment and the sounds of the long-drawn agony of the victims had filled the city for several days. Each naked man was suspended on a t-shaped cross so his feet rested just clear of the ground to die in yet another blasphemy against their faith; in the Torah it was forbidden to strip priests naked, let alone scourge them so that flesh hung in strips. Moreover, a death by crucifixion was cursed by Torah.

The following year Joseph Caiaphas became High Priest. He presided over a Temple which reflected a national anxiety that it could be polluted by some new idolatry, despite the new Procurator, Pilate, promising there would be no further acts of sacrilege, such as displaying Roman military standards within the city, or allowing his soldiers to peer into the Temple during its various ceremonies.

Caiaphas had reached these agreements by skilled and persistent negotiations, persuading Pilate that as long as the Temple remained sacrosanct, he would guarantee Jewish compliance with the wishes of Rome in all secular matters. The arrangement suited both sides.

In the nine years he had been in office, Caiaphas had maintained this balancing act at the cost of considerable personal odium. He knew the Romans looked upon him with contempt, as little more than their creature. His relationship with Herod Antipas was icy. To the Pharisees, Caiaphas' accommodation was seen as a further example of how far into bondage the Jewish people had sunk. To an increasing number of the population, he was also a figure of revulsion because of the way he had exploited his office for personal gain.

The High Priests had always benefited from the flourishing

trade in Temple sacrifices, but Caiaphas had substantially increased his percentage on the sale of each bird or animal. He had also raised the tithe on all profits made by those licensed to trade in the Temple. These sanctions had made him one of the richest men in the land. His office also appointed every priest in the Temple. It was another way for him to exercise control and be, at all times, fully aware of what was happening. His intelligence was reinforced by the reports of a small army of agents – spies – who constantly roamed the countryside and reported to him all that they had seen and heard.

But, for the moment, that would have been forgotten when his voice broke the complete silence in the Court of the Israelites and began to deliver the timeless words of the noon-day prayer, the *Shema*, which Moses, the giver of the Law, had first spoken.

Voices, piping and deep, wavering and strong, united in the responses.

The truly moving moment over, Joseph Caiaphas descended from the podium and walked back through the Nicanor Gate.

Behind him normal activity resumed.

Before entering his office, a number of interconnected salons, Caiaphas performed another ritual. He went to the purification pool adjoining his work place. Stripped naked, he immersed himself in a tub set in marble surrounds on which stood several vats containing holy oils.

His steward, Ithamar, poured an amount into the water so that once more Caiaphas would be spiritually purified after going outside the hallowed Courtyard of the Priests. Ithamar was another who bore, in the service of the Temple, an honoured name. The first to do so had been consecrated as a priest by Moses and given the task of listing the gifts for the first Tabernacle and supervising their transport out of Egypt. An Ithamar had attended every High Priest since the office had been created 800 years previously. The post called for a confidante as well as a flunkey.

In the time he would have soaked, Joseph Caiaphas may well have pondered that, despite all the contempt and revulsion directed towards him, under his influence the Temple remained tangible proof that a strict observance of the Law was essential. The Law was what separated the Jew from all pagans.

The calls for more autonomy; freedom from burdensome taxation; the religious divergencies which had always been there, but were now coming to the surface; renewed attempts by the Pharisees to redefine the organization's structure of the Temple so as to give them more say and power: all this could be resisted by a proper interpretation of the Law. Ultimately, that power resided in him. He was the final arbiter, God's own voice on earth.

As long as he stayed in office, the Sadducees would remain a conservative organization, defending the interests of the Temple against all comers. It was of no consequence that its members did not have a strong rural base, like the Pharisees. All that mattered was that the core of Sadducee power was the Temple. Joseph Caiaphas believed he had been chosen to ensure no one threatened that advantage.

He also believed the Pharisees failed to understand the socio-economic, political and ideological realities of living under an occupying power. To speak out, let alone condemn and anathematize Rome, could greatly affect the Temple's position – could even see it destroyed.

Equally, he accepted he ruled over a Temple polarized between irreconcilable tendencies. But as long as he remained the final interpreter of the Law, ultimately it would not matter. His lawyer's skills would tell him when to push, when to move ahead and when, most importantly of all, to do nothing. He knew when to reaffirm the ancient truths and yet appear to leave open the door for some other viewpoint; when to be authoritarian in the face of radicals.

Those who said he lacked the determination and decisiveness of his father-in-law, Annas, did not understand that Joseph Caiaphas operated by far more subtler methods. He was devious, manipulative and utterly ruthless. He had never been known to raise his voice. He did not need to. His authority was there in his eyes, in his every gesture. He could cow and terrify by a mere glance. He would do anything to make sure he did not go down in history as the High Priest who oversaw the dismantlement of the Second Temple.

His ritual ablutions over and dressed in the plain black robe he normally wore, Joseph Caiaphas moved to the next part of his structured day.

His chief scribe, Shem, had brought him copies of the verdicts handed down by the various lower courts. Shem, too, bore a legendary name. In Hebrew it meant 'renown'; historically, Shem was the eldest son of Noah.

The Little Sanhedrin court dealt with minor crimes – land disputes, cattle thefts and so on – in the eleven districts into which the Romans had partitioned Judaea. The Great Sanhedrin was the nation's Supreme Court of Jewish Law, not only in Judaea but throughout the Diaspora. Its competence and reputation had stood for almost four hundred years, admired first during the Persian and Greek occupations, and later by Julius Caesar himself when he had visited Jerusalem.

The Great Sanhedrin comprised senior members of the priesthood, drawn from both the Sadducees and Pharisees, together with Elders, sometimes called 'principal men of the people', and scribes. In all, the court numbered seventy-one members under the presidency of the ruling High Priest. It was rare for the Court to sit as a full body even in a particularly difficult case.

Joseph Caiaphas' work salon was a place of racks of scrolls in which were contained much of the history of Israel. The afternoon would have passed with Caiaphas reviewing the judgment scrolls, noting each one with his mark of approval. Only when that was attached was a verdict ratified.

From beyond his window opening came the constant sounds of drilling from the courtyard of the Antonia Fortress. Centurions daily practised the tactics which had made Roman soldiering the most experienced the world had known. The sounds of iron clashing with iron was deliberately meant to intimidate the occupied.

Towards evening, Joseph Caiaphas began the final part of his day. Accompanied only by Jonathan, he made his way through a number of passageways inside the very walls of the Temple up on to the roof. From where the horn-player had summoned the faithful to noon prayer, he walked first to the western corner of the building and peered out over the city and its environs.

Below him the pilgrims were streaming out of the courtyards, the flames on the Great Altar no more than glowing embers. Judges and scribes were leaving by the Royal Portico. In the Gentiles Court, Temple guards were shooing out the pagans, but not before they had paid their dues to the Levites. It was ever thus.

Beyond, Jerusalem was settling down for the night. Animals were being stabled and the first pinpricks of tallow lights were already visible in the Lower City. Outside the outer walls, the dusk was gathering pace, softening the hills.

For a moment longer, the sun burnished Caiaphas. Then, as it settled, the High Priest, on behalf of all Jews, gave thanks to the Lord for the day that was drawing to a close.

With the same measured tread, he walked to the eastern corner and asked God to bring forth another day that would bless his people. Next, he moved to the southern corner of the roof, then to the one opposite, looking north towards Galilee. At both points Caiaphas repeated the prayer.

From this great height as he looked out over the hills of Judaea, it would have been impossible to have seen the agent on his donkey who was making all speed on the journey from Capernaum. Or Mary Magdalene on her way to Nain.

Six

News of Jesus' healing of the boy and Peter's mother had preceded Mary Magdalene as she made her way towards Nain. In a world where word-of-mouth was the only means to spread news, the events had been imbued with a mystery and power which increased with each telling. Those who knew their Scriptures wondered whether the Nazarene, as people increasingly called Jesus, should be taken not as referring to his home village, but to the prophecy of Isaiah who had predicted that one day would appear a human *nezer*, 'a branch which will grow from the stump of a fallen tree and bring change the like of which the world has never seen before'.

For Galileans the presence of Jesus was also reassuring proof they were not the untutored people dismissed by sophisticated Jerusalemites. Had not the Nazarene shown those arrogant city folk the mettle of a true son of Galilee when he had gone to the Temple with his parents?

Jesus had been twelve at the time and, like every other Jewish male child of that age, he had reached the next stage of his induction into the Law. At the age of three, his mother had given him a tasselled prayer garment; at five she had taught him the first portions of Scripture, written down on Scrolls that had come down from Joseph's side of the family. On his twelfth birthday, Jesus had strapped to his left arm for the first time a phylactery, a small box containing a portion of Scripture. From then on he had worn it every time he recited his daily prayers.

The journey to Jerusalem after his twelfth birthday had been to celebrate the Passover: the Law demanded that every male must go to Jerusalem during one of the three great feasts, Pentecost and the Tabernacles being the other two. The family would have travelled with others from Nazareth, chanting processional psalms as they walked south. Like every other pilgrim, Jesus would have joined in reciting Psalm 121, rejoicing at their first sight of the Temple.

Within its walls Joseph did what every other head of a family did: choose a lamb for the Passover sacrifice. As proof that Jesus was now of legal age to partake in Temple ceremonies, he would have accompanied Joseph to the outer courts where the sacrifices were on display.

Together they would have watched the priest slit the lamb's throat and scatter its blood to the four quarters of the earth. That evening Jesus would also have watched Mary prepare the carcass for roasting by piercing it with skewers – one through the breast, the other through the forelegs, so that they formed a cross. Had a premonition of his own forthcoming fate as the Lamb of God not crossed his mind?

Next day Joseph and Mary had begun the long trek back to Nazareth. As usual, the youngsters of the village had been allowed to make part of their way home alone, yet another sign of their coming of age. They would meet up with their families a day or so later so that they could all then travel together into the foothills of Galilee, an area less than safe.

But when all the other village boys had rejoined their families, there was no sign of Jesus.

Mary and Joseph had returned to Jerusalem. There, in a training school for rabbis inside the Temple, they found their son. Jesus was not sitting among the pupils but 'surrounded by the teachers, listening to them and putting questions; and all who heard him were amazed at his intelligence and the answers he gave. His parents were astonished to see him there.'

The image of the boy Jesus sitting among the great doctors of the law – the school numbered Hillel on its faculty as well as the distinguished Rabbi Simeon – would be one of the most powerful to survive from his childhood. That he was being listened to respectfully by the teaching profession suggests that what Jesus had to say was sufficiently riveting to hold their attention. He was no pupil receiving instructions but someone who could also instruct. His parents' astonishment was understandable. Here was their boy who, only a few years before, had been taught the basic passages of Scripture, now dissecting its most complex meanings with an erudition which had amazed his learned listeners.

For Mary it was also a reminder how quickly Jesus was growing up, something she as a mother was reluctant to accept. It was there in her words, 'My son, why have you treated us like this? your father and I have been searching for you in great anxiety.'

She was telling him he was still Her child, born from her womb. To reinforce her feelings she included Joseph, 'your father and I.'

Jesus had then spoken his first reported words. He put them in a form of a question, one that contained a hint of frustration that his mother, of all people, should have forgotten the meaning of her encounter with Gabriel.

'What made you search? Did you not know that I was bound to be in my Father's house?'

The words were more than a rebuke. Jesus was reminding her that while he had been born of her, he was also the Son of God. In that moment Jesus had distanced himself from any claim of earthly parentage. It was the first indication of what he had come to achieve. In the Temple Jesus had laid down a marker for all his listeners. Now, twenty years later, Jesus – in curing the demented boy on the road to Nain and Peter's mother – had shown that what he had debated as a child with those Elders in the Temple was to be put into practice.

That the message had reached Nain cannot be in doubt. Why else would its most prominent citizen, the Pharisee Simon, had invited Jesus to dinner?

Geographically, Nain had the finest view across the Plain of Esdraelon, allowing its few hundred inhabitants to look out across what was once the private granary of the Pharaoh Neco when Egypt had ruled this land until the Babylonian Crown Prince, Nebuchadnezzar, drove him out in 609 BC.

Away to the right of the village was where Deborah had faced overwhelming odds against the Zealot general, Sisera, in 1200 BC. While she prayed for divine intervention, a thunderstorm had swept across the plain causing the usually sluggish River Kishon to overflow. Sisera's nine hundred chariots had been caught in a quagmire, enabling the fleet-of-foot Israelites to decimate them.

Nain was where the prophet Elijah rested after his own victory over the forces of Baal on the summit of Mount Carmel and, centuries later, was also the birthplace of Ohil, the officer who had been King David's camel keeper.

There were those who said that Nain and its people had not changed much in the intervening years. They were renowned for hard work, clannish behaviour and their commitment to the Pharisee way of life. Its men worked the friable loam of their fields and produced exceptional crops; Nain's olives and citrus fruits ripened a good two weeks before other crops in Galilee and were marketed for a good price to the caravan traders heading back and forth across the plain.

Strangers were given the traditional welcome but not encouraged to settle unless they were Pharisee. No man of Nain would marry into a family from elsewhere in the area unless his bride was a member of the sect. The villagers had embraced the austerity of Pharisaic belief after its founders formally declared themselves to be the 'Separated Ones'. Previously they were known as 'the Holy Ones' during their long struggle for religious freedom when the Greeks occupied the country.

There was not a farmer, shopkeeper or businessman who did not subscribe to the teachings delivered by their present spiritual leader, Theudas, the village priest. On every Sabbath he reminded his congregation of the importance of fostering synagogue life, studying the Law and its application to their own lives, constantly reminding them that was how God wanted them to show their rejection of Roman pagan rule.

This exclusion also extended to all other non-Jews who were considered to be 'outside the mercy of the God of Israel'. They were collectively known as Gentiles or *goyim*, from the Hebrew. Galilee had its Gentile enclaves which no Pharisee would ever enter.

While the Pharisees were represented in the Temple through the scribes and its quota of judges – most notably Nicodemus and Gamaliel – on the Great Sanhedrin, their influence was greatest in Galilee, where the majority of the three hundred thousand population were members of the sect. In the province's largest city, Sepphoris, Pharisees controlled the synagogues and the courts and, in the small towns, villages and hamlets on the Plain of Esdraelon, their authority was equally binding.

The self-righteousness of their views did not trouble Pharisees. Each one knew that, on every point of Scriptural interpretation, he was right. And, while they would do nothing to discourage the Zealots in their burning desire to gain Israel's freedom by force of arms, every Pharisee believed as an absolute act of faith that, when the time came, God would triumph through the Messiah.

No one held more closely to this view than Simon the Pharisee. Physically he was a man of the plain: short, dark-skinned and with eyes to match. Mostly he wore the black robes of his profession as a lawyer. His house was where the most important of Nain's Pharisees regularly met to reaffirm their own rigorous standards and decide who should be admitted to their inner circle after showing himself capable of the prescribed daily seven hours of prayer. That did not mean a man had to pray for seven hours in a synagogue, only be seen to pray, just as he must be 'seen' to fast twice a week and obey the complicated Pharisee code of food laws and Sabbath commands. Pharisees had their own belief in resurrection: at the end of time the body would physically rise from the grave, as intact as when it was placed in the ground.

Simon's voice had been heard in every court throughout Galilee, including the memorable time he had defeated the lawyers of the tetrarch in Herod Antipas' own courthouse in Tiberius.

The issue had been a land dispute. The tetrarch claimed title to a tract of ground to the west of Tiberius. There he planned to build a repository for the poll and property taxes he collected for Rome. The Pharisees feared that the tetrarch would then mint his own coin to breach the second of the Ten Commandments which prohibited not only the worship, but also the manufacture of a likeness, of any human being. Like the Roman denar which bore the ruling Emperor's face, Herod Antipas would do the same for his coinage.

While the tetrarch could simply have seized the land, that would most likely have provoked an outcry. Already the subject of deep anger among his subjects over his private life – he had discarded his own wife to live with Herodius, the wife of his brother, Philip, – Herod Antipas could not risk further confrontation into which the Romans would be drawn. That could have politically disastrous consequences for him. Herod Antipas had said he would abide by the ruling of the Court.

Simon had been retained to oppose the sale of the land to the tetrarch. For a whole day he had argued that the ground was part of the site of a cemetery; to build on such hallowed ground was a desecration against God. Citing legal tractates and Scripture, Simon had won his case. He had become the champion of all the Pharisees.

It would have been close to dusk when Mary Magdalene saw the setting sun softening the squat, white-walled houses, each with its roof dome. Compared to Magdala, Nain was small and with little to offer a traveller in the way of comforts. Dusty from her walk from Capernaum through countryside where the tetrarch's patrols were known to have their way with an unaccompanied woman, Mary Magdalene would have been eager to substantiate further reports about Jesus.

He had said, 'When you see a cloud moving from the East, you say rain is coming. When the desert wind blows, you know it will be hot. If you can read the signs in the earth and the sky, how is it that you cannot understand that the Kingdom of Heaven is upon you?'

Those who had asked what the words meant had been told, 'Unto you it is given to know that seeing you may see, and not perceive, and hearing you may hear and not understand lest at any time you should be converted and your sins forgiven.'

The Nazarene had made no further attempt to explain, beyond adding that if people could not work out the meaning, there was no place for them in the Kingdom he was proclaiming.

Another time Jesus had gathered everyone around him and, in the manner of a story-teller in a Jerusalem souk, had sat in their midst and spoken about a man who had two sons. The younger had asked for his share of his father's estate there and then. The father had promptly divided his entire wealth between his siblings. The younger son went off to various parts of the Empire and squandered his fortune on wine and women. When he had spent all he had, he was forced to work as a swineherd. For a Jew, no one could have fallen further down the social scale. The destitute youth had begged God to have his father take him back into the family, even if only as a servant.

His father threw his arms round his neck and kissed his son and told his servants to wash and dress the boy in the finest clothes. And while this was happening, the father ordered the finest fatted calf be prepared for a banquet. The elder son was on the farm. When he heard about the plans for the celebration he was angry. His father tried to calm him but the eldest boy said that he had worked all his life and he had never received so much as a kid to celebrate with his friends. The father said to his eldest son 'you are always with me. All that is mine is yours. But your brother was dead and has come to life again. He was lost and has been found. Understand that and you will understand the Kingdom of Heaven is upon you.

Jesus had asked people to apply what they had heard to their own lives. They must dedicate their lives to a credo of peace, harmony and neighbourliness, the foundation stones of the new Kingdom. But what he was offering could only be achieved through understanding that it needed more than the existing Law to be 'fulfilled.'

He was telling them that to enter upon the new life he had come to proclaim required a clear understanding and acceptance of the huge gulf between their present spiritual existence and the one he was offering. They had all been born from sin, but now they must experience a second birth, a cleansing spiritual one; without that, they had no hope of gaining admission to the new Kingdom. Each one must understand their earthly birth had made them the offspring of their parents. But their second, spiritual birth, could make them children of God.

That was exemplified by what the father in the parable had said to his earthly son. Jesus, the greatest of all teachers, had cast himself in the role of the forgiving father. It was the precursor of the words he would later speak from the Cross which would symbolize all he had come to do: 'Father, forgive them; for they know not what they do.'

But now, in the early stages of his ministry, Jesus was primarily concerned to remind everyone that they had found what they were seeking; that through him their spiritual thirst and hunger would be satisfied. It was symbolized in another parable:

When the farmer sowed, some seeds fell by the wayside and the fowls came and devoured them. Some fell upon stony places and forthwith they sprung up because they had no deepness of earth. When the sun was up they were scorched and, because they had no root, they withered away. And some fell among thorns and the thorns sprung up and choked them. But others fell into good ground that brought forth fruit.

Jesus was offering another example of how love can only be nurtured through faith; only then can its true glory and triumph be realized. Then redemption would follow as surely as the seed would flourish despite the failure of its sower.

Who then can challenge the sense of excitement which gripped Mary Magdalene as she walked into Nain? She may also have found the town agog with the news that John the Baptist had been arrested for publicly attacking Herod Antipas over his relationship with Herodius. The tetrarch's men had taken the preacher to the fortress of Machaerus, near the Sea of Salt. No prisoner had ever been known to leave the fort alive. In Nain they were saying what was being said elsewhere – in denouncing Herod's licentious ways, the Baptist had shown a courage which rivalled Elijah's when he had denounced Jezebel. John's last public utterance had been to quote the words of that other great prophet, Malachi: 'Behold I send my messenger, who shall prepare the way.'

The words, rich in implication, had triggered intense speculation in Nain, not least whether they could explain why Simon the Pharisee had invited the Nazarene to be his dinner guest.

Mary Magdalene would have known – who didn't? – that Simon did nothing by accident. He was a man who had spent his entire working life baiting traps. A few years ago he had travelled to Magdala in his horse-drawn carriage, one of the few Jews in Galilee to possess one. In the town's courthouse he had called upon a precedent dating back to Solomon to defend successfully a local businessman who had killed a thief who had broken into his home during the night. Simon had argued that a conviction was only possible under the Law if the offence had taken place in daylight when the robber could have been taken alive. Under cover of darkness, roused from his sleep, the businessman would not have known if the intruder was armed, and was entitled to kill him. Simon had won another case.

Yet even Simon could not have found a ready explanation to the one story about the Nazarene which baffled everyone. It concerned Jesus' birth.

It was at the time Herod the Great had ruled. Dying, he was gripped by a fear of betrayal, so much so that he murdered his favourite wife, her mother and two of his sons. Knowing he governed by the grace of Rome and was hated by every Jew, the more so because he was not even of their faith, his regime was so tyrannical that even Augustus Caesar had remarked it was better to be Herod's pig than his son.

In the twilight of his reign, Herod came to the conclusion there was yet another plot being fomented by Jewish nationalists. At its centre would be a first-born child who would present himself as the Messiah, the Anointed One. Herod asked his astronomers to tell him where the Expected One could be born. They had suggested Bethlehem as the most likely place, given a star had recently been seen over the town. Herod needed no reminding of the old biblical prophecy. 'A star shall rise out of Jacob and a sceptre shall spring up from Israel.'

Then, as if to confirm matters, three visitors had arrived at Herod's court, members of the ancient cult of the Magi. They too had followed the mysterious star.

Herod's interest had quickened as his visitors described how their large and well-armed caravan had crossed vast sandy wastes, scrambled through rocky gullies and forded swollen rivers along the way. They had fought off fierce attacks from the Kurdish mountain tribes and the warriors of the lowlands of the Tigris. They had passed by Babylon and crossed the battlefield where Alexander had conquered Darius. Turning north, still following the star, they had plodded on across the blistering desert of Mesopotamia, on through Aleppo and Palmeria, and on down into Syria. From there they had entered Judaea, keeping to the east of the Sea of Galilee, taking the well-trodden caravan route along the banks of the Jordan, crossing the river at the ford near Jericho. When they reached the opposite bank, the star had disappeared.

Despite his incipient brutality, Herod realized that to follow his normal custom and torture further information from the Magi would lead to a battle. Given his visitors' army was camped in his own courtyard, he could not guarantee victory. Instead he had summoned his own advisers to conclave with the Magi. After deliberating for several days, they all agreed that, according to the fifth chapter of the holy Scripture of Micah, the Anointed One would be born in Bethlehem. Herod had one question: had the Messiah yet arrived?

The Magi said they would find out – and return to tell him. Their caravan of camels loped out of Jerusalem to cover the scant few miles to Bethlehem. Leaving their force camped at a well outside the village – the same watering hole where Mary and Joseph had slaked their thirst during their unsuccessful search for a room at a Bethlehem inn – the Magi saw once more, faintly visible, the star which had brought them half-way across their world.

It seemed to be hovering over a cave a little distance away. Scrambling over the stony ground, past shepherds watching over their flocks, they reached the cavern. Inside they found Mary and Joseph and a new-born child. They had given gifts to the infant – the kind only offered to royalty. There was gold, the symbol of divinity; frankincense, the potent incense used only on the most religious occasions; myrrh, the spice used to embalm the dead.

It is not difficult to imagine the joy and relief of the Magi. Their long mission was over. Now a more earthly demand intruded, a need for sleep before preparing for the long journey home. As they curled up on the ground outside the cave, the Magi heard in their dreams the same voice telling them not to return to Jerusalem but to warn the parents that Herod intended to kill Mary's first-born. After the Magi had done so, they helped the family to prepared their escape. A donkey, supplies and money were provided for the family to hasten south, down beyond the Dead Sea, across the sands of Sinai and into the safety of Egypt. The Magi themselves headed back across the Jordan – whither, no one would ever be certain.

Back in Jerusalem Herod grew impatient for their return. He sent his court chamberlain to discover what was happening in Bethlehem. The official returned with news the Magi had vanished – and that Bethlehem was full of incredible stories about the birth of a very special child. Herod send his most skilled interrogator to ferret out more details. But the tight-lipped Bethlehemites, sensing trouble, denied all knowledge of the child. Herod ordered the immediate slaughter of all new-born male children in Bethlehem.

In all, some forty infants were massacred. It was this one heinous crime which would ensure the name of Herod would live on through history, forever mocking the epithet after his name 'the Great'.

The account would provoke very different responses. There were, at the time Mary Magdalene made her way into Nain, those who, whether from faulty memory or some other reason, would say the terrible slaughter never happened; that the story was a further attempt, not that it was needed, to reinforce the sheer wickedness of Herod. That claim would survive down the centuries.

Others would later insist the slaughter not only happened, but that it was the precursor for the blood Jesus himself shed; that from the very time of his birth, the shadow of death had loomed over him.

The very choice of delivery room, a filthy manger, was deliberate, intended to emphasize his own purity. Born among animals, he would later be killed by men behaving worse than any beast. In a cold cave, which shepherds used only when there was no other place to shelter their flocks, he was delivered. The Magi who called upon him had to stoop to enter the cave. It was a reminder of their humility and readiness to accept that before them, cradled in a mother's arms, was a foundation of the new Kingdom. That was why they showered him with gifts.

That cave became the bridge between heaven and earth, the place where, for the first time, people looked upon God in human form. 'So the Word became flesh and dwelt among us.'

The Magi were the first to understand that they were in the presence of the One through whom the human race would have a chance to start a new life.

Now, some thirty years after Jesus' birth, Mary Magdalene continued to take her own steps towards partaking in it.

Simon's home was in the northern part of Nain. The walls around the house were sufficiently high to keep passers-by from looking in, and the arched gateway was usually guarded to keep out intruders. Like everywhere else, the rich and powerful guarded their privacy.

That evening, however, the gates were wide open, an invitation for the people of Nain to witness the public debate between Jesus and Simon. It would be held over dinner, the traditional time for such an important discourse.

The finest foods and wines had been laid out on low tables in the centre of the courtyard. In a corner, Simon's wife supervised her maids preparing soups, meats and vegetables, the staple of all banquets. Nothing had been stinted to make this a memorable occasion.

By the time Mary Magdalene arrived, the area around the

tables was filled with spectators intently following the discussions between Jesus and his host. Likely their exchanges began with a subject over which there could not be any dispute; the latest excesses of the Romans and the tetrarch. It was a never-ending matter for discussion, how they used brutality whenever their power was challenged, bled the land for their exorbitant tribute, and gorged off every Jew like horseflies. But one day they too would be gone.

But how and when? It may have been Simon who had let the question drop into the conversation. Or one of his carefully-chosen guests. It would have been put casually, in the way such questions were. And it would have been directed at Jesus.

As the guest of honour he would have been placed opposite Simon. His disciples would have been among the onlookers.

There were Peter and Andrew, both with the swaying gait of fishermen who had spent their working lives in a boat as it criss-crossed the Sea of Galilee. James and John, like many a man of Nazareth, had broad shoulders and muscular torsos. The tall, spare-framed man was Thaddeus, and the one with the fairest of all beards, Philip, was fired with the impetuousness of youth.

People said it had been Philip who had planted the idea for Matthew to follow the Nazarene. But then other people said it was the other way around; that Matthew was already a member of the group and had enlisted Philip. Bartholomew had a face which appeared even paler because of his magnificent jet-black beard. James the Less lived up to his name, being of slight build. And there was Thomas, whom Matthew had nicknamed Didymus, the twin.

Towering over them all was Simon the Zealot; a good half-head taller than even Peter or John. Even in his bare feet, Simon looked as imperious as an emperor. Finally, standing a little apart from the others, dressed in a short-sleeved *kilbur*, the linen tunic which marked him out as a man from Kerioth, was Judas.

Jesus had chosen them all as a further proof he had not come to be served, but to serve. Through them he hoped to exemplify that the simplest way to salvation was to have the faith of a child. Belief in him was everything. Without such belief there was no possible hope of entering the Kingdom of Heaven. But, as he was about to show, belief required humility.

In the light from the dried reed torches and tallow burning in bowls, the apostles would have seen Mary Magdalene, sensing she was as much a stranger as they were, judging by the looks she attracted.

The villagers from Nain, in the instinctive sly way of those parts, knew that not only was she from some other part of Galilee, but how she earned her living. There may even had been men watching and listening to the unfolding events around the tables who had paid for her favours. It was a common practice for the men of the plain to journey to towns like Magdala to seek sexual satisfaction when their wives were ritually 'unclean'. Like Mary Magdalene they were all avidly following the intensifying debate between Jesus and Simon.

Did Jesus agree that the title 'Messiah' could equally well be applied to either the ruling High Priest or, if the Jews had one, to their king? When David had become king, had not Samuel also pronounced him to be a Messiah? And was that not also true of all the kings who had followed? Had not those vassals of Rome, the succession of High Priests, claimed the title, each being anointed as the Priest Messiah?

Did not the very word, Messiah, need to assume some wider meaning? Should it not, for example, be applied not so much to a corrupt High Priest like Caiaphas, but perhaps to a 'Deliverer' – someone who could rescue the Jews from being subjugated to the pagan power of Rome?

Once more the question would have been casually put by Simon, a lawyer's way of asking, to see how far matters could be pushed to test the mettle of the man seated opposite him.

Seeing that Jesus would not be drawn, Simon had developed his theme, one well-honed by frequent repetition. It was perfectly true that every self-respecting Pharisee believed one day God himself would save Israel. But was it not also equally true that the idea of a divine Messiah was sacrilege? Did not Moses forbid the worship of any human being? And had not this refusal to worship the pagan figures of the Ancient World, from the Pharaohs down to the deities of Rome, brought much suffering on the Jews?

Jesus had replied in a characteristic manner. 'They that are whole have no need of the physician, but they who are sick, do.'

Simon may well have smiled his lawyer's smile. What did Jesus mean by those words? The reply could also have sent a shiver of excitement through Mary Magdalene, 'I came not to call the righteous, but sinners to repentance.'

Simon pounced. Was Jesus saying he was against the Pharisee principle of casting out all sinners?

Jesus replied he was opposed to all narrow-minded puritanism which forbade the fullest freedom to prepare for the coming Kingdom.

Once more Simon pressed. 'This Kingdom – on whose priestly authority is this being proclaimed?'

'For therefore I am sent,' Jesus calmly replied.

'By whom?' Simon had sensed an opening.

Jesus would not be drawn.

Thwarted, Simon moved to another tack. Those words – 'For therefore I am sent' – had a familiar ring. The Baptist had used them often. Was his guest no more than an echo of a man most people thought was mad, and was now languishing in the tetrarch's dungeons for his pains?

Again Jesus remained silent, intent on his meal.

'Tell me, Rabbi,' demanded Simon, 'why do the followers of the Baptist often fast, but you eat and drink so freely?'

This time Jesus had not hesitated. 'Can you make the bridegroom's friends fast while the bridegroom is with them?'

The response could only have astounded Simon. Every Pharisee knew that the relationship between God and Israel was often depicted as that of bridegroom and bride. The prophet Hosea had heard God speak to Israel in unforgettable terms.

'I will betroth you to myself for ever, betroth you in lawful devotion and love; I will betroth you to myself to have and to hold and you can know the Lord.'

Incredulous, Simon had asked another question. 'Was Jesus saying he was God?'

But again Jesus would not be drawn.

The style of the lawyer, momentarily defeated by the response, survived with Simon's next question. 'Was Jesus' response a clever way to avoid really revealing what he thought about John the Baptist?'

Jesus replied with words he had used before when faced with a challenge.

'I say unto you, among them who are born of woman, there has not risen a greater one than John the Baptist; notwithstanding he that is least in the Kingdom of Heaven is greater than he.'

Simon knew the word 'Heaven' was synonymous with God. In the apocalyptic and prophetic passages of Scripture there were repeated predictions for the inaugurations of a new Order when God would rout the forces of darkness. But these prophecies were nowadays generally interpreted to mean the total destruction of pagan Rome.

Simon had once more pressed: was Jesus talking about insurrection? Was he a Zealot in disguise?

Where such questions might have led was interrupted by Mary Magdalene. She eased herself through the onlookers to stand before Jesus. By her very behaviour, boldly doing what no women of Nain would ever do, she confirmed she was one of those whom Pharisees contemptuously called a 'fallen woman'.

Simon's examination of Jesus had been ruined by her intrusion.

The silence was broken by the first whispers from the other guests. What was she doing here? Did she already know the Nazarene? And why didn't he send her away? A harlot had no place in the company of a rabbi!

Weeping freely, Mary Magdalene knelt at the feet of Jesus and allowed her tears to fall on his callused skin before drying them with her long hair. She produced a small alabaster box from a pocket, opened it and massaged his feet with some of the cream it contained. Finally, she reverently kissed one foot, then the other.

The shocked whispers continued. Why did the Nazarene allow her to touch him? To them her very touch was a brush with sin, her tears a sign not of redemption but of trickery; every prostitute in the land knew how and when to cry.

None of them, not for a moment, could understand the sweet truth of what was happening. Her very boldness in kneeling before Jesus was an entreaty to be accepted; using her most valued possession, the ointment, was her way of saying she was ready to sacrifice all she once held precious to be accepted by him. Mary Magdalene was showing she was ready to give up her old life.

But the scandalized onlookers no longer bothered to whisper. They loudly demanded that Jesus should send her away – otherwise he would be as unclean as she was.

Simon demanded, his voice suffused with an anger which would come down through the ages. 'Do you not know this woman? A whore! The whore of Magdala!'

For a moment the tableau was frozen. Mary Magdalene bent even lower over the feet of Jesus, her every gesture continuing to expunge her sins. Jesus looking at the others. Simon summoning up more damning words. Those around him momentarily mute. The apostles staring at each other uncertainly. It was a moment which would survive for all time in Mary's memory. Then, as Simon found renewed voice, Jesus stilled it.

'Simon, I have something to say to you.'

Forced by the courtesy expected of a host, Simon gave way.

'A money lender had two debtors. One owed more than the other. Neither could repay their debt, but the money lender forgave them both.'

Jesus paused, every moment establishing his control over them.

'The question is this. Which of the two freed debtors was the most grateful?'

Once more his eyes studied the faces around him. Men fell silent, pondering uneasily at the sheer authority with which the question had been put. They were used to Simon's legal traps. But they sensed here was something different.

Some may well have even begun to realize that the story was far more subtle than they had first realized. Underpinning it was the truth that God himself is a creditor, someone who trusted each one of them with his goods until the time when he would collect his debt. Though no man could pay the debt he owed God in terms of sin committed, God was all the same prepared to wipe clean the slate for all sins, however large or small, if there was a genuine desire to seek redemption.

Jesus rose to his feet and stood over Simon, pointing to Mary Magdalene.

'You see this woman? I came into your house and you poured no water over my feet, but she has poured out her tears over my feet and wiped them away with her hair. You gave me no kiss, but she has been covering my feet with kisses ever since I came in. You did not anoint my head with oil, but she has anointed my feet with ointment. For this reason I tell you that her sins, her many sins, must have been forgiven her, or she would not have shown such great love. It is the man who is forgiven little who shows little love.'

He was asking Simon if he could ever begin to understand that Mary Magdalene was no longer the woman she used to be, but the one she had just become. Her courtesies were tangible evidence that God had forgiven her.

Jesus turned to Mary Magdalene and spoke to her for the first time. 'Your faith has saved you.'

Jesus had revealed another facet of the love that was at the core of his teaching. Love could only be achieved through understanding and compassion; it could be found as easily in a whore as among those who proclaimed their faith loudly like Simon and his fellow Pharisees. Mary Magdalene may not have known a prayer word-perfect, or how to perform a religious rite correctly. But she had shown she was capable of weeping with those who weep, sorrowing with those who sorrowed, comforting those who mourned – and she had done all this without demanding or judging. For people like her the Kingdom of Heaven was ready to extend its welcome. Always.

Mary Magdalene must have left Simon's house with Jesus and his disciples. She returned to Magdala and may well, as some claimed, have sold her home and possessions and distributed the proceeds among the poor of the town.

More certain, she offered herself as a living example of the positive value of his love. In that moment she became as loyal to Jesus as any apostle, with an infinite capacity to love him in a way they never could. She became the woman who loved Jesus.

Shadow of the Cross

Seven

In those first months of travelling with Jesus, Mary Magdalene increasingly came to understand the liberating nature of all he said and did. It was a theme which underpinned his call to discard worldly values and acquire humility of the spirit. For her, all else would grow from that.

Geographically she had come to anticipate their route. It had two fixed points: the small town of Bethany just south of Jerusalem and, in the north, Capernaum. They usually stayed there for a few days at the home of Peter's mother-in-law. It would be a time for washing clothes, darning and patching, and mending footwear after trekking over rough terrain. Bethany was where friends of Jesus lived: Martha, her sister Mary, and their brother, Lazarus. Industrious and God-fearing people, they became early converts to Jesus' message after they had heard him preach in the town. Since then their modest home had become his base whenever Jesus came south.

On his journeys, Jesus preached from dawn to dusk, repeatedly challenging audiences to accept the truth he spoke. If they could not, they could continue to live meaningless and empty lives. The simplicity and repetition of the message did nothing to diminish its power. That, too, could only have had a profound effect on Mary Magdalene. Time and again she had seen how Jesus could change a person's long-held belief with a few well-chosen words which offered a new hope. He reserved some of his most powerful attacks for avarice and lust. Always his message faced people to think for themselves.

Those who rallied to his side were warned that 'All will hate you for your allegiance to me.' But they must take comfort because, 'you have been granted the privilege of not only believing in me, but also suffering for me.' For those who still hesitated, there was a further reassurance: 'those who hold out to the end will be saved.'

Time and again, Jesus had alluded to Mary Magdalene being

the perfect example of a wretchedly unhappy sinner who had shown the courage and strength to change. However, part of her former life as an astute judge of men would have helped her form her own judgment of the disciples.

Some friendships were closer than others. Peter and his fellow fishermen enjoyed contacts going back to childhood; nevertheless, even among this close-knit group, there were outbursts of anger, pettiness and jealousies. Each man vied to sit closest to the Master at mealtimes, to walk beside him, to place himself on the ground next to Jesus when they slept.

Simon the Zealot was the group's natural protector. With his knowledge of Roman tactics and those of the soldiers of Herod Antipas, he knew the safest routes through a countryside infested with the tetrarch's patrols and ruffian tax gatherers.

Judas Iscariot as treasurer slept directly at the feet of Jesus, his money-purse serving as a pillow. It contained shekels which paid for the group's barest necessities of life on the road. Judas was a relentless bargainer, his eagerness to drive a deal only equalled by sustained praise for the ministry of Jesus. But otherwise his views remained under careful lock and key. It had contributed to the dislike the other apostles felt towards him. Judas was still the outsider.

Mary Magdalene's own relationship with Judas was coloured by being the only woman permanently with the group. In a male-oriented society, she was expected to attend to the domestic chores while on the road. At night she slept a little apart from the men; in winter she bedded down on a straw pallet in a barn while the others huddled together on the ground outside. She may all too often have fallen asleep to the whispered voices of the apostles still quarrelling among themselves over the meaning of something Jesus had said. She may also have felt that each one was absorbed with his own self-importance. The more the Master chided them over such behaviour, the greater seemed to be their preoccupation with their own position in the group.

Exasperated by their bickering, Jesus had once delivered a sharp rebuke: 'I tell you this. You will never enter the Kingdom of Heaven.'

The disciples had fallen into sullen silence. Yet they continued to see him solely in human terms, identifying him with how they themselves would behave. This had been epitomised by John and James asking Jesus to wreak vengeance upon a group of Samaritan villagers who had abused them. Jesus had wearily answered: 'you do not understand what you are asking. Can you drink the cup that I drink, or be baptized with the baptism I am baptized with?'

He was once more reminding them why he was here: that vengeance had no place in the coming New Age. Mary Magdalene had seen that life here and now still mattered for her companions. They continued to speculate for instance whether Jesus, like them, had been even momentarily attracted to evil. He had reminded them that the person tempted was innocent until the moment of succumbing.

How quickly they had forgotten what had happened to him in the wilderness where he had faced such temptation. Mary Magdalene may well have been the only one among them who understood Jesus was proclaiming that confronting evil was the only way to overcome it. It would still buffet everyone all their lives, but it need not be feared. Only those who believed they could ignore evil and temptation simply by refusing to acknowledge their presence were at risk.

Being young and as robustly healthy as Mary Magdalene herself was, some of the apostles may well have speculated as to why she was among them. Had he chosen her as a visible reminder of earthly temptation?

Certainly, Jesus had spoken out against the sins of the flesh, lust and gluttony; of the mind, envy and pride; and of materialism, greed. He had explained how one led to another. During their younger years a man or a woman – he made no distinction – was sometimes tempted into adultery. Later, as the physical urges lessened, they all too often gave way to pride in worldly position. With that went avarice and acquisitiveness: the more people had, the more they wanted. They could expect to find no place in the Kingdom of Heaven.

Her own background would only have made Mary Magdalene better able to understand all this. And certainly, not by so much as a glance, had Jesus looked upon her in any improper way. Yet he undoubtedly had a strong attraction to women, and they to him. To them Jesus was almost always especially gentle and tolerant.

Other times he could respond almost imperiously to a situation. Shortly after they had left the home of Simon the Pharisee, John the Baptist had somehow managed to smuggle out of his cell at Macherus a question he wanted one of his followers to put to Jesus: was he really the Expected One?

Ignoring the second question that the follower had asked – would John soon be free? – Jesus had simply pointed out all he had already achieved: 'Tell John how the blind recover their sight, the lame walk, the lepers are made clean, the deaf hear and the dead are raised to life. Happy is the man who does not find me a stumbling block.'

Mary Magdalene had sensed the words were more than a declaration of Jesus being ready to stand on his record so far. Jesus understood what lay behind John's question. The Baptist knew it would be asked in public – and so provide Jesus with another opportunity to remind people who Jesus was and why he was there.

The most startling way Jesus used to demonstrate his purpose was through miraculous healing. Among the disciples his cures were seen as manifestations of his earthly power. But Mary Magdalene again may have been the first to realize that the miracles were vivid proof Jesus was doing God's work among people. In performing each wondrous cure, Jesus underpinned it with the reminder of the greatest miracle of them all – the miracle of the redemption only he could guarantee to everyone. The promise had still not altogether convinced the apostles or, for that matter, his mother. But where Jesus had continued to be exasperated with the disciples, he had remained unfailingly patient with the elder Mary.

By the time middle age had made her figure that much fuller, Mary's life was no different from that of any other widow in Nazareth: an endless round of housework, shopping, Sabbath candles to be lit and visits to other family members. At the beginning of his public life, Jesus had made it clear that there were some matters he could not share even with her, 'because the burden would be too great for you to know.'

Yet, with a mother's instincts she may well have realized where his ministry was leading him. His continuous promise of a new Kingdom, a new way of life, was in direct contradiction to everything the Jewish establishment and Rome represented. For either of them there would be only one solution to a trouble-maker. Remove him. The shadow of the cross darkened his every footstep.

It would be enough to make any mother fearful. But Mary had continued to maintain a heroic acceptance which had been there from his conception and birth, and was reinforced in that moment at the Cana marriage feast when Jesus first revealed his miraculous powers.

Jesus had made it clear he himself would never marry, even though he valued marriage as the most important of all earthly ties. 'What God has joined together, man must not separate, but only for those for whom God has appointed it. For, while some are incapable of marriage because they were born so, or were made so by men, there are others who have themselves renounced marriage for the sake of the Kingdom.' In that spiritual kingdom, men and women would have to clearly understand if a partner became tired of the other's body, he or she could not lightly take another. 'What I tell you is this: if a man divorces his wife for any cause other than unchastity, he involves her in adultery, and anyone who marries a divorced woman commits adultery.'

Who can doubt that Mary Magdalene had accepted her new life of celibacy? Having endured a life of the flesh, it could only have been a blessed relief to enjoy the joys of the spirit. It made it that much easier to avoid any friction with Jesus' mother, whose own life clearly revolved around her Son. For nine months she had protected him within her womb; everything she had consumed – the wheat, the grapes, the ass's milk, the wine and the lamb – had sustained him so that later he could proclaim he was the bread and wine that would sustain everyone in the coming new world.

As Mary his mother, and Mary Magdalene sat under a starlit

Galilean night, the younger woman's faith would have been further deepened by what she learned about the upbringing of Jesus.

His boyhood years had passed in Nazareth like those of any other child. Outside school there had been time to identify the crops in the fields, the animals in the woods. Standing in the doorways of workshops, Jesus watched how the skilled potters crafted jars and vases with light, caressing strokes; how sharp tools carved shapeless wood into exquisite objects. He observed the tanners and the dyers, listened to the cries of the shepherds, saw the care with which men sheared their sheep, led them to water, carried the smallest lambs in their arms.

So unexceptional were his formative years that to others in Nazareth he was the son of Joseph who, when the time came, began to learn his trade as a carpenter. Jesus developed to full manhood like any other young man but inwardly he was growing in divinity, developing a deep knowledge of the Scriptures and the Law. On the Sabbath he went to synagogue. Like every other place of worship in Judaea, the one in Nazareth was built along the same design: an unadorned hall between two colonnades of arches, and oriented so that the worshippers always faced the Temple in Jerusalem.

His vocation had begun at a time when political and social corruption flourished on a scale unknown in living memory. The Jewish Èlite and its priestly caste lived cheek by jowl with their Roman conquerors.

Both had become targets for Jesus' preaching. He did not attack them in the guise of a political agitator. Instead he constantly reiterated that real freedom was spiritual and could only be achieved by liberation from sin. But the urge for earthly liberation was foremost in the popular mind. Ever since Pompey had desecrated the Holy of Holies, every Jew had yearned and waited for the day of vengeance. Increasingly, they had begun to look to Jesus as the means of making that dream come true – especially when he spoke of the power invested in him.

He, of course, spoke of power not as an earthly, visible entity but as a spiritual invisible force anchored deep in the heart of those who believed what he said.

Mary Magdalene clearly did so believe. That was why she would have increasingly recognized that, among much else, the spiritual power of Jesus was infinitely greater than all the temporal authority of the Emperor Augustus Caesar and his appointed representative in All-Judaea, Pontius Pilate.

Eight

The one certainty in the life of Pontius Pilate, the fifth Roman Procurator of Judaea, Samaria and Idumea, collectively known by the Roman Administration as All-Judaea, was that he would awaken to the sound of military activity.

Some 50,000 soldiers lived in Caesarea, as well as Roman civil servants and their families and slaves. Their every action was determined by Pilate. To many he was no more than an imperious figure who rode on horseback through the streets in his Imperial cloak and helmet. Others who knew him said he was cruel, completely lacking in remorse, highly intelligent, ambitious and ready to seek an accommodation where he could. Equally he was prepared to use all necessary force to achieve what he wanted. More certain, he was cast from the mould which routinely turned out civil servants of his ilk. People whispered his wife was still childless because her husband was too intent on his own career to have time for her.

A new day in his fortress headquarters began when the level of liquid, released a drop at a time, reached the fifth marked division on the *cledsydea*, the water clock on a rampart walkway. A moment later a trumpeter's harsh and triumphalistic notes carried across the city of Caesarea. It had been so every morning since Pilate had first arrived there in the year AD 26.

His predecessors had all grown rich from governing and had returned home to comfortable retirement. But they had been considerably older than Pilate's thirty years. For him, ruling over All-Judaea and being answerable only to the Emperor was a stepping stone to higher office. It helped that his wife, Claudia Procula, was a woman who would do all in her power to ensure that would happen – and her influence was considerable.

Their sleeping and living quarters extended the full width of the palace-fortress. Interconnected salons, each furnished with the artefacts of the Empire, enabled Pilate to survey the sea port

135

on one side and, from the other, look down on the great inner courtyard of his citadel and the city beyond.

Built around an ancient Phoenician defence tower, the only remaining landmark in Caesarea to commemorate the world's most renowned seafarers, the palace was of a size and scale befitting the Roman administrative headquarters. Just as the Antonia Fortress in Jerusalem brooded over that city, so did the palace at Caesarea dominate the countryside sixty miles to the north-west.

There were over a hundred salons, several kitchens, and stabling for three hundred horses, housing for goods carts, open carriages and Claudia Procula's personal coach. There was also space for fifty chariots, together with barracks for the three legions who formed the permanent garrison. In all, over three thousand people worked and lived in the palace.

None did so in such comfort as Pilate and his wife. Their retinue included a personal valet and maid, several more handmaidens for Claudia Procula, clerks to write their letters, a food taster and, as they ate with their fingers the Roman way, servants to wipe their fingers clean between courses. It was a lifestyle in keeping with the Emperor's chief representative.

Like any senior Roman official, Pilate was rarely found in his office after noon. His afternoons were spent exercising with weights before entering the *caldarium*, a steam room. Next he immersed himself in a tub of cold water before visiting the *laconium*, a super-heated chamber. Afterwards he bathed in perfumed water before being massaged by a servant. Dressed in a toga he would spend the rest of the day reading or, if the mood took him, riding one of his stallions. Like most Romans of his station, Pilate was a fine horseman.

Claudia Procula would go through a similar bathing routine. Afterwards she would check on preparations for the next dinner party. Following Roman custom, Pilate entertained several nights a week, his guests drawn from senior staff officers, members of his administration and a sprinkling of merchants or officials visiting from other parts of the Empire.

Every year there was an inspection team from Rome to contend with. The system of checks and balances had been introduced by Julius Caesar. At the end of the visit there would be a magnificent banquet at which ostriches, boars' heads and imported oysters were served.

Claudia Procula would be responsible for the menu and the after-dinner entertainment. Another responsibility was to ensure there were sufficient bowls in the screened-off area of the dining salon for guests to make themselves physically sick after overeating. Afterwards they would return to the table to consume more. Such behaviour had long been a Roman custom. The night would conclude with a full review of the legions in the palace courtyard.

Jews were never invited to these banquets. To Pilate they were obdurate and arrogant, a conquered people who stubbornly refused to succumb to Rome's ways. They were prepared to die for their liberty, yet they deplored violence. Their heroes were lawyers and prophets, not warriors. Even their most revered king, David, had not been allowed to build their Temple, simply because he was a warrior. They called their capital city Jerusalem, 'the city of peace', yet of all the nations within the Empire, the Jews were the only ones to support a resistance movement which continued to nurture itself in that most inhospitable of all Judean provinces, Galilee.

For almost the three years he had been Procurator, Pilate had only passed through there on his way to Jerusalem to collect Rome's taxes and to keep an eye on the pilgrims during their religious festivals. An excitable people at the best of times, they could become even more so when Jews from all over the Empire came to Jerusalem. They were at their most volatile during Passover, when they believed their Messiah would come to liberate them.

Pilate now knew the festival was the holiest in their long religious calendar, an occasion which combined gratitude for escaping from Egyptian bondage with a reminder they only worshipped one God – and that he would free them again. This covenant God had made with Israel was annually sealed with blood and formalized the concept of its people being God's chosen. Each Jewish family offered a slain lamb and dipped a hyssop branch in the blood, then secured it to the door of their home. It was a reminder of how the avenging angel had passed by Jewish homes as it had gone on to smite the first-born in each Egyptian home to force the Pharaoh to let the Jews go.

In the two Passovers Pilate had already witnessed, the air had reeked from the blood of countless thousands of year-old lambs being ritually killed to commemorate that freedom, accompanied by prayers for it to happen once more. Those days the street echoed with the repeated cries that the city would not be 'rebuilt in its entirety until all the children of Israel will be gathered from exile'; only then would Jerusalem, 'the most holy of all cities, become the metropolis for all lands'.

Like any Roman, Pilate would have found such beliefs as unbelievable as the Jewish claim that their invisible God would surround the city with seven walls, one of gold, another of silver, four more, each made from a precious stone and, finally, an outer wall made of fire to ensure the existence of Jerusalem would 'radiate to the four corners of the world'.

Even Jupiter would not have dared make such a promise. Yet the Jews believed every word of the prophecy. That was what helped to make them so unpredictable. To a Roman their rituals were equally bizarre. There was the business of forbidding a private home in Jerusalem having an oven because the smoke would blacken their Temple: all baking was carried out in the Tower of Ovens, a huge edifice in the Lower City. Yet the bakery was close to the gate Jews regarded as especially holy. It had been built by their King Solomon for a single purpose. Every Jew believed the day would come when their Messiah would enter the city through its portals. For Pilate, whose gods were visible as statues, the idea would have been as far-fetched as another widespread Jewish belief that deep inside the Temple was a stone which miraculously hovered in the air and would only fall to earth when the Messiah came.

The Procurator would have well understood the need for such legends: to any Roman the Jews were essentially cunning, inflexible, stubborn, clinging to their blind faith to the very point of death – but weak.

He had thought so from the day he had stepped ashore from his galley and stood for the first time on their soil. His eyes had gone beyond the guard of honour to the silent watchful throng of Jews. His diplomatic training had taught him how to outstare any one. The onlookers had turned away. How great or small Pilate saw his victory, history does not record.

The time was approaching when he must return to Jerusalem for another Passover. With him would go one of his legions to display once more visible proof of Rome's capacity to crush the first sign of trouble.

This time he would take Claudia Procula with him. It would make a change for her from Caesarea, a city that mimicked Rome in every possible way.

Named by Herod the Great after his patron, Emperor Caesar Augustus, Caesarea was a considerable feat of Roman engineering. Massive stone blocks had been sunk into one hundred and twenty feet of sea to create an immense breakwater. Some two hundred feet wide, it extended seawards for over half-a-mile and provided one of the largest and safest harbours in the Eastern Mediterranean. Approached from the sea, the city was a vision of colonnaded buildings rising towards the distant hills of Galilee. Planned along the classic Roman grid system, the streets went either at right angles or parallel to each other.

Interspersed among the buildings were temples and triumphal arches – each celebrating a victory in battle – the city forum with its shopping arcades and the basilica which housed the law courts. Everywhere there were domed roofs, another Roman architectural invention. Towering above everything were the ramparts of the palace of Pontius Pilate. Walls a metre thick rose almost a hundred feet to crenellated walkways which, in turn, ascended to the main palace. From its window openings to the south-east was a clear view of the Roman road which ran straight and true to Jewish Jerusalem.

On any given morning, Pontius Pilate was master of all he surveyed. Looking out to sea he would observe galleys coming and going, the largest of them propelled by the combined brute strength of a hundred and more enslaved oarsmen. Even with a fair wind it could take a month to complete the journey from the port of Ostia, Rome's gateway to the Mediterranean. Protecting the bulky freight galleys were the Empire's warships, ranging in size from biremes, with their twin rows of oarsmen, to the quinquiremes, which had five tiers of rowers. With a complement of heavily-armed centurions and battering rams at the prow, a war galley was more than a match for the pirates of North Africa.

Inside Caesarea's harbours was berthing for thirty galleys to moor alongside broad quays along which dray carts came and went with the produce of Judaea: dates, olives and dried fish from the Sea of Galilee. Separated from the commercial side of the port was the berthing space for Pilate's personal galley. Crewed by two hundred oarsmen, it was used to carry to Rome the taxes levied on All-Judaea. Its next voyage would be after Pilate returned from Jerusalem.

Walking to the other side of his private quarters, Pilate could look down into the palace courtyard. From dawn to dusk it was filled with the sounds of drilling centurions practising with battering rams and siege towers, improving the time it took to load a catapult which fired small boulders or volleys of arrows. Other soldiers performed the classic tactical formation known as the 'tortoise'; head-to-foot shields formed a solid square which was roofed over with more shields held by the centurions beneath. A 'tortoise' was slow but formidable and was used to drive a wedge into the advancing ranks of an enemy through which the charioteers could rush.

Each of the garrison's legions consisted of ten cohorts, each in turn divided into centuries of one hundred men, each under its centurion. A legion was commanded by a legate who had his personal standard bearer and trumpeter. Under his command was also a troop of cavalry. Well paid, the men of the Empire's twenty-eight legions formed the most powerful fighting force the world had seen. Coarsened and hardened by battle experiences as far apart as Hadrian's Wall and the eastern shore of the Black Sea, the three legions under Pilate's command had little now to do in Judaea except physically remind people of their presence. Apart from going to Jerusalem, they rarely ventured beyond Caesarea. The Zealots never confronted them in open battle, preferring instead to use hit-and-run tactics against a patrol that did venture up into the hills. It created an illusion that under Pilate, All-Judaea was at relative peace.

Beyond the palace ramparts spread the city. To the left of Pilate's quarters were the twin temples where he and Claudia Procula gave thanks to their gods and goddesses. His shrine was larger, reached by a wide flight of steps and entered between imposing Doric columns which rose to a magnificent carved pediment. Before the door was an altar slab on which, on holy days, the procurator's personal priest sacrificed an animal to Jupiter, king of the gods, Mercury, the gods' messenger, or Mars, the god of war.

Claudia Procula's temple was circular, its domed roof supported by twenty-four delicate Ionic columns. Under the dome was her altar, a block of granite decorated with bas-reliefs of her personal idols: Minerva, goddess of wisdom; Venus, goddess of love and beauty; and Juno, Jupiter's wife, who was goddess of marriage and childbirth.

Beyond was the city theatre, standing in the centre of its own piazza, where plays from Rome were produced. Most of the actors were freed slaves. When not performing, the players lived in quarters beneath the stage. Built on flat ground, the theatre had arches and vaults to support the stone seats. Its exterior rose, one arch above the other, to sixty feet above street level. Supported by a combination of Tuscan and Corinthian pillars, the interior was even more magnificent. There were banks of seats, together enough to hold twenty thousand spectators. The procurator's box had been built into the natural stone of the hillside. From there Pilate watched the weekly chariot races, each one several laps of the oval track. In between the races there were boxing contests in which slaves wore spiked gloves to inflict fearful injuries. On high holidays, especially that for Lupercalia, to celebrate the founding of Rome, imported gladiators staged fights to the death. Predicting the winner was something he much enjoyed. But even his considerable judgment in such matters would have not helped him to influence the events taking shape in the hills of Galilee in the year that would become known as AD 30.

* * *

Pontius Pilate was the second son of a well-to-do Roman merchant. There were a number of such families in Rome who, because of their great wealth, exercised considerable influence at the Imperial court. In time of war they provided supplies for the army in the field and, when conquest was achieved, they developed new trading links with the defeated. Pilate's family may well have had links with the tin miners of Cornwall and the dealers in precious stones and silks in India and China.

Pilate was the product of a typical Roman education. A private tutor, usually a Greek, taught him to count on an abacus and write on wax tablets with a stylus; later he would have used a reed pen and ink on papyrus. His basic curriculum included Greek and Latin – the first language of the Empire – history, geography, arithmetic and the works of famous authors.

Every student spent a portion of his day in one of Rome's many libraries. When school ended Pilate, like any other boy from his background, took part in sports, including running, wrestling and fencing. As he progressed into his teens, he would have abandoned such boyish pursuits as rolling hoops in favour of learning how to be a charioteer by racing a small pony cart. Everything he did was designed eventually to prepare him for life in either the army, commerce, politics or the legal profession.

When the time came, there would have been the customary family gathering to decide what profession Pilate should follow. To join the family business would have been one option considered but almost certainly his skills in oratory and philosophy would have influenced the eventual choice of the diplomatic service.

At the age of twenty, Pilate had been enrolled in Rome's Imperial Academy for future envoys. Upon graduation, he was qualified to help rule the world's greatest empire.

Somewhere in his crowded curriculum, he would have learned that the Jews could trace their history back further than any other nation in the Roman world except the Egyptians. Ground between the feet of powerful armies for over a thousand years, Jews still saw themselves as a proud, self-governing people, supported by a religious belief that insisted they must never become a mere client-state, like so many other conquered countries. Driven into exile time and again, they had somehow always managed to return to their land. Even Pompey had said they were like no other people he had met in a lifetime of campaigns. That judgment had found a ready echo in Julius Caesar's decision to create the office of procurator for All-Judaea. These facts may well have been the deciding factor in Pilate's decision after graduating that, when the post next became vacant, he would seek it.

By then he had become involved with one of the most desirable young women in Rome. Claudia Procula was the granddaughter of the Emperor Caesar Augustus, a princess royal and, by all accounts, sophisticated, cultured and sensitive. They may well, as the story goes, have met during one of Rome's great festivals – perhaps the week-long celebration for Flora, the goddess of flowers, or during the feast of Saturnalia, held in December, during which slaves swapped roles with their masters.

Having fallen in love, they would most likely have married on that most auspicious of days, March the First, when the Roman New Year was celebrated by fresh laurel leaves being hung on the doors of buildings and the Vestal Virgins lit a new fire in their temple. Given the status of the bride, the wedding sacrifice would have been made at the Emperor's own altar. Afterwards Claudia Procula and Pilate would have consumed the traditional first slice of wedding cake.

After the celebrations ended, the question of Pilate's career would have loomed large in not only the young couple's thinking, but that of the Emperor. Now that Pilate had married into the Imperial family, he could no longer be treated as a commoner. Yet he was still too young and inexperienced to be appointed to the Senate or to a senior posting overseas. But there was one gift the Emperor could bestow: a procuratorship. The current holder of that office, Valerius Gratus, was abruptly summoned to Rome and Pontius Pilate was appointed to rule in his place from Caesarea.

Judaea as such was not exactly a jewel in the Imperial crown. Most Romans barely knew where it was; those who did regarded it as a pimple on the rump of Empire. Nevertheless, a governorship was several rungs up the ladder that might one day lead to the Senate, or even the highest office of all.

As a further sign of the favour the newly-weds had in the Emperor's eyes, Tiberius broke the rule he had introduced which banned a procurator from taking his wife with him on active service. Claudia Procula would become, in effect, First Lady of All-Judaea.

Her own education and training ensured she was suited for the position. Versed in music, dancing and the theatre, and familiar with poets like Virgil, Claudia Procula would also have had a working knowledge of the laws which laid down punishments for crimes by her personal servants.

Since childhood, she had learned the skills of looking beautiful: how long to keep on a face pack made of flour and ass's milk; how much coloured powder to rouge her cheeks; how to darken her eyebrows and lashes and apply eyeliner. Her cosmetics were made from the purest of vegetable and mineral dyes. Perfume was an essential, and she would have taken with her to Caesarea a wide selection of flasks containing the essences of flowers, spices and scented woods. Her make-up trunk would have contained a toothpowder of ground chalk, combs, mirrors and nail clippers, all made from gold or silver, together with a selection of wigs created from the hair of slaves, and several sets of tongs to curl her hair. For the long sea journey she would have followed the custom of wearing her hair in a simple bun. Among their retinue of servants would have been her hairdresser and Pilate's personal barber.

The couple had arrived in Caesarea in the late summer of AD 26, around the time, had they but known it, when Jesus began his ministry, and Mary Magdalene was hearing the first reports of his teachings. Almost three years later, the two very different women who would soon have an important role to play in his earthly life were separated by no more than a few miles.

The one great disappointment in Claudia Procula's life must have been that she was still childless. For a princess of the blood not to have conceived within a year of marrying was always a matter of concern. Like any Roman noblewoman, Claudia Procula would have sought expert advice and, along with everything else in Roman society, there was precedent for her to follow.

The first step would have been to consult her personal augur, the priest who interpreted cloud formations and the flight pattern of certain birds. From these he would try and decipher if the gods were angry with his mistress.

The next step would have been to go to her favourite astrologer; there were over a score on the Caesarea administration's payroll. He would spend time watching her sacred chickens, which no high-born Roman household was without. If the birds ate their grain quickly, it was a sign pregnancy was imminent. If they ate slowly, it was an indication the gods did not favour conception. She could then consult the palace *haruspex*, a soothsayer; he would invariably recommend a sacrifice to the goddess Juno. When all these experts had failed, Claudia Procula would understandably have looked elsewhere for the cause of her childlessness.

In her husband's behaviour since coming to Caesarea, the gods could have found much to criticize. From the very outset Pontius Pilate had miscalculated the behaviour of the Jews.

Days after he arrived in Caesarea, the procurator discovered there was no statue of the Emperor Tiberius in Jerusalem, making it the only city in the Empire where its inhabitants did not make obeisance to the Imperial presence. Pilate was told the presence of any statue or emblem was an affront to the One God of the Jews.

Riding at the head of a legion, Pilate had entered Jerusalem with drums beating and the images of the Emperor on the Roman battle standards. The Jewish devout had fled, hiding their faces in their hands, weeping at such sacrilege. For them this was worse than the time Valerius had crucified their priests.

With the sound of drumming reverberating around the city walls, Pilate had marched into the Antonia Fortress. A short while later a priest from the Temple had presented himself at the fort gateway with a scroll written by High Priest Caiaphas. It reminded

Pilate that the Emperor Augustus had guaranteed Jerusalem would be exempt from any threat to its sanctity. Caiaphas had concluded with the reminder that the One God did not even allow images of himself.

Pilate had kept the priest waiting for several hours. Then he had ordered the battle standards raised on the fortress's outer walls so that the emblems overlooked the Temple. He had returned Caiaphas' scroll to the priest having first torn it in half. In the world of Rome, there could be no greater personal insult.

Pilate had spent the night on the fortress ramparts, his centurions at battle readiness below in the courtyard with orders to kill any Jew who attempted to remove the standards. Soldiers were then to enter the Temple and seize the High Priest and all the other chief priests.

At dawn, Pilate had witnessed an extraordinary sight. The Temple gates remained firmly shut and its courtyards were filled only with patrolling guards. But thousands of Jews were fleeing out of the city: on foot, on donkeys, in carriages. And they were all heading back down the road to Caesarea. The only sound was of a horn player's plaintive lament. From the roof of the Temple, a solitary robed figure watched the exodus. Only when the music had finished did Joseph Caiaphas leave his vantage point.

Nothing in his diplomatic training had prepared Pilate for this. His legion commander, Quirius, a veteran of five years service in Judaea, said he had seen nothing like it.

Next day Pilate had returned to Caesarea. Along the way he had not encountered a single Jew. But, approaching the city, he was met with a second astonishing sight. Not only the thousands who had fled Jerusalem were kneeling outside his palace, but also all those they had gathered to them on the way. There may have been 5,000; there could have been more. Stunned, and uncertain what to do, Pilate had led his centurions back into the palace and ordered the gates locked.

This was the first test of his authority – but he instinctively knew that one mistake could be his last. For the moment, he faced only passive resistance. But that could swiftly change. Soon the entire Jewish population might converge on Caesarea. While three legions should be enough to triumph, there would inevitably be loss of Roman blood. And, in the process, the Jews could well put Caesarea to the torch. His own career would be engulfed in the flames.

Pilate summoned Quirius and called in his lawyers and his senior officials. To them all he put the same question: was this civil disobedience the start of bloody insurrection?

No one knew.

Outside, the crowd grew. They came from all over Samaria, from Decapolis and Perdea. They came from Galilee, from Sepphoris, and the towns along the lake shore. They came to kneel and pray for the soul of Pontius Pilate; that God would forgive him for what he had done to the Temple. By the second day their numbers had doubled, paralyzing Caesarea. Shops ran out of food, access to the port was blocked. Every building was an island – none more so than Pilate's palace.

Quirius suggested he should send out his soldiers to scatter the Jews. 'Kill a few hundred and all the other thousands will be frightened,' he told Pilate.

Instinctively, the procurator knew that would not work. Pompey had been right. These were like no other people.

On the third day, Pilate walked out of the palace gate to confront them. By now his original estimate of their number had doubled. There may have been ten thousand kneeling before him. He tried to reason and argue. His words were lost in the repetitive cry for God to have mercy on his pagan soul.

Once more defeated, Pilate retreated into the palace. Four more days he waited, the crowd growing by the day. All work had ceased in the city; its inhabitants were besieged in their own homes.

On the morning of the seventh day, Pilate once more emerged. Drawn up behind him was his entire force of centurions with their troops – ready to commit mass butchery should the order be given.

Pilate displayed his most Imperial manner. He told the crowd they should disperse now or face the consequences. Behind him the soldiers unsheathed their stabbing swords and spears that could skewer a body to the ground with one swift jab.

Every Jewish man, woman and child in unison called out they

were ready to die rather than see their Temple further desecrated. They continued to kneel down and wait for the blows that would end their lives.

The terrible silence stretched. Then, defeated and humiliated, Pontius Pilate walked back inside the palace.

Next day he sent a written message to Caiaphas promising there would be no further breach of the Imperial undertaking to preserve the sanctity of the Temple.

It was the first step in an uneasy alliance between the procurator and High Priest which now, almost three years later, was moving slowly but inexorably towards an unholy climax.

Nine

In those first two years only Jesus, the disciples and Mary Magdalene had travelled together along the pilgrims' paths. But now, in the weeks before the coming Passover – the onset of the third year of his ministry – Mary and Martha of Bethany and his own mother accompanied them.

The presence of his mother would have helped to reduce the bickering which still continued among the apostles. Jesus continued to warn them: 'Look, I send you out like sheep among wolves.' He was telling them he understood the risks they were taking by being with him but they must weigh them against the future he promised. Tragically, they still failed to understand the glorious reality of what lay ahead.

They still had not bonded together, even though Jesus had told them they were to be 'the light of the world' and 'the salt of the earth'. Using examples they would understand, he tried to show that, in the Kingdom he was creating, they would have prized roles: the fishermen who would fill the nets, the sowers of crops, the reapers of the harvest, the shepherds who would protect their flocks.

Resolutely working men, they all too often took Jesus' imagery at its face value, especially when it came to protecting themselves. 'He that has no sword, let him sell his garment and buy one.' The words had been part of the same injunction that they must be ready to defend themselves through their new-found faith against the hatred they would attract for believing in him. It was not an earthly call to arms, any more than his request, 'He that has ears to hear, let him hear,' was a call to spy on the Romans.

Yet those demands, as Mary Magdalene would surely have attested, had played a part in the petty bickerings and jealousies which so often still coloured the day-to-day life of the men around her. The apostles came from a background where keeping a lookout for anyone trying to take advantage was a recognized way of self-survival.

When Jesus had singled out Peter for special attention, the others had not bothered to hide their resentment. Why him, they had protested? Just because Peter – once called Simon – had been the first to answer the call, 'Come, follow me,' surely did not give him special status? All of them believed they were equally worthy; pointing out not one had hesitated when his turn had come to be asked to give up *everything* – wife, family, home, and a secure job. Each had followed Jesus blindly into the unknown, and collectively became his 'fishers of men'.

But, nevertheless, Jesus had chosen Peter to be their first among equals. He had given Simon a new name, *Cephas*, the Rock (or *Petrus*, Peter). In calling Simon Peter the Rock, Jesus was acknowledging more than the apostle's courage in leaving his wife and home to follow him through Galilee for the past three years. Jesus was saying that of them all, he had seen in Peter the very qualities needed to found his Church.

Peter possessed more than his share of human failings. He was impetuous and boastful, often promising what he could not deliver. He had a readiness to pick a fight, and language which could be as coarse as the salt he had once used to cure his fish. With it went impatience and bouts of pique. But Jesus had also seen that those very failings would one day lead to Peter becoming the firmest of foundations on which faith would grow and spread. Peter had that one essential quality, the capacity to seek and be given redemption. That was why he was the disciple with whom Jesus most closely united himself on earth, using the word 'we' when he spoke to Peter.

It did not make Peter any easier to live with for his younger brother, Andrew. Barely out of his boyhood, Andrew was quiet and sensitive, content to live in the shadow of Peter's volcanic personality.

The brothers James and John remained close to each other, presenting a common front of stoicism against the others. But between themselves they bickered and sometimes came close to blows.

Philip had changed little in the time he had been with the group. His curiosity was usually hidden behind a painful shyness.

Matthew, Bartholomew and Thomas had formed their own

closed group, each drawing from the others strength they did not possess. Matthew was the former tax collector – the most hated of all jobs to his fellow Jews – who had redeemed himself by following Jesus. Bartholomew's inborn humility had helped Matthew come to terms with his new life as a penniless mendicant. In turn Matthew had lifted the pessimism which so often gripped Thomas.

The others had remained shadowy figures, prepared to join in an argument but never the ones to start one.

Judas Iscariot had never told anyone when and where he had answered the call, 'Come, follow me'. He had simply appeared one day. Jesus had never said why Judas had been chosen to be treasurer, and Judas had never elaborated. He had remained truly a man alone.

He usually walked behind Jesus, the accustomed position for a treasurer, ready to be on hand to buy anything his Master required, and at night he slept at his feet. Had he originally been chosen to fulfil the symbolism of Scripture: the twelve patriarchs of the Book of Moses, the twelve tribes of Israel, the twelve spies who had originally explored the Promised Land, the twelve stones on the breast of the High Priest?

No one would ever know.

The apostles' day-to-day lives and habits would remain beyond record, especially on the question of how they coped with the constant presence of a woman in their midst. The only clue that survived was the observation of Philip:

'But Christ loved her more than all of us. And we were offended by it and expressed disapproval.'

No doubt they did so to each other as they followed in his footsteps across Galilee, or settled down for the night. But they would never have dared openly challenge Jesus on the matter. Instinctively they would have realized the stern rebuke that would have drawn.

Mary Magdalene's own response to such human jealousy would also go unrecorded.

Apart from Peter's now clearly defined role, it would have been doubtful, even with her undoubted foresight, if she could have envisaged the roles Jesus had in mind for the others; these past three years had been preparation for what they would do after the shadow of the cross had finally darkened their landscape. Mary Magdalene could well have been forgiven for thinking that they had still so much to learn before they could become the gatekeepers to the Kingdom of God.

Over and over again he told them that only by being humble could they expect to become exalted.

'You know that in the world the recognized rulers lord it over their subjects, and their great men make them feel the weight of authority. That is not the way with you; among you, whoever wants to be great must be your servant, and whoever wants to be first must be the willing slave of all.'

Jesus had offered himself as an example. 'For even the Son of Man did not come to be served, but to serve.'

And still the disciples had not grasped why he had 'come' into the world; that Jesus had once more deliberately chosen 'come' rather than 'born' because he wanted them to realize the act of human birth was most certainly not the beginning of his existence. Long before he had assumed the form of flesh, he had planned every meticulous detail which was now steadily moving towards its inevitable and triumphant conclusion.

That the disciples did not understand would, not for a moment, change the course of events. Their very failure to grasp reality was also part of his plan.

From time to time, the presence of his mother and the Bethany sisters would have made Mary Magdalene's own life on the road easier. Unlike the disciples, they were not jealous of each other. Each awaited her turn to walk for a while with Jesus, perhaps to share with him how they were trying to live their lives through his teaching. Perhaps they were the first to sense the deepening shadow of the Cross across their path.

In turn he reminded them that all those who stayed true to him would, themselves, become outcasts, often even within their own families. He also explained why he had not come to remove the Roman yoke, its coinage, and its every demoralizing subjugation of their people. Others before him had brought them a short-lived earthly freedom. What he had come to offer was a different freedom, one that everyone could keep in their heart. He could do so, 'because my Father and I are one'.

For Mary Magdalene, the very certainty of those words held her in thrall as they criss-crossed the countryside.

Since Cana, Jesus' own human relationship with his mother had changed. Until then she had been someone to be listened to and obeyed as the matriarchal head of the family. But the miracle at the wedding feast had altered everything: not only had he changed water into wine; so had his perception of her altered. He no longer called her 'mother' but 'woman' – a symbol for those he had come to redeem. The ever-looming loss of her Son could only have been made more bearable by the presence of Mary Magdalene, the first sinner to have received his redemption. Her own faith must have helped his mother prepare for the coming time when her Son's death would pave the way for the sins of everyone to be forgiven.

Each woman, in her own way, would have tried to calm the disciples' fears. At every turn there seemed to be someone waiting with a verbal snare. Why did Jesus associate with the outcasts of society? Was he no better than a sinner himself by mixing with such dregs?

Once more he had given the same patient answer. 'I did not come to invite virtuous people, but sinners.'

Mary Magdalene had been with Jesus long enough now to understand the subtleties of his words. He had come offering salvation to all those afflicted with sin – but only if they wanted his help. He was not forcing it on anybody, only showing it was available. The choice was there for people to take. Always.

During their journeys, Jesus had deliberately led them into Samaria, a small province separating Judaea from Galilee. The Samaritans were a hybrid race, created centuries before when the Israelites had been once more enslaved and their Assyrian captors settled pagan people among them. They brought their idols and, when intermarriage followed, diluted the purity of Judaism. The Samaritans created for themselves a new religion. Loosely based on the five books of Moses and some of the writings of the Prophets, it rejected the other books of the Bible and the authority of the Temple in Jerusalem. For Jews, Samaria was a place to be avoided. Those who had to travel through the province did so as swiftly as possible.

On their own journeys through Samaria, Jesus told the disciples they would take their time, stopping at towns like Jericho, Ephraim and Arimathea. The inhabitants, no doubt surprised to see them, were nevertheless welcoming. They listened to what Jesus said and debated with him in a vigorous but open-minded manner. Jesus and his entourage became familiar visitors. On one particular journey they had reached the outskirts of the small town of Sychar, close to the River Jordan. It was at Sychar where Jacob had experienced a vision of a host of angels welcoming him as he slaked his thirst at a watering hole. On the day Jesus arrived, there was only a woman carrying a waterpot to the well. Clearly she had not expected anyone else to be there in the heat of the day; water was usually only drawn at dusk. Her surprise may have been eased by the presence of Mary Magdalene. Instinctively she realized why the woman was there at that hour. She had been forced to do so because of who she was, a whore. In those now gone-forever days in Magdala, Mary Magdalene had sent her own serving girls to fetch water when they would not encounter the disdain of other women.

Jesus had politely asked the woman, 'Give me a drink.'

'What! You, a Jew, ask a drink of me? A Samaritan?'

The woman's mocking, insolent, voice further hardened Mary Magdalene's suspicions. She herself had used such a tone to her clients; it had been her way of showing that, though they had rented her body, they did not own her mind.

But Jesus gave no sign of being offended by the woman's response. Instead, he began a dialogue that was rich in meaning.

'If only you knew what God gives and who it is asking you for a drink, you would have asked him and he would have given you living water.'

Understandably the woman was perplexed. Living water was a concept outside the daily existence of someone so earth-bound she had no grasp of spiritual values. She may well have sensed this stranger already knew who she was, and that his words were a prelude to withering dismissal, the usual fate for those in her profession. In that case she was determined to deliver some home truths of her own.

'You have no bucket and this well is deep. Are you a greater man than Jacob our ancestor who gave us the well and drank from it himself, he and his sons, and his cattle too?'

Pointing to the well and, in a voice that brooked no challenge, Jesus replied: 'Everyone who drinks this water will be thirsty again, but whoever drinks the water I shall give, will never suffer thirst any more. The water that I shall give will be an inner spring always welling up for eternal life.'

Once more with a powerful economy of words Jesus had restated the core purpose of his ministry. Believe and accept and he would guarantee a life beyond comprehension.

Who can doubt that Mary Magdalene would have silently urged the woman to understand that, instead of the well water she had come to draw, an altogether more powerful slaking was being offered? But the woman was not yet prepared to let go her earthly way of understanding.

'Sir, give me that water and then I shall not be thirsty, nor have to come all this way again to draw.'

In the silence there is a sense of the apostles nodding to each other: what the woman had said made perfect sense. For them the spiritual lesson Jesus was unfolding was also rooted in earthly aspirations.

How long the silence stretched and whether the woman's fear gave way to puzzlement are mere digressions in the unfolding drama.

'Go home, call your husband and come back.'

Mary Magdalene could have been the first to understand the deeper meaning behind the command. Jesus' choice of comments – 'go', and 'come' – were deliberate. Jesus was giving the woman two choices: 'Go and face the truth of the life you now live; when you have done so, you will be forgiven, then come and make a new start.'

But all the woman still only really understood were the physical parameters of a home and a husband – in which Jesus

155

had deliberately chosen to encase the redemption on offer. The irony of this would not have been lost on her. This stranger who spoke riddles, yet seemed to know so much about her lifestyle, would surely also have known that in her profession, women had no marital support.

Across the well, the woman and Jesus faced each other. 'I have no husband.'

The shock of the confession as the disciples realized who she was; what she did for a living; the encouraging look of Mary Magdalene urging the woman to go on; the whore once more silent and increasingly uncertain; the images would be forever burnished in their minds. She was away from her natural surroundings where guile and sensuality were her stock-in-trade, where soft candlelight hid the truth in her eye. She was out in the open, under the searing light of the noonday sun, held in an unflinching gaze, the like of which she had never before encountered.

Jesus had located in the depth of her soul the spark which showed she was ready for redemption. Yet she still had some way to go: there was a need to instil in her more than an admission of sin. He wanted an absolute promise it would not be repeated.

'You have five husbands. The man with whom you are now living is not your husband: you told me the truth there.'

He needed to remind her how far she had fallen into degradation. But now – still clinging to her worldly ways – she did what others had done when Jesus had forced them to confront their past: the woman attempted to change the subject. She fell back upon her old wiles, using flattery to try and escape. 'Sir, I can see that you are a prophet.'

The coquettish smile, the turn of the head, the renewed challenge in her eyes: they are all there in her words which now followed. 'Our father worshipped on this place, but you Jews say God should be worshipped in Jerusalem.'

Jesus would not be diverted. Old religious squabbles held no interest for him. What mattered was here and now.

'The time approaches, indeed it is already here, when those who are real worshippers will worship the Father in Spirit and in truth.'

The woman could do nothing but abjectly admit she could no longer go on evading. 'I know the Messiah is coming. When he comes, he will tell us everything.'

In one short sentence Jesus left her in no doubt. 'I am He, I who am speaking to you now.'

Stunned, then dropping her bucket in her excitement, the woman turned and ran to tell everyone she met that the Messiah was here. In no time a steady procession of Samaritans made their way to the well. There Jesus explained again the meaning of salvation and redemption.

No doubt as stunned as the woman, they had listened in wonder to a promise they would never have heard in their own temple. Gathered around Jesus at their own sacred well, he had not converted them by any miracle or act of healing. Only by words had he opened their eyes. 'The Samaritans pressed him to stay with them, and many became believers because of what they heard from his own lips.'

To the once fallen woman, now risen in purity, they said. 'It is no longer because of what you said that we believe, for we have heard him ourselves, and we know that this is in truth the Saviour of the World.'

This was the first time Mary Magdalene and the disciples had heard the Master so described. Yet in that moment the shadow of the Cross would also have darkened a little more.

At first the opposition had been confined to the Pharisees, led by Simon of Nain. Within their closed-minded community, they had fulminated that the Nazarene had abrogated the power of God. Their anger had spread to other parts of Galilee and then south to Jerusalem. There, for the moment, the miraculous claims attributed to Jesus had largely been received with little more than curiosity. Nevertheless, the Temple had sent its agents to investigate. High Priest Caiaphas could have done no less.

In Galilee the opposition had grown, spurred by such incidents as had happened in Capernaum. A family had brought their paralyzed father to Jesus. Instead of immediately helping the man, Jesus had forgiven his sins.

Once more scandalized, the Pharisees had condemned Jesus for blasphemy. He said to them: 'Why do you harbour thoughts like these? Is it easier to say to this stricken man, "your sins are forgiven", or to say "stand up, take up your bed and walk?" But to convince you that the Son of Man has the right to forgive sins, I say to this man, "take up your bed and go home".'

The man did, offering vivid proof of the power of God. But the opposition grew apace with the thirst of the people to learn more of what Jesus had to offer.

They came to listen from as far north as the port of Sidon in the province of Phoenicia, from the villages of Decapolis to the east, the port of Joppa on the coastal plain, where pilgrims landed after their long sea voyages before going on to Jerusalem. They walked all the way from the edge of the wilderness. At first they came in small groups, then in their hundreds, then, these past few months, in their thousands.

They came during the month of Adar when the nights were so cold the law required a creditor to return any clothes taken as a pledge before darkness. They braved the winter *qadim*, the great winter wind which howled from the east, icy and dry, cleansing the air and chilling every bone marrow with its blast. And, when the broiling heat of summer was heralded by the *khamsin*, the sand storms roaring in from the desert, filling the sky with gritty greyness which stung like a rasp on skin – they still came.

They had done so in ever-increasing numbers since Jesus had preached what would become his most memorable sermon.

Standing on the lee side of Mount Hattin, the disciples squatting around him, with Mary Magdalene standing among the other women in the crowd, Jesus began to deliver a succession of unchallengeable and inviolable maxims. They would be a prescription for the future, their passport into the Kingdom of Heaven. Those who followed his instructions would have in their grasp what was required to include God into their daily life, and to accept that, beyond their life on earth, was a far more rewarding tomorrow.

Each time he used two key injunctions. The first was 'you have heard'. He would then state the Law. Then, voice rising, he would emphatically add one word 'But'. They would have heard that no one can be happy unless they had sufficient money. But – 'blessed are the poor in spirit'. They had been told the world loves to laugh: – 'blessed are those who mourn'. And, of course they would have heard that the way to success was to seek power and popularity. But: 'Blessed are you when men revile you and persecute you and speak all manner of evil against you falsely because of me.'

Jesus promised help to all who endured persecution and afflictions; those who were exploited; the meek and mild; those troubled in their search for peace or were poorly rewarded for their generosity and, above all, mocked and reviled for the faith in their hearts. To all those multitudes he promised a new way forward.

For some listeners, what became known as the Beatitudes had a familiar ring. Similar guarantees could be found in the books of Moses with their promises that poverty and suffering would one day end, and *all* people would enjoy all the good things of the earth. But Jesus welded together these expressions of optimism and presented them as *about to happen*. He was promising no mere illusory hopes which might come true at some vague time in the future. The promises were to be fulfilled here now, on the very spot from which he spoke.

The effect of such certainty had been galvanizing. His audience, as always, were the downtrodden, those who had been exploited all their lives. There was probably not a rich man among them. Yet, to them all, Jesus had offered incomparable richness; a great beacon lit up his every promise. In every one was his declaration of having no interest in earthly power politics. The only change he had come to launch was to make hearts beat faster to a new rhythm of joy.

Yet what he said challenged powerful and powerless alike in a revolutionary way. The intention to commit a sin was just as great as actually doing so. 'You have heard...' 'But I tell you...' Time after time the words thundered forth to condemn adultery, theft, greed, bribery, and corruption of all kinds.

Next he dealt with revenge. 'You have heard what they say. An

159

eye for an eye, a tooth for a tooth. But I tell you. Do not set yourself against the man who wrongs you. If someone hits you on the right cheek, turn and offer him your left. If a man wants to sue you for your shirt, let him have your coat as well. If a man in authority makes you go one mile, go with him two.'

For Mary Magdalene, Jesus' every word was a powerful reminder of the world she had given up: where violence was the norm, where sex was a commodity; where men had flattered her for their own ends. She had hated them all. But hatred, too, was a sin, Jesus reminded her, all of those people on the hillside of Hattin.

Expressing himself from the background of his own impoverished background in which there had been no luxuries, Jesus continued to lay out a brave new world, a utopia where people could live in perfect harmony.

Choosing words that would deliberately satisfy a thirst for personal justice – a constant demand of an oppressed people – he ignored grandiose prospects of national prosperity and political revival, and focused on the most humble perception.

Blessed are the poor in spirit: for theirs is the Kingdom of Heaven. Blessed are they who mourn: for they shall be comforted. Blessed are the meek: for they shall inherit the earth. Blessed are they who do hunger and thirst after righteousness: for they shall be filled. Blessed are the merciful: for they shall obtain mercy. Blessed are the pure in heart: for they shall see God. Blessed are the peacemakers: for they shall be called the children of God. Blessed are they who are persecuted for righteousness sake: for theirs is the Kingdom of Heaven. Blessed are you when men shall revile and persecute you, and shall utter all manner of evil against you falsely, for my sake.

He was synthesizing what he had come to do: save humanity and show his oneness with them. Until this moment it had been the Law which governed people's religious lives as they patiently waited for salvation. It was finally here. Through him, they could be committed to a new life and go forth to tell others.

To all those standing before him, Jesus was saying what they so badly wanted to hear and see happen. For them, he was now not just another prophet, offering momentary hope or an unattainable vision. He was saying he was here to end their misery, to fight social injustice through the principle of neighbourly love.

The words were yet another rebuke for the disciples. They still believed the Kingdom Jesus spoke of had earthly delights within its invisible borders, which they would reap. How else to explain the words of Thomas: 'For you have there, in Paradise, five fig trees which change not winter or summer.' Or the expectation of Philip: 'The brooks softly run, the palm trees and the dates every tree bears.' Or Bartholomew's: 'The wheat shall grow as high as the cedars of Lebanon and God can cause grain to fall from heaven so that every man shall gather it in his hands.' And Andrew's vision: 'A place where man shall no longer have to tread out the grapes: he need only carry in great clusters into his house, and leave it in a corner thereof, and he shall have wine in abundance for all the years.'

Those fanciful and understandable images after the miraculous event at Cana, Jesus now wanted to eradicate from the minds of his followers.

Next he dealt with how to pray. From now on, even to be *considered* as worthy of admission into the Kingdom of Heaven, people must give up praying like hypocrites, striking pious poses and ensuring everyone saw and heard their piety. Instead, they should pray alone. God would hear: that was all that mattered.

This deliberate attack on the Pharisees would send a further shock-wave through a religious party who believed they represented the very ethos of Jewish religiosity in their meticulous fulfilment of the existing Law. For them it was an article of faith that divine protection had to be earned by presenting continuous proofs of devoutness through a prayer life that no one could fail to notice.

Now, in a few sweeping sentences, Jesus charged the Pharisees with hypocrisy, of being the grand-masters of error when it came to a true understanding of what God required.

Their faith was one of sterile conservatism; they were people who mortified religion; their sole concern was only to preserve their customs and traditions.

It was a full-blown onslaught on their sniping, their poisonous challenges and opposition to the new morality and doctrine he had brought. He wanted the Pharisees to know that all those years ago, an infant in his mother's arms, the old man, Simeon, had seen who he was: 'A light to enlighten the pagans, and the glory of your people Israel.'

Now, on that windswept hillside, Jesus proclaimed he was 'the light of the world. No follower of mine shall wander in the dark; he shall have the light of life.'

He used such eloquent language that people were surely moved to tears as he tried to link his own fate with the benefits it would bring to them.

Through the Beatitudes ran a constant theme: love. Love was the key to everything. People should not judge, but love; not condemn, but love; not reject, but love. Yet, it must not be a possessive love. It must always strive to come as close as possible to God's love.

But the prime illustration of how Jesus intended to fulfil the Law was how he expanded the Mosaic commandments forbidding murder.

'You have learnt how it was said to our ancestors: *You must not kill*; and if anyone does kill he must answer for it before the court. But I say this to you, anyone who is angry with his brother will answer for it before the court.'

Not only murder was to be punished, but even an uncalled-for, angry outburst. Once more Jesus had broadened the existing code of Moses by adding new strictures to make everyone live a life of personal accountability. This was synthesized in a compelling declaration.

'So then, if you are bringing your offering to the altar and there remember that your brother has something against you, leave your offering there before the altar, go and be reconciled with your brother first, and then come back and present your offering. Come to terms with your opponent in good time while you are still on the way to the court with him, or he may hand you over to the judge and the judge to the officer, and you will be thrown in prison.'

Jesus was saying that in everyone there is an inherent sense of morality; if it was not obeyed, punishment could follow. But for those who listened to his message, there was a promise of new life. Mary Magdalene's own life was striking testimony to that. More than anyone on the hillside, she already had a better understanding of what the Kingdom of Heaven really meant. It would not be an easy place for anyone to enter, let alone survive within its spiritual boundaries unless their faith remained constant. Hers most certainly did.

As if sensing the need to provide a final reminder, Jesus told the crowd the story of the man who built his house on a peak. His neighbours laughed at him, at all the extra effort it had taken to raise the home on such a foundation. But when the annual storm and floods came, the other houses, built on sand, were swept away. Only the house on the rock remained intact.

For Mary Magdalene the message was clear: those who believed in the Master would, like that house, survive. Non-believers would be consigned to spiritual oblivion.

Spell-binding preacher that Jesus was, it is not hard to envisage him drawing to the end of the Sermon on the Mount, with the wind tugging at his robe. Spreading his arms, he raised his voice to offer a final promise. 'Seek and you will find. Knock and it shall be opened unto you.'

For Mary Magdalene, those words could only have been striking confirmation that she was daily coming closer to witnessing the imminent creation of a new world. The cross that would precede it would have also been that more sharply defined.

Ten

The three years of endless walking in all weathers had toughened Mary Magdalene's skin and hardened the soles of her feet. Her fine silk robes had long been replaced with a coarsely-woven voluminous *istomukhuim*, the robe of the desert women.

Hood pulled close to her face against the wind and sun, she had become a familiar figure emerging from a wadi or trekking against the early morning light along a ridge, matching her pace with that of the others. In the evenings she could be seen fetching water with the other women of the house where they were invited to stay overnight. Later, she would help with cooking the evening meal. They ate simply; Judas put a price on everything and challenged the smallest expenditure.

In his mind the treasurer could have been saving the money for the day it could be used to purchase weapons for an earthly revolution.

The others shared this hope, not least because they had been raised in the tradition that only force of arms could prevail. And had not Jesus, early on in his ministry, bluntly stated: 'Do not think that I am come to bring peace on earth. I came not to bring peace but a sword.' And there was his equally unforgettable injunction: 'If you have no sword, sell your cloak and buy one.'

Over those past three years such earthly exhortations had confirmed their belief that Jesus *had* come to raise rebellion, *had* come to sweep away the hated Romans, *had* come to establish a new Kingdom on earth where all Jews could live in freedom; Gentiles would be welcome but it would predominantly be a new Israel. So they believed and so they interpreted his every word and action to support that misconception.

For them a sign of his intention was the increasing way in which Jesus challenged the authorities, preaching against both the Pharisees and Sadducees. At those times his anger was as real as Scripture recalled had been the rage of the great warriors of Israel. They, too, had called upon God to protect their forces –

just as the Master now promised that God would do the same for all those who helped to found his new Kingdom.

Mary Magdalene had long realized it would be pointless trying to persuade them there would be no earthly revolution. In their world women did not express their views on anything outside domestic matters. She knew there would have been no point in reminding them that the Scriptures were filled with strong-willed women: Eve, the mother of all life; Sarah, Abraham's wife; Hannah, the mother of Samuel; Delilah, whose fatal attraction ensnared Samson; Ruth and Rahab, the ancestors of Jesus. But the disciples were the product of a male-dominated society. Their every thought and action reflected no less.

For herself, Mary Magdalene had come to understand the real meaning of the message Jesus expounded, and the way he had chosen to do so. he used parables and allegorical discourses because he wanted only those with 'ears to listen'. He was also sufficiently aware of the religious divergence among the Jews to know he must deal with that first before tackling Roman paganism. While both the Sadducees and Pharisees worshipped the same One God, they did so by very different rules. The people could not be unshackled from Roman domination until they were freed from the crippling sectarianism of their faith. To show them how to achieve that was also part of his mission.

Yet the longer Mary Magdalene remained in their company, the greater the separation of views between her and the disciples. This had led to a clash between Mary Magdalene and Judas. At issue had been the remains of her jar of precious ointment she had used to anoint Jesus' feet in the courtyard of Simon the Pharisee's home. Judas wanted her to sell it to raise further funds. She refused. The other disciples sided with the treasurer. Matthew asked her what was the point of holding on to the jar's remaining contents when it could be sold and the money put to better use, perhaps to clothe the poor and feed some of the hungry who dogged their every footstep. As she calmly continued to refuse to hand over the jar, their anger increased. They accused her of being selfish and in danger of reverting to her old ways.

Jesus had followed the exchanges intently, but not

interfering, satisfied that Mary Magdalene could more than hold her own. But, as the sniping and sneering from the disciples had become more objectionable, his own anger had surfaced.

'Leave this woman be!'

Knowing they had gone too far, the apostles fell into sullen silence. Then, ramming home his point, Jesus added: 'you will have the poor among you always, but you will not always have Me!'

The apostles had become fearful. Was the Master saying he was about to leave them? For how long and where to? Well into the night Mary Magdalene had heard the whispered questions for which they had no answers. Neither would she explain why she was keeping the last of her precious ointment. That was between her and the Master.

Increasingly there was a quiet confidence about Mary Magdalene. Undoubtedly part of it was a woman's intuition: she knew what to say and do at the right time. But there was also her now deep-seated faith that gave her a secure place in the Master's entourage. She had been returned to purity and goodness. Jesus had shown her he would forever be identified with sinners and absorb their guilt.

Increasingly she was coming to understand the reality of where their endless trekking was leading the Master. Winter and summer they criss-crossed the countryside, Jesus preaching, as was his right, in every synagogue, speaking in apocalyptic imagery of the coming of a new age. Preceding it would be disaster, war, the emergence of false prophets, and the persecution of those who believed in him. Mary Magdalene saw that Jesus scrutinized the disciples carefully to see how they received his words and later she could hear the debate among them as they once more tried to fathom what exactly the Master meant.

Jesus continued to use her as a further means to get across a point. He would, for instance, ask her to fetch him a drink. Thirst quenched, he would explain there must always be a thirst for repentance. After the incident at Jacob's Well, he often used water as a common denominator between sin and salvation.

He reminded them what was of the world, the world would never oppose. But what came from God, the world would not only reject but malign, mock and ultimately persecute. He told his listeners they had the capability to recognize the truth, but a lifetime of old habits, ingrained dishonesties and base passions stopped them from doing so.

They were like a sick person who would not seek help because he feared the doctor would impart even worse news. But just as a good physician should never flinch from the truth – for without it there could be no meaningful diagnosis leading to a cure – neither would he hold back. To purify the human conscience he must first arouse and disturb it. To deny they were sinners could only extend the time they were. There were only two kinds of people: those who had found God and those who were still thirsting for him.

Mary Magdalene had come to understand that if she had never sinned, she could never have been saved. It did not mean she would never again be tempted: that possibility would always be there. And now she had the faith to resist. Increasingly she needed it to help her cope with all those who, in their city clothes and cultured Jerusalem accents, asked ever more questions designed to entrap Jesus.

They had been waiting when, late in the Sabbath afternoon, Jesus had stopped at a watering hole at Bethsaida. Peter, Andrew and Philip had all grown up in the hamlet before they moved to Capernaum. Around the pool were the usual number of people who had come in the hope of being healed by Jesus. Among them were several Temple agents, for the moment silent and watchful.

Mary Magdalene was struck by the condition of one disabled man. He could not walk but had dragged himself on a wooden pallet to the pool. He immediately pleaded with Jesus to heal him.

'Do you believe in the coming of the Kingdom?' It had become axiomatic for Jesus to ask the question before performing a cure.

When the man said he did, Jesus replied, 'Rise. Take up your bed and walk.'

Uncertain at first, the man struggled to his feet, the delight on his face matched by the joyous cries of the others. Slowly, gaining in strength, the man began to walk, a step at a time, one foot after the other, gaining confidence all the time. His steps grew faster until he could run, lapping the edge of the pool before returning to pick up his pallet and hoist it on his shoulder. As he began to thank Jesus, one of the agents intervened. 'It is the Sabbath. You are not allowed to carry your bed on this day.'

Suddenly, confused and uncertain, the man was about to put down the pallet, when Jesus ordered him to go to the nearby synagogue and give thanks for his cure. As the man hurried away, no doubt relieved to be spared from the confrontation everyone around the pool sensed was developing, the agent put his first question to Jesus: 'By what right do you order such things on the Sabbath?'

Six times already since Mary Magdalene had been with Jesus, she had witnessed him heal on the Sabbath. He had cast out evil spirits, restored the withered hand of a man, made a crippled woman walk, cured a woman of the dropsy, and opened the eyes of a man who was blind. For her, the cures were not only evidence of Jesus' thaumaturgic powers and testimony to his rabbinical authority, but compelling proof that through faith came renewal. The feats were tangible evidence of the truth of what he preached.

Performing those other miracles, he had ignored the probing questions of the Temple agents. But after watching the man stride away with his pallet, Jesus rounded on the agent. Just as the agent had grounded his question in Scripture, so did Jesus do so with his response. He reminded the agent that the teaching of the prophets was clear: religious observation was of secondary importance when it came to offering help.

For a moment there was silence. Another agent, with all the slick skill of a lawyer, spoke: 'Rabbi, are you saying you are greater than the Sabbath?'

Jesus rebuked him with a question which would be readily understood by the villagers of Bethsaida. 'Is there not a single one of you who does not remove his ox or donkey from the manger and take it out to water on the Sabbath?'

Through the laughter of the villagers had come yet another question from the agent. Had not God rested on the seventh day from his creative work?

Without hesitation, Jesus answered. 'My Father has never yet ceased his work, and I am working too.'

For Mary Magdalene, for all who understood, the Master was once more affirming his unique affiliation with God. Through him, God was showing that the Word had indeed 'become flesh', it *was* acceptable to perform acts of mercy on the Sabbath; God had always said so.

For the agents, all that mattered was that, by implying direct kinship with God, Jesus was also claiming equality with him. And that was blasphemy. Yet Mary Magdalene knew nothing would sway Jesus from preaching and healing.

A few days later, they were making their way southwards again, following the flow of the Jordan, when once more misplaced expectations were used to try and trap him. In spite of Jesus' persistent disclaimers, people still continued to find a powerful nationalistic undertow in his preaching, one they believed was the precursor to sweeping away Roman rule. Such a prospect had an enduring and overwhelming appeal to the passionate commitment to liberty which burned brightly in the heart of every Jew.

From time to time, to cool their expectations, Jesus retreated into the hills beyond the River Jordan. There he continued to try and instil in the disciples that what he meant by true freedom was a spiritual liberation from sin. For Judas the words could only have held a very different meaning. The miracles and the growing crowds were enough to confirm that Jesus was capable of achieving anything, including, when the time came, issuing the call to rise against the Roman occupiers and their vassal, the tetrarch. That could be the only way to launch the coming Kingdom. David and Simon Maccabeus had shown what armed struggle could achieve. The Master was only biding his time. All his miraculous feats were no more than a prelude to the greatest miracle of all – the unifying of the people into a cohesive force to drive out the occupiers. Every day brought closer the prospect because the Master had himself said the Kingdom was coming ever closer. And, of course, after all the people had endured, he was right to call it a Kingdom of Heaven. It would indeed be like living in Heaven after these long years of earthly hell. So Judas believed, and so he would act.

When Jesus led his entourage back across the Jordan, the expectation that he would create an earthly paradise was on the faces of the crowd waiting on the track leading to Shechem. They had deliberately chosen a historic place. This was the ground on which Abraham had stood and heard the Lord's voice, and where Saul, in defeat, had walked to fall upon his own sword on Mount Gilboa.

At the back of the crowd, where they always lurked – 'like serpents', Philip described them – were the Temple agents. As so often nowadays, there was a sprinkling of Pharisees in the crowd. 'Waiting their opportunity in the guise of honest men.'

It was not long in coming. Two of the Pharisees stepped forward and told Jesus they were in dispute with the tax authorities in Tiberias. Rabbis were often called upon to suggest ways to reduce a tax obligation. One of the Pharisees began by praising Jesus. 'Master, you are an honest man. They say you teach the way God requires.'

Jesus waited, patient as always, for the question. It was couched in the circumlocutory language favoured by the Pharisees.

'This tax which we Pharisees resent so much having to pay, but which our tetrarch insists must be handed over: should we pay or not?'

Then in the next breath came the sting in the tail. 'Which of us is right – we Pharisees who loathe and resent the tax, or the tetrarch who justifies it for Rome?'

How many times had Mary Magdalene heard her own clients yearn for the day when they would be free of tax burdens? But that wishful thinking had been done in the privacy of her salon, knowing their grumbles would never be repeated beyond its walls.

But the Master was being asked to state his position publicly, with all the risks that could entail. If he said it was not lawful to pay taxation to the Herodian administration, Jesus faced the very real possibility of being reported to the Romans, accused of conspiracy against the Emperor. Every year hundreds of Jews who protested their tax demands were crucified on such a charge. Yet if Jesus said the tax was lawful, he would not only earn the further enmity of the Pharisees, but run the risk of seeing the very people he wanted to help turn from him in disgust. No Deliverer or Saviour would ever have agreed the people should continue to bear such an onerous burden. Upon his reply Jesus would either become an open rebel against Rome – or an enemy of the people. Yet how could he provide an absolute standard which could be equally applied to God and Caesar?

The impossibility seemed to be in his angry response. 'You hypocrites! Why are you trying to catch me out?'

The triumphant quick look between the two Pharisees and the Temple agents would also have been there. These were indeed serpents. Not even branding them as hypocrites – a damning word in their lexicon – could take away their sense of impending victory. After all those times of seeing their traps spring uselessly open before their very eyes, they had successfully baited one.

Suddenly Jesus demanded, cold anger reflected in his words: 'Show me the money in which the tax is paid.'

One of the Pharisees handed over a coin. Pressing forward, the silent expectant onlookers saw Jesus examine one side of the denar, then the other, first the face of the Emperor, Tiberias Caesar, then on the reverse side, the word Pontifex Maximus. Finally, Jesus held up the coin between finger and thumb. 'Whose head is this and whose inscription?'

The Pharisees answered. 'Caesar's, of course.'

Then came his response. 'Pay unto Caesar what is due to Caesar, and pay to God what is due to God.'

The sense of relief Mary Magdalene felt, then the wonderful feeling of once more witnessing another victory for the Master must have swiftly followed each other. Jesus had understood that the real issue was not God or Caesar, but God *and* Caesar.

The coin's inscription confirmed the Jews were not a free

nation in earthly terms. But, by adding the caveat they should also pay to God what was due to him, Jesus was saying his Kingdom was not of this world. If they accepted that, they would realize the national freedom they yearned for was not the only one available to them. He was telling them he was here to promote only the rights of God. When they took full account of that, they would achieve the earthly freedom they so urgently desired. Jesus had once more not only escaped a clever trap, but reinforced the one reason he was on earth.

Leaving his entrappers speechless, he led his small band on towards the next staging point. There would be more crowds. More Temple agents. But Mary Magdalene could be confident the Master would deal with them all. And she could only marvel at the way he did. Time and again she heard him include epigrams which contained a new kind of truth. 'He that finds his life shall lose it.' 'What shall a man give in return for his soul?' Phrase by phrase Jesus reinforced his principles. 'Whoever exalts himself shall be abased, and he that humbles himself shall be exalted.' 'A man's life consists not in the abundance of the things which he possesses.' Worldly power and authority meant nothing when God was not the forging link. Yet the disciples continued to see Jesus only in human terms.

Shortly after she had sold up in Magdala and they were walking through the foothills of Galilee, Jesus asked the apostles what people were saying about him. A woman in a male group, Mary Magdalene waited for others to speak first. But the disciples remained silent, clearly none of them anxious to be the first to answer.

Finally Thomas had blurted that some were convinced Jesus was the reincarnation of Elijah, the great prophet about whom an ancient king of this land, Ahab, had bitterly cried: 'Art thou he that troubleth Israel?'

The sheer possibility they were in the presence of such a revered figure as Elijah, who had predicted so much, provoked further suggestions. Thaddeus said people he had spoken to wondered if the Master was actually Moses returned to earth.

Andrew said the talk out on the coastal plains was that Jesus was really Jacob who, even before Moses, had promised to make this land one for God's chosen people.

Bartholomew said people wondered if Jesus was Joshua – whose very Hebrew name meant 'God is salvation'. Philip revealed they thought he could be Samuel, holder of an equally revered name – 'name of God' – and whose moral stature was so great that he had direct access to the Lord.

Jesus had listened without comment.

Finally he turned to Peter and repeated the question in a slightly different form. 'Who do you say I am?'

In that broad Galilean accent outsiders found so hard to understand, Peter replied, 'The Messiah'.

In the sudden, stunned silence, Jesus had quietly praised Peter for his perception. It was the first time Jesus had confirmed his divinity. No doubt sensing the excitement his words had understandably produced, he warned them to keep the knowledge secret: the world was not yet ready to learn such a momentous truth.

Once more Jesus turned to Peter.

'You did not learn that from mortal man; it was revealed to you by my heavenly Father. I say this to you: you are Peter the Rock, and on this rock I will build my Church, and the powers of death shall never conquer it. I will give you the keys of the Kingdom of Heaven; what you forbid on earth shall be forbidden in Heaven, and what you allow on earth shall be allowed in Heaven.'

Jesus then gave the first clear indication that he expected to die. Peter, filled with the authority he had just received, took Jesus aside and, in an almost angry tone, insisted: 'No, Lord, this shall never happen to you.'

With a woman's grasp of how little men understood about pain, Mary Magdalene realized that for Peter, indeed all the apostles, suffering would be a sign of failure. Jesus was also saying that following him was never going to be easy. But that did not mean relinquishing all earthly values; it was a matter of placing them in a proper spiritual context. 'What does a man gain by winning the whole world at the cost of his true self?'

For Mary Magdalene, those words were another confirmation of how right she had been to renounce her worldly ways. For her, Jesus was no longer a man of God, but the Son of God.

A few months after Mary Magdalene had left Simon the Pharisee's house, they had once more approached Nain. It was late afternoon and the fierce heat of the day was easing. The long walk out of Samaria had left them tired and thirsty. But there was a way to go yet before they would reach one of the farmhouses on whose flat roof Jesus preferred them to spend the night. Over a simple supper there would be further discussion about the latest healings he had performed: the cure of a paralytic; a leper; a man's withered arm and exorcising demons to make people sane again. Every cure was an example of how steadfast faith could overcome adversity; each thaumaturgic act symbolized the illumination of faith and victory over evil.

Approaching the outskirts of Nain, a woman named Anna came running towards them, wailing the cries of the newly bereaved. Mary Magdalene recognized her: Anna had been one of the serving women at the fateful dinner given by Simon the Pharisee. Then, she had been cold and contemptuous of the Master. Now, through her broken sobs, she begged Jesus to revive her daughter.

'She is dead, rabbi,' Anna cried, falling to her knees and clutching at the dusty hem of Jesus' robe.

Reaching down, Jesus helped Anna to her feet, his eyes searching her face.

'Do you have faith that the Kingdom is upon you?' he asked.

Unable to speak through her grief, Anna nodded.

'Go on believing! Have faith! Come!'

With those words, Jesus strode into Nain. Mary Magdalene would have seen the sheer purpose on his face and sensed something more than a physical energy which seemed to come from a wellspring deep within the Master. It was as if his own faith was sufficiently powerful to impart confidence and courage in others.

Reaching Anna's house, Jesus found the courtyard filled with

Nain's professional mourners. They were in full lament, accompanied by flutes, pipes and death gongs.

'Be silent!' Jesus commanded. 'There is no one dead here! The child only sleeps!'

Accompanied by Anna, he went to where the girl lay in her burial shroud.

In the courtyard and the street beyond, there was total silence. It was as if life itself held its breath.

Suddenly, from inside the house came a child's cry, then shouts of joy from Anna. Moments later she and her daughter appeared in the courtyard.

Excitement and relief swept over the crowd. They had seen or heard nothing like it. The musicians who had been mourning death, now celebrated rebirth.

As Jesus left, he told Anna to say nothing of what had happened in the room where her child had lain lifeless. But Mary Magdalene had been with him long enough to know such miracles could never be kept quiet.

And, even as they had walked out of Nain into the darkness of a Galilean night, the whispers had started that what had happened was sorcery.

Early on, Mary Magdalene saw that Jesus' teaching ministry and healing miracles were at their most powerful after he had spent lengthy periods in prayer. Afterwards he had explained the importance of having God continuously in their lives as a vibrant, living certainty. She came to understand that when the Master spoke about clothing the naked, nursing the sick and feeding the hungry, he was describing a God committed to help every human situation, a selfless God whose one wish was to share himself first with her and his disciples, then through them, with all people.

Jesus constantly found new ways to engage their interest. On yet another long trek south, he told them the story of the rich man who gave his servants money and how only one, through diligent application, multiplied the sum. The message reinforced a constant theme: effort and common-sense were essential for anyone embarking on a new spiritual life. Such parables were a good way to focus attention on the *evangelion*, the gospel of good news, Jesus brought. He wanted all of them to understand that removing injustice and helping the under-privileged would be a constant challenge, for the poor and oppressed of the world would indeed always be there.

On a clear summer's day, Jesus began another missionary trek out of Capernaum. Shortly afterwards they took a boat across the lake to the port of Gergesa. They landed in the lee of cliffs and were met by a local swineherd, Shim. Gergesa was the only town where pigs were raised and sold to the Romans. Dispensation to do so had been granted by the Temple.

Shim, with the slow-speaking manner of a man used to long silences and solitude, warned them to stay clear of the burial caves to the sides of the cliffs. They were the refuge of a madman. At that moment there was a truly terrifying scream from the graveyard and the wretch emerged, filthy dirty and naked, his hair and beard matted with dried blood. Seeing Jesus, he ran forward with threatening gestures and cried: 'What do you want with me, Jesus, son of the Most High God? Swear by God you will not torture me!'

Motioning for the others to remain still, Jesus walked toward the man whose screaming grew louder and even more demented. Jesus stood before the wretch, staring fixedly into his eyes. The man stopped in mid-scream. Anxious moments followed; the only sound was the lunatic's heavy breathing.

Loud and clear, came Jesus' question: 'What is thy name?'

The reply was a madman's: 'My name is Legion, for we are many.' An allusion, no doubt, to the hundreds of demons that possessed him. Once more, the wretch howled, his screams even more terrifying.

Jesus remained calm and passive.

The madman fell silent and sat down before Jesus.

The peace was broken by a sudden new screaming, louder and even more fearful, coming from the top of the cliffs. Shim led the rush up the scree slope. Jesus and the madman remained in silent communion.

Reaching the clifftop, Mary Magdalene saw a sight which would remain with her, with all of them, for the rest of their lives.

The sound came from scores of pigs racing towards the cliff edge. Still squealing madly, the animals plunged to their deaths in the lake below. They went on and on, wave after suicidal wave. Matthew gave up counting when he had reaching two thousand. Then, just as suddenly as the self-destruction began, it was over. There were no more pigs to hurl themselves to death. There was only silence.

Down below, Jesus was leading the madman to the lake's edge. While the others watched, he bathed the man and covered him in an old robe from the boat.

Shim had become frightened; nothing in his simple life had prepared him for all he had just witnessed. It was there in the question he put to Jesus. 'Who are you?'

Jesus gave a response Mary Magdalene was now familiar with: 'I am the way.'

In those words Jesus was again saying his miracles were not only manifestations of power, but proof of human deliverance from sin. Yet, once more, incredulity had underpinned the words of Shim – as they had done with others who had witnessed other miracles Jesus had performed. There were so many that they would become referred to collectively as 'he cures the sick, the blind, and the lame.' To which could be added Jesus calmed the sea and made the wind his servant.

To Mary Magdalene those actions could only have provided strength as the earthly clock of Jesus' time moved slowly and inexorably towards his final hour.

Eleven

Darkness came like a thief in the night to the Herodian fortress prison at Machaerus, first obscuring the towering sandstone cliffs on the eastern shore of the Dead Sea, the immense sink-hole whose waters had long become a witches' brew of chemicals, bitumen and the asphalts which Egypt's pharaohs had used for embalming. Then, fleeing across the water, the last of the day vanished into two gorges, before finally reaching the massive walls of the castle. Originally built to guard the highway from Cairo to Damascus, it was where Herod Antipas now kept his prisoners. They never numbered less than hundreds. None was as famous as John the Baptist.

The cells and torture chambers extended beneath the ground on several levels. Condemned prisoners were often shackled by having their feet fixed in hollow stones filled with molten lead. When the time came for them to die, they were thrown into a pit to be mauled and eaten alive by starving wild dogs. Others were drowned in vats of oil. There were hinged human effigies made from wood and iron and lined with spikes. When a hollowed-out shape was closed, the spikes slowly penetrated a man's body, resulting in a slow and excruciating death. But the most favoured form of execution remained the axe. Its blade made of unpolished iron was crude in appearance as in action, and epitomized the tetrarch's warning to behave or be beheaded. The axe's partner, the block, stood in the centre of the beheading chamber. Made from hardwood, it was stained with blood and scarred from blows of the blade.

The execution area separated the two tiers of cells. On the upper level were those for the lesser offenders awaiting judgment. They might escape with no more than a flogging or confiscation of property or land. On the lower level were those accused of more serious offences: tax evasion or open opposition to the tetrarch. For them their last journey was to the execution area.

John was incarcerated on the lower level. His cell was no more than a barred hole in the rock-face, its dank, stygian darkness briefly lit once a day from the rush-torch of a guard bringing him food and water. A hole in the floor served as a toilet. From time to time he had been dragged up flights of stone steps to face Herod Antipas. Each time the tetrarch had demanded John must withdraw his attacks about the tetrarch's relationship with Herodius.

The scandal continued to shock every Jew. To have coveted his brother's wife was a crime against the commandments of Moses. Banishing his own wife and finally marrying Herodius had done nothing to mitigate the offence. To the Pharisees the tetrarch was a religious heretic, and thought little better of by High Priest Caiaphas. Matters had worsened when Herod Antipas had begun an affair with Herodius' own daughter, a voluptuous fourteen-year-old called Salome. Clever and devious like her mother, the girl had played on her step-father's carnal passions to become his favourite in court. Rumour had it that Herodius tolerated their relationship because it secured her own position.

A striking woman, as bejewelled as any Egyptian princess, Herodius was as ambitious and calculating as she was cruel. At times she appeared almost mad in her capricious behaviour, as on the day she had casually ordered a group of her husband's slaves to be slashed with swords and thrown into the Sea of Salt to see how long they would float. It had taken them several hours to bleed to death.

She had shrugged off the condemnation of Caiaphas and the Pharisees. But the continued attacks of John were a different matter. His presence at Machaerus was a living reminder that Herodius was not undisputed mistress of all she surveyed. Long ago she had lost patience with her husband's attempts to persuade John to desist: threats and physical torture had not stopped the Baptist from repeating his reproaches. Even in his cell John had continued to fulminate that Herod Antipas should set an example to his people.

John continued to say so as once more Herod Antipas and his court arrived at Machaerus. The occasion was to mark the tetrarch's forty-ninth birthday. For Herodius it was a further opportunity to try to rid herself of the Baptist. She may well have thought of little else on the journey south from Jerusalem before concluding she would do so by exploiting her husband's desire for Salome.

Herod Antipas had kept John alive for two reasons. It was a matter of personal pride for the tetrarch to force him to apologize before having him killed. However, as time passed, the tetrarch had become increasingly aware of the widespread support the prophet continued to attract. Herod Antipas had realized that to execute John could trigger violent repercussions. While his troops would quell it, his own standing would be seriously damaged in the eyes of the Roman administration. Pontius Pilate regarded Herod Antipas as a barbarian who did not understand how to be subservient and to accept that nothing could be achieved without the procurator's approval. Instead, the tetrarch displayed an increasing arrogance and had begun to develop some of the more manic traits of his father: a laugh which seemed to verge on the edge of madness, mood swings and unpredictability and a conviction he was surrounded on all sides by plotters. His paranoia may have been caused by syphilis; his adult life had been notorious for its licentious ways.

Matters had not been helped with the latest reports from Galilee about Jesus. While still outwardly dismissive of them, Herod Antipas had become sufficiently alarmed to have moved his court from Tiberias to Jerusalem. Even behind its ramparts and protected by a sizeable army, he had not felt entirely at ease.

All his life the tetrarch had believed his father's ordering the slaughter of the new-born at Bethlehem had not eliminated a threat to the Herodian dynasty; that waiting to emerge was a figure who would bring to naught the other abiding belief Herod Antipas held: that one day Rome's rulers would eventually destroy each other, leaving him to rule over All-Judaea.

Herod the Great had instilled in his son the need to move swiftly and ruthlessly at the first hint of trouble. He himself had executed a wife and two of his sons when he felt they could usurp his authority. Not only had he built a Second Temple to try and mitigate his unpopularity, but he had created a succession of palace-fortresses across the land in which he could be protected should the people rebel. One citadel was the Antonia Fortress in Jerusalem which, in a typical grandiose gesture, Herod the Great had handed over to the Romans for a headquarters.

Herod Antipas had acquired from his father the same combination of cunning and extravagance when dealing with the occupiers. Essential to maintaining that relationship was ensuring that no Jew created a problem.

When the tetrarch had first heard about Jesus almost three years ago, he had not associated him with any threat. The Nazarene was the son of a carpenter, with only a small band of permanent followers. Unusually, one of them was a woman, a whore from Magdala. However, over the past year Jesus' ministry had become more outspoken, attacking the Pharisees, then the Temple, to the point where Caiaphas had despatched agents to check on what was happening in Galilee. Still the tetrarch had not been unduly alarmed. Travelling rabbis had always vied with one another to claim their reinterpretation of the Word was the correct one.

But increasingly, Jesus had focused his preaching on one particular aspect – the creation of a new Kingdom. That had finally fuelled the tetrarch's paranoia.

He had repeatedly questioned John on the matter, but the Baptist had only insisted the tetrarch must seek repentance through baptism before it was too late. Instead Herod had sent his troop commander, Molath, to investigate Jesus. He had returned from Galilee with news that the Nazarene still had only a handful of permanent followers and the Magdala woman. There were claims the Nazarene was descended from any one of the puritanical prophets, though his mother insisted he was from the House of David. He had done a great number of healings – but again the rabbis of Galilee had had a reputation for effecting some remarkable cures since the days Elijah had wandered the hills. While the Nazarene now attracted huge crowds, they were overwhelmingly women and children; the men were mostly aged and infirm. Hardly a force capable of launching a new Kingdom, Molath reassured the tetrarch.

Nevertheless, Herod Antipas decided that for his birthday

celebrations he would travel to Machaerus, the southernmost point of his fiefdom, and remain there until custom demanded his presence in Jerusalem for Passover, less than a month away.

There would be over a hundred thousand pilgrims from all over the Diaspora. Would the Nazarene use the occasion to reveal more of his plans for this Kingdom?

It had taken days for what happened at the tetrarch's birthday banquet to emerge from inside Machaerus. As the details were passed from mouth to mouth, people could not be certain they had heard correctly, so shocking were they.

The evening began normally. A hundred roast lambs, together with delicacies from as far away as Cairo and Damascus, were served to the guests seated in the torch-lit fortress courtyard. The wine flowed freely. At the height of the revelry, a drunken Herod Antipas ordered Molath to bring John from the dungeons.

An expectant silence settled over the guests. Few had seen the Baptist; everyone knew his stubbornness had inflamed Herodius beyond reason. She and her daughter, Salome, saw John emerge into the courtyard. Captivity had done little to weaken his imposing physique. John had the body of a gladiator; resolute and unflinching eyes showed he was still far from broken. For a moment Herod Antipas and John faced each other. Who knows what was in the tetrarch's mind. A new way to finally humiliate John and break him in front of the guests? Instead the tetrarch invited his prisoner to preach. The guests would vote on the sermon by a show of hands.

John may well have sensed he was being offered an escape. All he need do was choose a safe subject, one that did not challenge the morals of his host, and he could be set free. But John was not interested in pleasing his audience, only God. Pointing a finger first at Herod and then Herodius, John once more cried out: 'you have no right to your brother's wife.'

John's faith had not wavered after months of incarceration. How easy it would have been to choose the easy way, the earthly way. Instead he had decided to remind everyone – the women with their painted faces, the men in their finest robes; the musicians and the dancers – the truth that God had decreed marriage was holy and indivisible.

The fury of the tetrarch remained in his scream. 'Take him back to his hole.'

Bored and disappointed – displaying the joylessness of the jaded – his guests demanded new entertainment. He beckoned to Salome and asked her to dance. The child, a descendant of the noble warrior Maccabeus, but already debased and corrupted by her degenerate mother and step-father, pirouetted slowly at first then, gaining speed, swirled barefoot, skilfully removing one silken veil after another, tossing each one into her audience.

With one last fling, Salome threw herself into the tetrarch's lap and whispered in his ear. He shouted: 'Whatever you ask I will give you, up to half my kingdom.'

The guests laughed and cheered.

Herod Antipas repeated his offer. Once more Salome whispered to him. The tetrarch recoiled, visibly shaken. Salome murmured a third time, this time looking towards Herodius. Her mother nodded. Salome continued her beguiling, suggestive whispering. For Herodius, John was a thorn, pricking what little conscience she had left. Already some of the guests were calling out that Herod Antipas must not break his promise.

Herod Antipas sat transfixed. Salome continued to flaunt herself before him, daring him to refuse. A combination of the wine, the promise of her almost naked body, the growing calls not to refuse her, combined to tip the balance. Slowly, reluctantly, then more firmly, Herod Antipas nodded. He ordered Molath to carry out Salome's request. In the beheading chamber, John's head was severed from his body with an axe. Molath returned with Salome's gory gift on a platter.

She recoiled from the bloodied, bearded head and ran from the courtyard.

On that starlit night, at the bidding of the child of an adulteress, Herod Antipas murdered the forerunner of the Messiah.

When the news finally reached Galilee, Jesus gathered his small band together and praised John for being steadfast to the end. 'They failed to recognize him, and did what they wanted to him; and in the same way the Son of Man is to suffer at their hands.'

For Mary Magdalene the words were all too prophetic. Just as John had willingly died to fulfil his role in Scripture, so Jesus was preparing for his own fate. Such supreme selflessness could only have deepened her own belief and commitment.

To try and instil this in the disciples, Jesus had taken them northwards through the Galilean brushwood and myrtle, up to the scree slopes which marked the foothills of Mount Hermon. Already he had used a mountain setting to preach the Beatitudes, the ways through which people could find God in their lives.

Now Jesus intended to use a similar setting for an even more momentous occasion. All day they climbed, until at some point Jesus ordered Mary Magdalene and the others to rest. Only Peter, James and John would be allowed to accompany him on up the slopes of Hermon.

The day was drawing to a close and the sun sinking behind the summit. The four men had only climbed a little further when, from below, Mary Magdalene saw a brilliant ray dazzle the eyes of the three apostles. She saw them throw up their hands to avoid the piercing light. At that same moment Jesus, who was a little further up the slope, appeared to vanish in the glare.

When he next appeared: 'he was praying and the appearance of his face had changed and his clothes were dazzling white. Suddenly there were two men talking with him, Moses and Elijah.'

In that moment, the Old Testament was conjoined with the New: Moses, the author of the Law, and Elijah, the chief of all the prophets, were accepting that Jesus had come to finish what they had started. While they spoke, the mountainside was momentarily transformed into the very vestibule of heaven. A cloud formed above them, from which a voice called from the cloud, 'This is my Beloved Son on whom my favour rests. Listen to him.'

In her time with Jesus, Mary Magdalene had learned that a cloud was a sign of great importance. At the Master's baptism by John, there had been a cloud from which the same unearthly voice had spoken. Now, at this moment of his transfiguration, the voice had once more confirmed Jesus' work of salvation, and that his life was drawing ever nearer to its earthly close.

Through those moments on Hermon, Jesus was telling his followers they must fear nothing, for he would always be with them, there to guide and direct them; that one day they too would embark on the journey he must soon make to prepare the Kingdom. Before making their journeys to enter it, they must each let go of the past and embrace the new Truth. To do so they must go forth and live the life he had guided them towards. He would always be there for them to make sure they did.

Yet, despite the voice testifying to the unbroken and undivided union of God and his Son and of the presence of Moses and Elijah, a reminder that 'God would raise up in Israel One like Himself,' it was left to Peter to express the misunderstanding over what he and his companions had just witnessed.

'Master, how good it is that we are here! Shall we make three shelters, one for you, one for Moses, and one for Elijah?'

That moment of transient glory for Peter was no more than a manifestation of Christ's earthly power. He and the other disciples had once more failed to understand they had witnessed the very divinity of Jesus.

For Mary Magdalene, the dazzling display she had witnessed on the side of Mount Hermon was accompanied by the realization that soon it would be followed by a darkness more terrible than she had ever experienced.

Then only faith would protect her from the plots being hatched in Jerusalem.

Many other accounts about Jesus had followed the original one brought to the Temple by the agent who, almost three years previously, had ridden from Capernaum on a donkey to report the exorcism of a young boy and the equally miraculous healing of Peter's mother-in-law.

That first report had been processed through the Temple administration. Its office dealt with keeping track of tithes due, tax payments payable to Rome, fees received from every animal sacrifice at the Great Altar, and the percentage to be credited to the High Priest. Such matters were dealt with by several hundred scribes and their clerks who recorded the daily minutiae of Jewish life in All-Judaea. Every birth and death was entered in ledgers, as was every marriage solemnized and a record kept of every Jewish boy's *bar mitzvah*, the moment when he declared his submission to the commandments of the Law and accepted the Temple's right to control his religious obligations. Within the vast labyrinth of underground vaults were filed details of every Jew in the land; when and where they were born and lived, the profession they followed, the date they died. At the end of each century the scrolls were burnt to make space for new entries.

Few outside the upper echelon of the administration realized all this data was available to Pilate as part of the accommodation he had made with Caiaphas. The arrangement had been worked out during a number of secret meetings between the High Priest and the procurator. Behind this arrangement was a common need by the two most powerful men in the land. Neither had a liking for the other, but both had come to realize the importance of a society in which every Jew would live by the rigid principles the Temple demanded, and Rome could rule without trouble.

Caiaphas had used an underground passageway linking the Temple to the Antonia Fortress to meet Pilate in the Procurator's private quarters. Normally the covered way was only used to transport the Temple tribute into the fortress, so avoiding the need to carry it past the gaze of an understandably resentful population.

That first report from Capernaum would hardly have posed a threat to the arrangement between the High Priest and procurator. The details provided by the agent were written down by a clerk before beginning their journey through the labyrinth of offices behind the Nicanor Gate. Jesus would have been referred to as 'of Nazareth', or the Nazarene.

The village itself was so small that even the rapacious merchants of Greece thought it not worth visiting. There was even confusion over its name. Galileans called it En Nasiba, Natzrath, or even Notzereth. In Aramaic it was called Nazira, in Syriac, Nasaya, which means 'protected by God'.

There was nothing in the records to indicate that Nazareth had been singled out for divine protection. Historically there was no Temple record of when the village had even been established, which may account for why it was also referred to as a *netzer*, Hebrew for a sucker which suddenly appears on the stump of a tree. Centuries before, Isaiah had predicted a spiritual netzer would come forth from the roots of the nation and would initially make little impact, and indeed many people would despise it before realizing its true significance. To the scribe responsible for the village records, Nazareth was just another of those small and insignificant places in Galilee.

At each step the report gathered more paperwork, perhaps details about Peter's mother-in-law or the background to some of the Capernaum eye-witnesses the agent had interviewed. As his report progressed through the system, still more data was attached to it from the ledger entry of how Jesus had been brought to the Temple by his parents, a note confirming the rites governing the consecration of a first-born had been fully observed.

Not for a moment had the High Priest been aware that an old man, standing in the Courtyard of the Israelites, in the sunset of his own life, had spoken of the dawn of a new world as he held the infant from Nazareth in his arms. If a record had existed of the meeting with Simeon, it would most likely have been dismissed as of no consequence. Not a day passed without some person prophesying in the Temple courtyards that the Messiah was about to appear. Since becoming High Priest, Caiaphas had discouraged such speculation: it would anger the Romans.

At some point, a clerk reviewing the paperwork had spotted something. It may well have been the account of Jesus' encounter, when still a boy, with some of the Temple teachers. What may have caught the eye of the clerk was the reported response of the young Nazarene to his mother's understandably somewhat surprised question as to where her previously untutored son had found the knowledge to debate with his elders: 'Did you not know I was bound to be in my Father's house?'

The clerk might well have taken the words at face value: the newly bar mitzvahed boy was saying that, as a devout Jew, where else would he be expected to be found other than in the Temple? The clerk may also have been new to the job, eager to follow the rule that when in doubt, consult. He may have spoken with colleagues, perhaps even a scribe. Any one of those possibilities would explain why the paperwork on Jesus had been referred to Shem, the High Priest's Chief Scribe.

Joseph Caiaphas' outer office, where Shem sat, was the busiest in the Temple. Literally anything and everything which impinged upon the High Priest's authority eventually ended up in the spacious salon. Shem had a staff of a dozen scribes who dealt with the continuous flow of scrolls. They came not only from All-Judaea, but far beyond its borders; from Alexandria with its community of some 300,000 Jews; from Jewish settlements as far east as India and as far west as Spain and Gaul; from the old empires of Carthage, Babylon and Persia; from every outpost of the Diaspora, daily came a variety of problems which eventually ended up in Shem's office. Permits to build a new synagogue; licences to trade in holy oils; export and import tariffs; marriage announcements; death notices; authority to function as a *mohel*, a practitioner trained in the delicate art of circumcision: there was a need for everything to bear the stamped approval of the Temple. In practice this meant obtaining the signature of Shem or, if the matter was sufficiently important, that of Caiaphas.

When reports from the Capernaum agent and its attendant papers reached his desk, the Chief Scribe, himself a lawyer with considerable autonomy, dealt with the matter without recourse to Caiaphas. Shem despatched more Temple agents to Galilee to gather more information.

Enquiries were to be made of those who had been present on the bank of the Jordan when John had baptized the Nazarene. Witnesses should be asked to remember exactly what they heard after the dove descended and urged to recall how long the Nazarene had been in the wilderness and what he claimed happened there. In Nazareth, members of the congregation were to be questioned about the incident in the synagogue which had ended with Jesus fleeing.

In Capernaum, more questions were to be put to neighbours of Peter's mother-in-law; what sort of woman was she? Had she been seriously ill before she was 'cured', or was this another example of Galilean folklore? And her son-in-law: what manner of man was he who could abandon his wife and work to wander the hills of Galilee? The others with him: what was there to say about them?

Simon the Pharisee and his other dinner guests were to be spoken to, respectfully in their case, for Simon had power. But everything they said should be noted down, not least the Nazarene's claim to be able to forgive sins – exemplified by the whore from Magdala.

Agents would go there and ask yet more questions. Had the Nazarene any previous contact with Mary Magdalene before she had given up a profitable way of life and sold her home to travel with him? Did anyone know what was their relationship? Could anyone ever recall a rabbi consorting with a whore? Always the questions had come back to Jesus.

The agents had spent weeks in Galilee before returning to report to Shem. More weeks had passed while he studied their findings. There was still not sufficient to lay the matter before Caiaphas. But Shem, with a lawyer's instinct, sensed that the Nazarene could become a problem.

There was evidence that five of the Nazarene's closest followers had previous links to the Zealots. By themselves that guerrilla force could hope to achieve little. But if the Nazarene was to order those five men to train his own followers in military tactics, he would have at the Zealots' disposal a sizeable force, and one that was no longer comprised mostly of women and children and the infirm. A growing number of able-bodied men were also attending his meetings. Mobilized, they could threaten the relationship between the Temple and the Roman occupiers.

Shem sent the agents back to Galilee with instructions they were to stay close to the Nazarene, listen to what he said and observe what he did. Whenever the opportunity arose, they were to question him, everything they asked must be with a view to entrapping the Nazarene over his carefully-worded claims. What right did he claim for himself to call sinners to repentance? What did he mean by saying he could cast out devils? What was his authority to challenge the traditional regulations of the Talmud over the Sabbath?

The same questions were to be put to the Nazarene over and again. Each time his answers were to be checked against previous ones. Every healing was to be carefully recorded and, if possible, challenged as sorcery.

For over a year the agents had gathered their details.

Finally, in the month before Passover and the onset of Jesus' third year of ministry, Shem decided there was a *prima facie* case to place before the High Priest.

The relationship between the two men was more than a working one. Shem had his own living quarters in the Caiaphas household. Like any good assistant, he knew when to listen and when to speak.

The symbolism of the number of disciples Jesus had appointed was not lost on Joseph Caiaphas. Were they a reminder of the dozen precious stones sewn into the undergarment he himself wore against his skin? Was the Nazarene somehow signalling he claimed for himself the authority of the office of High Priest? Was another sign the way the Nazarene called those closest to him 'apostles': the word came from Greek and meant 'envoy' or 'messenger'. Was that another coded signal from the Nazarene?

The agents described him as presumptuous, that at times 'his mind wanders', especially 'when he is dizzied by the ideas he puts forth'. The most frequent descriptions were a 'fanatic' and a 'dreamer'. 'A man almost never seen to laugh', but 'quick to anger and scorn.'

However, the reports on the Nazarene's cures were what Caiaphas would have expected: they were very much in keeping with the methods used by other Galilean healers.

For centuries they had successfully demonstrated that some were hysterical in origin, often as a result of severe emotional stress. That could explain the Nazarene's curing of the crippled man who had been ordered to pick up his sleeping mat and walk. Hysteria could also induce blindness and an apparent inability to speak.

The Temple's own physicians over the years had examined a number of such alleged cures performed by other healers. In each case they had found the patient had no conscious awareness of feigning symptoms: yet in each case the doctors were convinced that a 'cure' had been achieved when the root cause of the hysteria had been identified and removed, usually by inducing a trance state. That would explain the Nazarene's reported success with exorcizing evil spirits. The Temple physicians had discovered that many Galilean healers used a sharp, authoritative manner in dealing with such conditions. The agents had repeatedly reported that the Nazarene frequently used similar injunctions to people alleged to be possessed. 'Be quiet, demon!' 'Come out of him!' 'Be free!'

While the number of claimed healing successes for the Nazarene was without equal, it only confirmed the sheer power of his personality. This seemed to come from two sources. Firstly, people had an unshakeable conviction that God was speaking and working through him in a way unknown since the days of Moses; secondly, there was an equally strong belief that the world as they all knew it was about to end. Only those who accepted what the Nazarene said would survive; all others would face eternal damnation. Given that, it was understandable why he continued to attract such huge numbers to witness healings and miracles.

In the case of a deaf man, the Nazarene had inserted a finger into each ear and established there was a blockage. He then wet the tips of each finger with his own saliva to free what was possibly only hardened wax. At the same time he called out 'be opened!' In the case of a mute, the Nazarene had followed the recommended practice of working the man's tongue between his own thumb and finger until, in an agent's words, 'the string of the man's tongue was loosened, enabling him to speak.' In a third reported case, the Nazarene had repeatedly massaged a blind man's eyes with a finger once more bathed in saliva before mixing some spittle with earth. He had applied the mud pack to the man's eyes. Moments later the man had said he could see.

For Caiaphas, claims the Nazarene had performed miraculous cures still fell short of the burden of proof. What degree of deafness, muteness and blindness had been present in the victims? What previous treatments had they received? Some of the miracles seemed bizarre – none more so than how he had supposedly calmed a storm when he and his followers were crossing the Sea of Galilee. The Nazarene had fallen asleep, no doubt lulled by the monotonous rhythm of the oars. Suddenly, so went the story told later to one of the agents, he had been awakened by the disciples, terrified by a sudden tempest that was about to sink the boat. The Nazarene had reprimanded them for lack of faith, then stood up in the boat and commanded the wind and sea to be calm. They were stilled. In the retelling of the story, the Nazarene's action was linked with the way he had similarly stilled the demons which possessed men. For Caiaphas there was a more prosaic explanation. The storm had been one of those brief ones that from time to time swept over the great lake. Not all the Nazarene's men were fishermen versed in the ways of the water and, what they thought as a storm was really only a squall. By the time their panicky cries had aroused their Master, the worst had passed. But, to reassure them, he had made the theatrical gesture of ordering the waters to become calm.

Time and again, Joseph Caiaphas had found a rational explanation for what was being described as a miracle.

The Galileans had always been a superstitious people, ready to ascribe all manner of ordinary events to some mysterious supernatural intervention. The so-called miracles were probably no more than that. But at some point, Joseph Caiaphas had begun to see how he could use the reports to his own advantage.

For some time the Pharisees had been calling for a more concerted opposition to the idolatrous, exploitative and merciless Romans. And, despite his own accommodation with Pilate, Caiaphas deeply resented the procurator's measures of control over the Temple.

Could the Nazarene's increasing popularity be mobilized to deal with that? Caiaphas had despatched still more agents to Galilee. Their reports had taken on a more definite theme. The Nazarene spoke with increasing fervour of a coming new Kingdom. People increasingly saw him delivering them from Rome. In preaching about the 'Kingdom of God', the Nazarene was also catching perfectly the public mood of the people by appealing to the well-known Galilean fervour and patriotism. That could spread.

If the Romans could be driven out, the tetrarch's army would likely desert him; Herod Antipas would be lucky to escape with his own life. Once victory was achieved, Caiaphas' position as High Priest would be unassailable, and the Temple saved for the Sadducees for the foreseeable future. He could then afford to be magnanimous; the Nazarene would be offered some fitting post within the Temple hierarchy, on the understanding he would accept the authority of the High Priest. Such thoughts were surely not far from Caiaphas' mind.

With the approach of Passover now almost upon them, the High Priest could only have felt his expectations continue to rise. The great festival had always been a time when the people felt most keenly their need for freedom. With their numbers swollen by tens of thousands of pilgrims from the Diaspora, they could launch what had once been unthinkable – a successful revolution.

Joseph Caiaphas would do nothing openly to encourage that happening; that was not his way. There must always be a loophole for him in case things went wrong. But equally, he decided he would also do nothing to stop Jesus from going ahead with his plans to launch his Kingdom.

Twelve

In April of the year AD 30, three full years since Jesus had begun his public ministry, he led the disciples and Mary Magdalene once more south out of Capernaum.

Their eventual destination was Jerusalem. In a little over two weeks, he told the disciples, they would all attend Passover. They had never before celebrated together the climax of the great festival when a roasted sacrificial lamb would be eaten. As if sensing her disappointment, Jesus explained to Mary Magdalene that he wanted her to enjoy the occasion with his mother, but he would spend time with them before joining the apostles for the formal Passover meal.

The promise the two women would have their own separate celebration with him was yet a further sign of the high regard in which Jesus held them. He loved both equally; one had brought him into the world, the other had been faithful to the very core of what he had come to do. Steadfast and true though both had been in their time with him they would, nevertheless, need a special strength to face what shortly lay ahead for him and for them.

If Mary Magdalene had felt a deeper significance behind the arrangements, she did not say so. She had learned there was a time to question and one to accept. But her intuition would surely have alerted her that events were moving to a climax. A hint of that had been in the almost casual remark Jesus made as they were about to leave Capernaum. 'It is unthinkable for a prophet to meet his death anywhere but in Jerusalem.'

Jesus was laying down another benchmark: nothing, and no one, would stop him going to the one city which for every Jew held a special significance. But for Jesus it was not its past history which drew him there but the knowledge he was about to change the future. That very morning as he watched them prepare for their momentous journey, Jesus had spoken heartfelt words which he would later repeat when they finally drew in sight of the city: 'O Jerusalem, Jerusalem, the city that murders the prophets and stings the messengers sent to her! How often have I longed to gather your children, as a hen gathers her brood under her wings, but you would not let me.'

The portent of the words had gone unremarked by the disciples; the excitement of being together in Jerusalem for the festival was all that mattered for them. Simon the Zealot had been sent to collect Mary, Jesus' mother, from Nazareth: they would meet up at the point where John had performed his baptisms.

Jesus had chosen a familiar route south. First they would walk along the Galilean lakeshore, passing through its small towns and villages. At each one Jesus would preach. Beyond the lake they would follow the course of the River Jordan.

They had left Capernaum on one of those mornings Galileans said was proof God smiled on them. Early though it was, the air was pleasantly warm and there was not a cloud in the sky, the weather of a Galilean spring. The lake banks were awash with colour from flowers and the trees were already in leaf.

Since dawn friends had brought food and fruit for the journey to the home of Peter's mother-in-law. Judas, as treasurer, had divided the items between the group, making sure that Mary Magdalene carried her share, including a pitcher of water she would balance on her head and replenish *en route*. Women had always been expected to do the heavy work on any journey.

Her own position within the group had been further secured from that day Jesus had asked her to walk beside him. The decision had astonished the disciples; no woman had previously been accorded such a privilege.

Once more sensing their resentment, Jesus had taken yet another opportunity to remind them that in answering his command – 'Come, follow me', he hoped they had done so without thought of reward or position in his entourage. After they had made their commitment, he had also promised them they could expect compensation. Glorious it would be: 'I tell you solemnly, when all is made new and the Son of Man sits on his throne of glory, you will yourselves sit on twelve thrones to judge the twelve tribes of Israel.'

But again, whether they grasped that their thrones would be symbolic was problematic. Their lack of understanding was all too clear when Peter had once asked if in the promised new Kingdom he would be able to keep his boats, failing to realize that he had been given a far greater role as a spiritual helmsman, to steer the church Jesus wanted him to build.

Most of Capernaum had turned out to see them leave; despite being widely called a Nazarene, the townspeople had long claimed Jesus for their own. In the time he had lived among them, they had become protective towards him and the disciples; warning them of the presence of Temple agents; 'like horseflies', James had once called the spies from Jerusalem. Capernaum's tavern-keepers had refused to rent rooms to the agents, forcing them to sleep outside the town limits. Being a Temple watchdog in Galilee had become an uncomfortable assignment.

It had also made the spies more cunning and determined to entrap Jesus in some branch of the Law. But the more they had plotted and schemed, the more he confronted them head-on. For Mary Magdalene, his behaviour was yet further proof her beloved Master was preparing himself for an even greater confrontation. Increasingly, he showed a breathtaking ferocity towards the opposition as if he was daring them to do their worst.

She could still remember that day when Jesus had led them on a Sabbath morning back towards Capernaum. After passing through the aptly-named Valley of the Roses, they descended towards the lake, walking beside a field of ripening corn. As usual, Temple agents and several Pharisees were dogging their footsteps. A relationship had developed between the spies and the sect, conjoined in a common purpose to catch Jesus out.

Some of the disciples, hungry, began to pluck ears of corn to chew. The Pharisees pounced, accusing Jesus of allowing them to flout the Sabbath. Strictly speaking, the Pharisees had the Law on their side. It was emphatically forbidden to do any work on the Sabbath – even picking ears of corn.

Perhaps tired from their long walk and certainly exasperated, Jesus rounded on his detractors. Once more displaying a magnificent sense of history, he reminded the Pharisees that David, before he became king and was a fugitive on the run from Saul, had entered a priestly sanctuary on a Sabbath and eaten the 'shewbread which was forbidden to all save the priests'. If David had escaped censure for doing that, why shouldn't the disciples?

Voice rising – for justifiable anger was one of Jesus' earthly traits – he turned to the agents and demanded: what about all those who worked in the Temple on the Sabbath? The priests and their assistants who lit the lamps, prepared the sacrifices and carried out all the rituals necessary for the Sabbath service. Were they in violation of the Law? And what was more important: lighting candles or satisfying a genuine hunger? Then in one telling phrase, Jesus had stunned the Pharisees, 'I tell you there is something greater than the Temple here.'

He was telling them that just as the lamp-lighters were guiltless because they were in the service of the Temple, so the apostles were beyond reproach as they were in the presence of God himself.

Leaving them for the moment with no response, Jesus had led the others down into Capernaum.

Later that day, in the town's synagogue, he had healed a man's withered hand, saying: 'Suppose you had one sheep which fell into a ditch on the Sabbath: is there one of you who would not catch hold of it and lift it out? And surely a man is worth far more than a sheep? It is therefore permitted to do good on the Sabbath.'

The hatred these words had generated among the ever-present Pharisees was so great that Matthew believed Jesus' life was in danger. The well-meaning disciple asked him for a sign that he would deal with their enemies.

Jesus had shaken his head. 'It is a wicked, godless generation that asks for a sign.'

He was saying they had no need to seek reassurance: it was there in everything he had told them. He then gave them an indication of what the future would hold, this time, choosing to do so through the story of how Jonah had been swallowed by a whale and 'spent three days and nights in its belly. In the same way the Son of Man will be three days and nights in the bowels of the earth.'

Once more they failed to grasp the reality of the message: that just as Jonah had been expelled from the whale's stomach, so would Jesus rise from the cold grave and complete the final part of his mission on earth. But the truth of that was still beyond the comprehension of his disciples.

During the past three years, Jesus had come to know many of the townspeople as friends, eating in their homes and regularly preaching in their synagogue. It had been there that he had first warned of the suddenness with which apocalyptic events would occur: 'The sun and the moon shall be darkened and the stars shall withdraw their shining, and the heavens and the earth shall shake. And whoever shall call on the name of the Lord shall be delivered.'

All others, the Romans and the pagans of all races would perish: 'in the great and terrible day of the Lord'. Therefore it was important that 'the lost sheep of the house of Israel' heeded the promise of repentance, 'For you do not know when your Lord will come.'

In a dozen and more thrilling sermons Jesus had promised the people of Capernaum that they would be safe if they answered his call to seek salvation urgently. Always, he expressed God's mercy and the efficacy of repentance in recognizable scenes such as fishing in the lake, harvesting and taking in the corn.

Jesus had promised salvation in the first sermon he had preached, demanding a rejection of sin and a turning to God. He had gone on saying it: in the Place of the Spring, and out on the Plain of Esdraelon; on the slopes of Mount Gilboa and in the Valley of Manasseh. He had promised redemption a hundred and more times in all these and many more places. But only a complete change of heart would achieve it. Only then could he welcome them into his new Kingdom.

Little wonder that those who saw Jesus set off on his final journey to Jerusalem believed they were witnessing the start of an inaugural tour of that eagerly awaited Kingdom.

The people of Capernaum had been the first to hear what had happened on the upper slopes of Mount Hermon and, for them, the event was the coronation of the longed-for Messiah. There could be no other interpretation in their minds.

The words which had emerged from the cloud – 'This is my beloved Son' were part of the Coronation Psalm, recited at the crowning of every Jewish King for over a thousand years. The presence of Elijah and Moses was another proof of his kingship; the two greatest prophets in Jewish history were bestowing their benediction. Peter's offer to build them tabernacles may, after all, have been an inspired gesture: symbolically providing the shelter of a cloth awning for a newly-crowned king and his closest supporters was an integral part of the Jewish coronation ceremony. Since David, kings had been crowned in the open, usually on the upper slopes of Mount Hermon; the mountain had been sanctified by the psalmists as appropriate for all anointing ceremonies.

Together, these pointers added up to one overwhelming conclusion: Jesus *was* the Deliverer, the Anointed One, the Messiah. He was no longer only a rabbi and prophet. He was their King, come to inaugurate his rule on earth, and his entering on a donkey would fulfill the prophecy of Zechariah: 'Rejoice heart and soul, daughter of Zion! Shout with gladness, daughter of Jerusalem! See now, your king comes to you; he is victorious, he is triumphant, humble and riding on a donkey, on a colt, the foal of a donkey.' A donkey was both a gesture of abject humility and a very public reminder that the king was no higher, in spiritual terms, than the lowliest of his subjects.

Certainly, the people of Capernaum could have sensed that humility as Jesus said his farewells and led his entourage out of the town. On the face of Judas was also recognition of a very different kind: the culmination of all he had waited for during these past three years was about to come true. No matter what Jesus had said, in the treasurer's mind the Master was going to Jerusalem to launch an earthly revolution.

Judas continued to show he was a man of action – quick to challenge anybody who confronted Jesus. Where the other disciples remained silently angry at the verbal attacks by the Temple agents, Judas displayed in public an almost obsessive belief that Jesus would emerge victorious from any confrontation. More than any of the other disciples, the treasurer was convinced Jesus was a brilliant strategist who intended to fulfil the prophecies of Isaiah, Joel and Zechariah, who had envisaged a great climatic battle in which the Messiah would lead the nation to victory.

Mary Magdalene saw that the more Jesus tried to explain this was not his mission, the more Judas cried out in his guttural desert patois that he welcomed the forthcoming battle in which their enemies would be swept aside. In his voice could be heard the authentic longings of Jewish Messianic hopes, dreams and expectations. Judas was a founding supporter of the tragically misguided idea that Jesus was destined to be an earth-bound all-conquering hero. In spite of all Jesus had said before leaving Capernaum, the treasurer could not begin to see that shortly Jesus would face the lonely agony of the Cross.

Within the group, Judas remained a man apart. During the day he walked on the right-hand side of Jesus, the appointed place for any treasurer. At night he still slept at his Master's feet, head on his money satchel, knife to hand, ready to repel anyone who attempted to steal his moneybag.

The journey along the shore of Lake Galilee was slower than usual. The paths were filled by pilgrims making their way to Jerusalem for Passover. At various points, crowds waiting patiently for Jesus to preach. He offered familiar reminders, unfolding once more his vision of salvation. From time to time he healed someone, aware that his every word and action was being carefully observed by Temple agents and the Pharisees.

A blind man was brought to him. Jesus knelt and spat in the

dust from which he kneaded two pellets. He placed them upon the man's sightless eyes and ordered him to go to the lake and wash off the mud. One of the agents had followed. Shortly afterwards the man had returned, shouting he could see. Behind came the agent, shaking his head in disbelief. His protests that what had happened was sorcery were lost in the excited roar from the crowd.

So the journey continued, with Jesus being acclaimed and the agents trying to ensnare him. Outside Magdala Jesus concluded a sermon with the reminder: 'you must know that the Son of Man has the power on earth to forgive sins.'

An agent noted the words: the prophet Daniel had referred to 'the Son of Man descending through the cloud of Heaven'. The expression was widely taken to mean the Messiah would one day appear in human form. Was that what the Nazarene was claiming for himself? Jesus had told the agent he must believe what he wanted. The crowd had cheered loudly.

A few miles further on, another agent had been waiting, this time with a group of Pharisees. One of them came forward saying, 'you should leave this place and go on your way. Herod is out to kill you.'

It was not sudden concern for Jesus' safety which had prompted the warning. It was an attempt to panic Jesus – and to show the crowd he was a man of no substance. Nevertheless, the threat was not groundless. Reports emanating from his court revealed that Herod Antipas had become increasingly concerned about the popularity of Jesus.

Jesus calmly told the Pharisee, 'Go and tell that fox that today and tomorrow I shall be casting out devils and working cures.'

No threat could stop Jesus. He, and he alone, would chose the time and the place when he would stop in an earthly sense.

His every word and action as he drew closer to Jerusalem also continued to darken the shadow of the cross.

On the twelfth morning before the start of the Passover festival, a new day in Jerusalem was heralded by the sound of a trumpet. At this hour all was in shadow except for the Temple and the Antonia Fortress. From its ramparts the trumpeter continued to blow harsh and triumphalistic notes. Mingling with the strident blasts came the mournful wail of a horn played by a priest on the roof of the Temple.

Moments later the city gates opened and pilgrims, traders, camel and donkey caravans entered. The air was filled with the sounds of bleating animals and birds to be sacrificed in the Temple. Accents from the furthest parts of the Diaspora filled the streets. Rather than pay the exorbitant charges the city's tavern keepers demanded at Passover, many pilgrims had camped out in the surrounding hills.

Since daybreak the smoke from thousands of fires cooking food for the day had drifted into Jerusalem. Now, the morning sun revealed thousands of encampments, tent shapes and colours from every corner of Rome's empire and even beyond, from India and China and the deserts of Central Africa. By the onset of Passover there could be up to half-a-million people camped around the city.

Because of the long journeys many had taken through areas infested with thieves and other enemies, the men were heavily armed. Often travelling in large groups, they had the fighting power of small armies, capable of fending off most attackers. Camped around Jerusalem, they now made a formidable force.

That realization, at this time of the year, was never far from the minds of the two most powerful men in the city: Joseph Caiaphas and Pontius Pilate. Both knew that, more than with any other, Passover was the festival when people expected to be delivered from their long history of suffering. It would also be the time when all other nations would finally acknowledge the One God, and that the Temple would become the centre of all faith with its High Priest revered above all others. Those who resisted his word would be destroyed by the Deliverer, the Messiah.

To Joseph Caiaphas, such beliefs were articles of faith, never to be challenged. To Pontius Pilate, the expectations were to be tolerated as part of Rome's accommodation with the High Priest.

Neither man could be certain how the Anointed One would convince the people he had finally come. But both knew that if he succeeded, their own lives would be changed forever. Caiaphas, because of his increased unpopularity among his own people, could expect to be removed from office. Pilate knew he could face an uprising which he could not be certain of quelling. Defeat would end in his disgrace; the Emperor and Senate were unforgiving of those who failed their mandate.

Pilate regarded Caiaphas as a creature of Rome; the High Priest saw the procurator as the representative of a loathsome pagan empire which every Jew would like to be rid of. Until now, how to achieve that goal had, for Caiaphas, been an impossible dream.

The news from Galilee had offered a possible resolution. If the Nazarene continued to attract people driven to despair by exorbitant taxes, subjected to constant humiliation and violence, sustained only by despair, apocalyptic yearnings and helpless resentments: those same people would believe the Nazarene was the Deliverer.

It might well be that the son of a carpenter would even put himself at the head of an army to drive out the Romans. If he succeeded, the Temple would embrace him.

Caiaphas understood enough of his people's fickle behaviour to know he could convince them he had been the power behind the Nazarene – just as he expected to bring the Galilean under the control of the Temple. All the reports on what the Nazarene said and did suggested the man was different and provocative. But the Temple had dealt before with rabbis like that.

If the Nazarene did proclaim revolution under the banner of his 'Kingdom of God' and failed, Pilate would certainly crucify him: the Nazarene would join the martyred hordes of Jews who had tried and failed to lift the yoke of occupation. The Temple would continue as before.

On this twelfth morning before Passover, Joseph Caiaphas may well have sensed the festival could be the most momentous he had presided over.

In the dressing room of his private quarters in the Antonia Fortress, Pontius Pilate followed a routine which had not changed since his appointment as procurator. On went his toga, then a leather breastplate, accompanied by a tug of its straps and the tightening of a buckle. The movements were swift, a reminder of the soldier he had once been, his manner imperious, speaking of the politician he now was. Tug on a boot, stamp it on the floor; on with the other and stamp again. Quick, purposeful movements. Next he put on his Imperial cloak and helmet, the outward symbol of his authority.

The competing sounds from the trumpeter and horn-player continued, carrying through a latticed window into the robing room of the High Priest. Even in his undershirt and bare feet, Joseph Caiaphas was clearly a man used to the world revolving around him. Ithamar, his steward, took a robe and reverently placed it on the High Priest, then used a ceremonial purifier to spray the garment. Custom demanded no less. Next Ithamar positioned a ceremonial waist sash, then fitted gold-tasselled bootees on Caiaphas' feet and sprayed them.

From the Temple roof the horn lament died; the trumpet gave a final riff, then it was also silent.

A new and altogether more piercing sound came through the dressing room window. In the courtyard of the Antonia Fortress the centurions responsible for mobile siege towers, battering rams and stone-hurling catapults were supervising their daily tests. Horses were being groomed and legionnaires checked their weapons. In the centre of the square a centurion inspected the rack of whips near the scourging post where miscreants were flogged. He had done so for the past three mornings since two legions, Pilate at their head, had arrived from Caesarea to reinforce the permanent garrison in case of trouble during Passover.

Since sunrise the Temple's Courtyard of the Altar was the centre of activity, focused on the massive slab of polished black stone and its ramps and walkways which led to the roaring furnace at the top. Around the base, merchants and vendors sold birds and lambs to pilgrims, who handed them to priests. They passed them to sacrificers walking around the furnace. The air was redolent with the stench of burnt flesh.

Suddenly, from the Temple roof the priest blew a long sonorous note on his horn. All activity ceased and everyone bowed obeisance toward the courtyard gate as a procession swept past – protected by the shields of the Temple Guard, led by their captain, Jonathan. Behind, isolated even in this tight-knit group, came Caiaphas, followed by several score priests. At the rear were more guards, each carrying a sack on his shoulder. The sacks contained the Temple tribute to Rome.

The very choice of the day on which it must be handed over, twelve days before the onset of Passover, was deeply offensive to Jews; the number was sacred to them, symbolized by the dozen precious stones woven into a vestment Caiaphas wore representing the twelve tribes of Israel. Rome's demand when the tribute must be paid was seen as yet another humiliation.

The High Priest's procession swept through the Nicanor Gate and made its way down steps leading to the vast subterranean world beneath the Outer Temple.

At the main doorway to the Antonia Fortress a centurion emerged, bearing a standard topped by a bronzed Imperial eagle. Behind walked Pilate, accompanied by Lentinus, the commander of all his Legions, and Quirius, the garrison commander. History records that, 'about Lentinus there was a feeling of natural authority', while Quirius was 'very much the soldier's soldier'. Escorted by centurions, Pilate and his commanders descended steps in a corner of the courtyard and disappeared from view.

Beneath the Temple the High Priest's procession moved past arched openings where the artisans worked: bakers at their ovens; candlemakers, perfumiers, dyers and weavers at their vats; gold and silversmiths at their tables. All stopped to make obeisance. The sound of marching was strong, like a heart-beat and found its echo. In another passage, where Pilate's group swept past the fortress' brewers, armourers and blacksmiths toiling in their alcoves, no man paused in his work.

The ringing crash of Pilate's boots were a counter-point to the soft fall of Caiaphas' bootees; the clink of Roman body armour contrasted with the swish of priestly robes.

The Temple procession halted before a wall that seemed to indicate the end of the passage. Jonathan stepped forward and rapped on the stonework with the hilt of his sword. The wall cantilevered open.

On the other side stood Pilate and his group.

Who can doubt both men stared at each other for a long moment, or that Pilate glanced beyond Caiaphas to the Temple Guards and their sacks, then turned and his escort wheeled with him? Or that perhaps after a moment's hesitation, that the High Priest and his procession followed into the bowels of the fortress? And it would have been normal for Caiaphas at least to show silent distaste at having to pass close to many of the symbols of hated Rome: battle pennants suspended from the roof, statues of gods and goddesses and busts of Emperors in carved silence. Instinctively Caiaphas drew his robe about him as if to be protected from such paganism. Any Jew would have done the same.

The group halted before a door fixed with two imposing seals. One bore the Roman eagle, the other Hebrew words. As the guards opened their sacks to reveal the tribute, Jonathan and Quirius moved to the door. Both drew their swords. All eyes were on them. With a single blow, they each smashed a seal that had been placed there after the last handover of tribute. The broken pieces, Rome and Israel, mingled on the floor.

Pilate stepped forward and, with his boot, moved to one side the shattered Roman emblem. Then, with studied casualness, he crushed a piece of the Temple seal beneath his heel. The moment would not have been lost on the High Priest, or on legend.

With the same slow deliberation Pilate had shown, Joseph Caiaphas turned on his heel and walked back down the passageway, followed by his priests. The only other sound was the start of handover of the Temple tribute, the coins being tipped out of the guards' sacks into those held by the centurions.

Thirteen

To the north of Jerusalem, a shepherd boy went about his daily work of herding sheep down into a valley where he would watch over them while they grazed. At dusk he would drive them back across the track that led to Bethlehem.

Soon a drover would arrive, assess the flock, haggle with the boy's father, settle on a price, and load the animals into crates. The sheep would then be taken to Jerusalem to be sold for the Passover meal. It had been so since Jews had settled the land.

Down that track came the unmistakable sound of a horse and chariot being driven at speed. It swept past the boy in a cloud of dust, giving him only a glimpse of the woman holding the reins. But everyone in All-Judaea knew that only one horsewoman rode like that: Claudia Procula.

A few days ago she had sat in her covered coach behind her husband as he led two legions into Jerusalem.

The coach had arrived with her from Rome and was decorated with figures of her personal gods and goddesses. Its windows were hung with lace curtains to keep out the dust. The interior had a single wooden gilded throne, its armrests ending in carvings of the Imperial eagle at rest. The journey had been long and uncomfortable, and her quarters in the Antonia Fortress were almost spartan in comparison to the accommodation at Caesarea. But these drawbacks had been balanced against the Arabian stallions in the fortress stables; they were reputed to be the finest in All-Judaea.

Like her husband, Claudia Procula was an excellent rider. As soon as she had bathed and rested, she had selected a team of horses and a racing chariot. Accompanied only by her personal maid, Miriam, the procurator's wife had every day ridden through the hills beyond Jerusalem. To the ever-growing number of encamped pilgrims, she was a striking rather than a beautiful woman, dressed befitting her station, handling her stallions with consummate skill.

The startled bleating of the sheep was lost in the thunder of hooves, with Miriam clinging to the chariot's guard-rail as it continued towards Jerusalem under Claudia Procula's skilled handling.

Immediately behind the Nicanor Gate was the roofed-over purification pool of the High Priest. Before Caiaphas could proceed further into the Inner Temple, he must first immerse himself in sanctified water. Little bigger than a large tub, the bathing area had two entrances. One he used when he was unclean, this time after his encounter with Pilate.

Inside the pool area he undressed. His clothes were taken away by his steward, Ithamar, to be washed in water into which had been sprinkled sanctified oils. Having watched the High Priest submerge completely in the tub, Ithamar then dressed Caiaphas in clean robes, once more spraying each item with the purifier. Caiaphas then used the other 'clean' door to reach his personal quarters. On a busy day he repeated this ritual a dozen times.

Caiaphas' work salon was deep within the Temple, close to the Holy of Holies. It was a lawyer's room of racked papyrus scrolls. Between them they contained the history of Israel and the judgments which had made the nation a byword in jurisprudence.

As on any other workday, waiting for Caiaphas were verdicts handed down by the Great Sanhedrin, the highest Jewish court in the land. As its president, Joseph Caiaphas was required to ratify them.

For four hundred years the Great Sanhedrin had not only tried the most serious cases, but had also reviewed judgments handed down by the courts of the eleven provincial districts into which Rome had divided the land. The supreme court had the power to change a sentence. It also examined candidates for the priesthood.

Its present seventy-one members consisted of three groups. The first were the chief priests of the Temple, many of whom were selected from the house of the current High Priest; eighteen relatives of Joseph Caiaphas served on the Great Sanhedrin. They formed a powerful bloc and exerted considerable influence on the other judges. When Caiaphas was not present, they supported the judgment of his father-in-law, Annas.

Though no longer High Priest, having been removed by Pilate's predecessor, Annas still had his own special responsibilities within the Temple. He controlled the collection of levies imposed on sacrifices and fixed the daily rate for the moneychangers. The image of the stoop-shouldered Annas hurrying through the Temple has survived down the centuries. From time to time he would disappear on some secret mission for Caiaphas. Over the years these had taken him to Alexandria, Athens and even Rome. What he did and who he saw were matters he shared with no one except his son-in-law.

The second group – the Elders – consisted of the twenty-four leaders of the weekly religious instruction courses run by the Temple. The Elders traced their lineage back to the original twelve ruling tribes of Israel: those families had led the people into Canaan and later out of exile in Babylon. For centuries the Elders had played significant roles in the nation's affairs. One of their members who currently sat on the Great Sanhedrin was Joseph of Arimathea, a rich landowner. Though his family came from Samaria, he had long settled in Jerusalem, establishing his right to be buried there by building a family tomb.

A tall, middle-aged man, Joseph was widely regarded as the most liberal of the Elders, renowned for his debating skills and an ability to listen. Originally trained to be a lawyer, he had opted for the priesthood and, through family connections, had been appointed to the Great Sanhedrin. He had sat on its Bench of Judgment for nine years and had dissented on a number of verdicts which Annas had endorsed. Joseph of Arimathea sat beside Gamaliel and Nicodemus.

The third group were the scribes, the specialist lawyers who interpreted the Law. Before the exile to Babylon, their predecessors had been merely public writers who, for a fee, would draft a petition or write a plea of mitigation. Often they had copied out relevant portions of the Law and, through doing so, they became its acknowledged interpreters.

Returning to Israel from Babylon, they found their knowledge much in demand; they became, together with the Pharisees, the defenders of the Law against pagans like the Greeks. Each success enhanced scribal reputations. Many were granted the title 'rabbi', teacher. Shortly after Pompey desecrated the Temple, the scribes were invited to serve on the Great Sanhedrin. Their ultimate authority was the Mishnah, a collection of edicts. Rich in language, its prime aim was to interpret the Law 'so that humanity can be saved from transgression'.

In the popular mind they were linked to the Pharisees of Galilee, sharing the same narrow religious outlook. However, in the Great Sanhedrin, they leaned towards the Sadducee viewpoint.

Among the scribes who sat on the court bench in what became known as the year AD 30 was Disham, brother of Shem, the High Priest's Chief Scribe.

Disham comes down through the centuries as a man not just physically short, but also short in patience, compassion and humility. He boasted that few could match his encyclopaedic knowledge of the Law or the rigid way he interpreted it. For him justice was a precedent – and Disham always seemed able to find one.

The reports brought back by the Temple agents from Galilee had undergone scrutiny by the scribes. What they read infuriated them.

Jesus had consistently attacked the Pharisees for their failure to understand the spirit of the Law. Worse, he had recently begun to launch an attack on the scribes themselves, accusing them by their rigid approach to the Law of actually robbing ordinary people of any freedom of interpretation. In Capernaum and elsewhere, he had said the scribes had 'set a fence around the Law'. The words had been the prelude for a sustained attack on scribal hypocrisy and their inability to temper justice with mercy. He had called them 'blind' and 'without compassion', steeped in their own choking codification. It was an attack without precedent.

Coupled to it was Jesus' claim to be able to forgive sins.

For Disham this was a declaration of war on all the Law represented for him.

But now, on the morning twelve days before the onset of Passover, there was one sin which required Joseph Caiaphas to study another verdict of the Great Sanhedrin. It concerned the case of a young married woman, Hannah of Hebron, who had been caught in an act of adultery. If upheld, the only penalty was death by stoning. Once more the High Priest must decide if the sentence should be carried out.

After returning from receiving the Temple tribute, Pilate had gone to the counting room of the fortress. The open area occupied the entire upper floor of the fortress and was filled with chests of coins and tribute of all kinds. Every shekel and other valuable was carefully noted in their ledgers by clerks brought from Caesarea. They marked payments against scrolls containing tax demands and handed out receipts stamped with a Roman eagle.

The collector waited until a chest was filled and sealed, then carried it to the despatch area in the courtyard. There the chests were loaded on to carts and taken, under heavy escort, to Caesarea. They were then stowed on board Pilate's galley. When fully loaded, it would sail to Ostia. From there the tribute would be taken by road to the Imperial Treasury in Rome.

Until the onset of Passover, the counting room was the focus of all activity in the fortress from dawn until dusk.

Here, as everywhere, Pilate's authority was absolute; his relationship to all those around him of total master to absolute servants. The arrival of a collector with an usually heavy satchel would always attract his attention. He would order the bag emptied on the floor before him, a clerk would sift the contents into piles of coins, jewellery and other objects seized in lieu of shekels. Often an item – a brooch, a piece of silverwork, a gold amulet, a belt encrusted with precious stones – would catch his eye. He would order the item to be placed in a chest set apart from the others. This contained the procurator's personal tribute. By such means, Pontius Pilate increased his wealth. It was the Roman way of occupation.

* * *

For Mary Magdalene the journey south from Capernaum continued to be broken by Jesus stopping wherever a crowd gathered. He preached, answered questions, performed acts of healing and fended off the barbed attacks of Temple agents. The process was repeated at the next place along the route where people had assembled.

Those Jesus had ministered to would often accompany him, so that he could have a group of several hundred people by the end of a long day. At night they would camp out. They sat around camp fires, sang psalms and discussed all he had said and done.

Mary Magdalene could not have failed to sense a new purpose about Jesus. Increasingly he was like a man who knew there was only a certain time left and much still to say and do. During the day he cut short rest periods and meal times and he preached in every small town and village along the west bank of the River Jordan.

At the site where John had baptized Jesus, they had met up with Mary, his mother. As always, Jesus was gentle and protective towards her, once more displaying his unwillingness to allow her, of all people, to assume the burden of his forthcoming suffering. He knew only too well that no other mother would ever send a son to his death: yet that is what she had done at the marriage feast at Cana when she had told him to turn the water into wine. The miracle had been the first tangible proof of his ministry. She was the mother who had brought the Saviour into the world, a woman like no other. Yet how much she understood of all this was debatable.

That Mary Magdalene tried to explain to her cannot be in doubt as they made their way towards Jerusalem, where the wine he would drink was to be changed into the blood of salvation. Three years with Jesus had given the woman of Magdala insights others did not possess. She perfectly well understood the antiphon of his life: 'All others come into the world to live; he came into the world to die.'

A week after leaving Capernaum, they moved inland to Samaria. They spent a night at Shechem, where Abraham had heard the voice of the Lord. Another in Bethel, where Jacob had his dream of a ladder rising up to heaven and, at the top, waited

God who had said, 'Behold, I am with you and will keep you wherever you go and will bring you back to this land.' A third night had passed at Ramah, where Deborah had dispensed justice under the palm tree, 'and the people of all Israel came to her for judgment'.

For Judas Iscariot, gripped by the delusion that Jesus had come to launch an earthly kingdom, these portents could only have been confirmation it would happen soon. Ever more isolated within the group, he had little to sustain him except his fantasies. In every twist and turn of their journey through Samaria, Judas increasingly saw only bloody revolution, with him standing shoulder-to-shoulder with the Master, ready to kill or be killed. It would be an image that would survive long after the real purpose of their journey to Jerusalem had become so gloriously clear.

One day Jesus had preached close to where Gideon had threshed wheat in the hamlet of Ophrah, nestling in the hills of the Jezreel Valley. That had been a time when Israel was under the pagan power of the Midianites. Gideon's work had been interrupted by an angel 'in human form', who told the young man that God had chosen him to rescue Israel. Gideon had answered he had no force to defeat such a powerful enemy. The angel had then asked for food. Mindful of his lapse of hospitality – he should have offered a meal at once – Gideon had prepared a small feast: a broth, unleavened cakes and grilled goat. His visitor had told Gideon to place the meal on a rock. The angel then touched the food with his staff. Fire sprang from the rock and consumed the meal. At the same moment the angel vanished. But Gideon was convinced the visitation had been a reminder he too could achieve the impossible. He put together a force of some three hundred men and led them against the Midianites, shouting, 'A sword for the Lord and for Gideon'. He achieved a momentous victory.

In reminding the people of Ophrah of the story, Jesus had further raised Judas' expectations. The Master was saying that a small, well-led force could triumph against supreme odds. The salvation the Master promised would be achieved through military intervention. That the Master had no experience in such matters was not a problem. Judas had those skills. So did others in their group, notably James and John, the sons of Zebedee. And, to be sure, others who came to listen and stayed had similar experience. When the time came, the Master would have a force every bit as committed as Gideon's. So Judas continued to believe; so the terrible misunderstanding deepened in his mind.

For Mary Magdalene the story of Gideon was Jesus demonstrating the power of belief. He had shown them all the authority of love, how it could be used to achieve the seemingly impossible. But that kind of love was only possible through belief. The knowledge could only have deepened her love for Jesus and strengthened her for what he would soon face.

Leaving Ophrah, they had walked the short distance to the city of Sebaste. The fortress town had originally been built by King Omri. His reputation as one of the great Jewish strategists had been blighted by his close links to the pagan Phoenicians. No longer welcomed by the other leaders of the tribes of Israel, Omri had set about building his own citadel. With its commanding view west to the sea and deep ravines on three sides, Sebaste had been as impregnable as any Herodian fortress. The city walls were up to thirty-two feet thick at the base and, behind them, had stood some of the most magnificent palaces in the land. It was these treasure houses which had been its downfall. Well-equipped Assyrian armies had laid siege to the city for three years before starving the population into surrender. Later conquerors, the Babylonians and the Persians, had rebuilt the city in their own architectural images.

Finally, when Jesus had been a small child, Herod the Great had turned Sebaste into a Roman city, encircling it with a two-mile wall and erecting an enormous temple in the city centre to honour the Emperor Augustus.

Outside this pagan temple, Jesus had reminded the large crowd this was the very place where Omri's successor Ahab had confronted Elijah with the words: 'Is it you, you troubler of Israel?' Once more Jesus had reached into the historical past to remind them why he was there. 'The righteous will always be here to trouble you.'

Who can doubt the thrill those words of Elijah's stirred in all those around Jesus? People who had become used to accepting

Jesus as a prophet had increasingly, on this journey to Jerusalem, come to regard him as a king. They now joined together to make him in their eyes the first King-Messiah. He was the Anointed One, so long expected, so eagerly awaited, the Expected One who could not only heal broken bodies but the pain and suffering of an entire nation. Yet the more Jesus tried to show them the reality of how that could be achieved, the greater was their refusal to understand. Nowhere was this more evident than with his disciples.

Leaving Sebaste, Jesus led them between the twin limestone massifs of Mount Gerizim and Mount Ebal, the highest and holiest mountains of Samaria. It was here that Abraham had heard the word of God. 'To your descendants I will give this land.' It was through here that Samuel had walked on his annual circuit as judge, holding court in every town. It was from here that the prophet Amos had denounced the vain piety of Israel. It was near here that Saul, with his army in flight and his three sons dead, had committed suicide and it was between these same mountains that King David, from whom Jesus' mother traced her lineage, had first marched forth to lead the nation. Now, centuries later, people found a similar hope as they followed Jesus through the path between the mountains.

Like Mary Magdalene, the women among them would have refilled their waterpots from the spring at the foot of Gerizim. Legend claimed it to be the sweetest-tasting water in the land.

It was here that Jesus re-stated another of the themes of his ministry, marriage. In a society where divorce was commonplace, Jesus reminded them, 'What God has joined together, let no man separate.'

Once more, the words held a deeper significance. Jesus was not saying that divorce was always out of the question, only that there had to be good grounds for it. It was a direct attack on the two rival schools of Jewish theology, one headed by Hillel, the other by Shammai. The former argued that divorce was permissible for comparatively trivial failings – among them being a poor provider or housekeeper, and drunkenness. The Shammai school held that only adultery could justify divorce – a moot point given the offence was anyway punishable by death.

Jesus was saying there could be no hard and fast man-made law; that each case must be judged on its merits.

A further opportunity for him to remind the crowd of another truth came when a young man made his way to the front. With his expensive clothes and well-bred manners, he was a cut above the others – a man of substance who clearly believed there was a way to achieve anything he wanted. He asked Jesus, 'what good must I do to gain eternal life?'

Mary Magdalene would have sensed the young man was not being used to spring yet another trap, bribed to do so by the Temple agents or the Pharisees. They were as surprised as everyone else by the question. The man's sincerity was not in doubt; he was searching for how to spiritually better himself. A few words of guidance was what he hoped for, reassurance that would fit neatly into his existing life.

Jesus had something very different in mind. He began by pointing out that people often knew the answer to a question but were never prepared to do enough to resolve it for themselves.

All eyes were on the young man. He rose to the moment in the only way he could. His voice filling with pride, he said that since his bar mitzvah, he had kept the commandments and done all he could to be true to his faith. 'Where do I still fall short, Master?'

His plea for an explanation was echoed in the murmurs of the crowd. Many of them were equally devout, yet they had detected that Jesus expected more. He spoke gently to the young man.

'If you wish to go the whole way, go, sell your possessions and give to the poor and then you will have riches in heaven; and come, follow me.'

This time the words held no hidden meaning for his listeners to fathom out by themselves. Jesus was not rejecting wealth and extolling poverty, any more than he condemned outright the failure of a marriage. Once more what he was saying was that it was possible to attain a more worthwhile life if people were willing to let go of the past.

Jesus had seen the unspoken reality behind the young man's question: he had really hoped to have confirmation that as he already lived by the Mosaic commandments, he had little more to do to achieve 'eternal life'. To continue as before would be no hardship. The commitment Jesus demanded called for real sacrifice. He had put the young man to the test: could he give up his fine clothes, luxurious life, all his worldly goods, everything by which people judged him? Yet only by abandoning them would he find the redemption he was after. It would be hard to do so but there could be no other way in his case.

Mary Magdalene well understood what Jesus was demanding. The more she had given up, the greater was his forgiveness and, in turn, the more she had grown in purity, goodness and holiness. She was the perfect example of how earthly wickedness could turn to spiritual love. From that encounter in the courtyard of Simon the Pharisee, she had gone the whole way in the sign of her heroic commitment to acquire true understanding of the meaning of salvation.

That the young man could not accept what was required was reinforced by the reaction of the disciples as he walked out of their lives and back to one he had not the courage to relinquish.

Jesus turned to them, sadness in his voice: 'How hard it will be for the wealthy to enter the Kingdom of God. It is easier for a camel to pass through the eye of a needle than for a rich man to enter the Kingdom of God.'

The apostles did not trouble to hide their astonishment. The analogy of the camel and the needle was once more seen by them in purely earthly terms – an impossibility. Like the young man, they had been brought up to revere the commandments and to be God-fearing members of the existing religious system with its well-honed beliefs: that people were successful in business, in all they did, because God favoured them. Conversely, that the poor were a grim reminder of what happened when God did not smile kindly on a person.

Mary Magdalene had heard them argue among themselves.

Hadn't they shown their willingness to put meaning into his command – 'Come, follow me' – by giving up their own secure lives, their fishing boats, their income from tilling the fields? They had even given up their wives and families: given up, in earthly terms, everything. Yet the Master was telling them all that was still not enough: like the camel they could not yet get through the narrow gap into salvation.

Sensing their mood, Jesus looked at them. 'For human beings this is impossible, but everything is possible for God.'

But they would not let it go. As they had done in the past, they looked to Peter to articulate their concerns. In his usual blunt way, Peter reminded Jesus, 'We here have left everything to become your followers. What will there be for us?'

Jesus told them, a hint of exasperation in his voice, that they were going to be the foundation stones of his new Kingdom. But they must remain truly committed; the persecutions they had seen him continually face would increase. Yet these would be small when measured against their eventual rewards.

For the moment reassured, they had no further questions to put through Peter.

Their progress towards Jerusalem brought them on to the plateau of Judah. There the pilgrims from all over the Diaspora had set up their encampments. Tied to a stake outside each tent was a *mezuzah*, a small cylinder holding replicas of the commandments God had given Moses. Each encampment was like the rest: tethered camels and donkeys; women grinding corn between millstones carried from distant parts and pummelling the dough in wooden kneading-troughs whose shape had remained unchanged since the Exodus. As Passover approached, the camps would move closer to Jerusalem.

The pilgrims could only have been excited at the sight of Jesus approaching in the midst of a sizeable crowd. They had heard the reports as they entered Galilee that a prophet had emerged to prepare people for the coming of great events. And now here he was, preaching impassioned promises.

For many, his message carried a political undertone: the

changes would be swift and only those who were prepared to accept them could survive. All others would perish. People who had been raised in the brutality of the Roman empire increasingly put only one meaning to the urgent words. They should prepare for earthly revolution.

Into this climate of expectation came an event which further heightened their mood.

On the twelfth day before Passover – the day when Joseph Caiaphas was reviewing the sentence on the adulteress, Hannah of Hebron, and Pontius Pilate watched the tribute arriving in the counting room in the Antonia Fortress – the walls of Jerusalem came into view for Jesus and the others.

Built of the local limestone that reflected a golden hue in the sun, the city stood on a high promontory, protected to the west by high precipitous hills and, to the east, the Mount of Olives. Most of the city faced eastwards, towards the inhospitable Jordan Valley and the wilderness. The Temple and Antonia Fortress towered over all other buildings.

Close to Jerusalem lay their next destination, Bethany, the home of Mary and Martha and their brother Lazarus. They were still a few miles from there when a neighbour of the family found them. The man was agitated and the reason became quickly clear. Lazarus, never physically robust, had been struck down with a sudden severe illness. His sisters had nursed him, praying that Jesus would arrive in time. They had sent the man to find him.

Such faith moved Mary Magdalene deeply. She had seen how devoted Mary and Martha and their brother were to Jesus. Yet, having heard the news, he made no immediate move to hurry to be with them. Instead Jesus preached to the crowd. The disciples were upset, grumbling among themselves that Jesus should at least cut short his sermon and go to Bethany. Once more he had shown his exasperation: 'Are there not twelve hours of daylight? Anyone can walk in day-time without stumbling because he sees the light of this world. But if he walks after nightfall, he stumbles because the light fails him.'

Early in his ministry, Jesus had called himself the Light of the World; now he was telling them that, just as the sun followed a set cycle, so what he had come to do had its own time and place. Delay would change nothing he would do at Bethany.

When Jesus had finished preaching he went there. Beside him walked his mother and Mary Magdalene. Behind came the disciples. The presence of the two women beside him was a further reminder his time was coming and they would have an increasingly important part to play in the hours left to him on earth.

With the village in sight, Jesus stopped. From Bethany came the sound of the laments for the dead.

'We are too late, Master,' said Peter.

Jesus calmly replied, 'This illness will not end in death; it has come for the glory of God, to bring glory to the Son of God.'

'But they already mourn, Master,' protested Matthew.

'Then be glad I was not there so that you may now believe,' answered Jesus.

He turned on his heel and strode ahead of them without saying another word. Mary Magdalene followed. For her, Jesus could never be too late to intervene; time and again he had shown the truth of that.

His remarks to Peter that he was glad not to have witnessed the earthly passing of Lazarus were not to be taken as a lack of sympathy. Jesus loved Lazarus like a brother; they had spent many an hour together.

Martha saw them approaching and came running out of the village, passing its cemetery filled with white-washed tombs. Through her tears she said Lazarus had been dead for four days now and lay in the family sepulchre. Struggling to hold on to the belief she had in Jesus, Martha added, 'If you had been here, my brother would not have died.'

Jesus gently took her by the arm and guided her towards the cemetery.

'In truth, in very truth I tell you, a time is coming, indeed it is already here, when the dead shall hear the voice of the Son of God, and all who hear shall come to life; all who are in the grave shall hear his voice and come out.'

Like most Jews who were not Sadducees, Martha believed in a resurrection on the day the Messiah would finally come. Just as the woman at the well in Samaria had not realized, neither did Martha grasp he was there beside her.

Pausing before the boulder which blocked the entrance to Lazarus' tomb, Jesus took Martha by the hands, willing her to look at him and stop crying. In a ringing voice he announced, 'I am the resurrection and the life; he that believes in me, though he were dead, yet shall he live.'

The others drew back, stunned at the words. He was promising what no one had ever done before: death was not the end; it was the beginning of a new life for all those who believed in the promise Jesus held out.

In those words, 'I am the resurrection', he was also telling them that he did not fear his own earthly end because it would enable him to fulfil the promise he had given to Martha, to all the others with her in the cemetery, to all people on earth and the unborn generations: Through his death they could have eternal life.

Martha's words reflected her sudden hope: 'Lord, I believe you are the Christ, the Son of God, the one who was to come into the world.'

Mary Magdalene led the chorus of 'Amens'.

Jesus told Martha to fetch her sister, for she too must bear witness. In the waiting silence he stood apart, eyes intent on the boulder guarding the tomb entrance.

When Mary arrived, she promptly fell at the feet of Jesus, crying that he had come too late to save Lazarus. Unlike her sister, she had not heard the promise Jesus had given. Now others, who only moments before had chorused their acceptance at his words, began to have doubts. They called out, anger replacing their tears.

'You have opened the eyes of the blind, made the lame walk, healed the infirm. Why did you not come in time to keep Lazarus from dying?'

Jesus 'sighed heavily and was deeply moved. He wept with them and for them.' With those tears he wanted to wash away the disbelief of those who had the capacity to believe. Instead, around him the taunts increased: 'If you are who you say, show us.'

From the time of the confrontation in the wilderness with Satan, there had been repeated demands for Jesus to show his powers. In the beginning he had often refused to do so because 'his appointed hour had not yet come'.

But now there was a need to reveal who he was, knowing it would draw closer the hour of his own death: the final proof that in coming into the world to die, he could guarantee eternal life.

Ignoring the taunts, Jesus turned to Martha and told her to have the stone removed from the tomb entrance.

Now even her belief began to waver. 'Lord, by now he will smell; this is the fourth day.'

In calling him 'Lord', Martha had continued to accept his deity, yet still she hesitated. Within the tomb Lazarus' flesh should indeed have started to rot.

Once more Jesus gently reminded her, 'Have I not told you that if you believe you will see the glory of God?'

Martha ordered the boulder rolled aside by several of the village men. Then, fearful of what they had done, for no one tampered with the resting place of the dead, they withdrew from the tomb. Only Mary Magdalene, Martha and Mary remained close by. No stench came from within the sepulchre.

Jesus walked to the entrance, raised his head skywards and called out, 'Father, I thank you for hearing my prayer. I knew indeed that you always hear me.'

Once more he identified himself as united with God.

For a moment time itself seemed to stand still. Then, in a thunderous voice, Jesus called into the cave:

'Lazarus! Come forth!'

From inside the sepulchre came a movement. Slowly, bound in a shroud that he unfolded as he emerged, holding the burial cloth which had covered his face, Lazarus emerged.

Mary and Martha came forward and covered their brother's nakedness with their shawls. A corpse which had been entombed for four days had been fully restored to life.

To many it was a miracle beyond their understanding. To the Temple agents it was an act of sorcery. They hurried to Jerusalem to report what had happened.

Mary Magdalene may well have been alone among Jesus' followers in realizing that, by this act of ultimate redemption, Jesus had accelerated the rush to judgment against him.

Rush to Judgment

Fourteen

The usual expectant silence filled the court room of the Great Sanhedrin. It was the hour when sentences were ratified by the High Priest, Joseph Caiaphas. The first verdict to be delivered this morning was the case of Hannah of Hebron.

Massive, circular and windowless, the chamber was hewn from the very rock on which the Temple was built. Lit by oil-burning lamps, it was dominated by the Bench of Judgment, made from a single piece of marble. Behind it sat the judges, each on a throne-like seat, unadorned and carved from the cedar wood of Galilee. Many of the men were elderly and frail-looking, their unrelieved black robes emphasizing the pallor of those who spent their working lives in salons at the rear of the court, poring over texts. They only left their desks to attend the noon prayer at the Nicanor Gate or to try a case.

The judges included Nicodemus and Gamaliel. Both were lawyers of great personal conviction and honesty, tough but fair, no detail escaped them; with a few questions they could destroy a defendant. Equally they could get to the core of a case which had little basis in law and argue for an acquittal. Younger than their colleagues, they had a reputation for showing mercy. In the absence of Caiaphas, Nicodemus as its vice-president presided over the court.

Behind the judges stood the scribes, eagle-eyed men who, during the trial had provided the judges with precedents and other points of law from their books stacked on the floor. Among them was Disham.

In the centre of the chamber sat Temple priests and privileged spectators. The charge of adultery against the accused ensured the seats were filled. At the opposite end of the Bench was the public area, also crowded; crimes of passion always guaranteed that.

Hannah stood inside a white-painted circle on the floor. At its edge, on her left was Jonathan, one hand on the hilt of his sword, the other holding a rope attached to her waist. This was the prescribed position for the Captain of the Temple Guard: the hand on the hilt symbolized punishment would be swift, the rope represented the binding finality of the law upon Hannah.

She had appeared before the court without the benefit of a lawyer to argue her defence: she had been unable to find the fee, a common occurrence.

Adultery was a capital offence for a married man or woman; if the partner in the act was a single person, he or she did not face the same supreme penalty; only imprisonment.

Hannah's husband had discovered her affair with the unmarried brother of their neighbour and reported the matter to their rabbi. A Temple agent had travelled to Hebron and interviewed the husband and the neighbour. Satisfied there was a *prima facie* case, the agent had interrogated the accused. Finally, Hannah had been questioned. Faced with the burden of evidence, she had confessed. The adulterous couple had been brought to the Temple and held in cells beneath the Great Sanhedrin. The case against the man had been quickly settled; he was judged to have been seduced by Hannah and sentenced to a term of imprisonment.

Hannah had been brought up from below to face the judges. Her husband and her neighbour were the chief prosecution witnesses. She had been given the opportunity to question them but had decided not to; the accused often preferred to avoid exacerbating their situation and hoped the court would be influenced to show mercy. A judge called for a character witness. None was forthcoming. There almost never was one willing to testify.

Nicodemus reminded Hannah she was entitled to make her own final plea of mitigation. This was heard in the customary silence. When Hannah came to a faltering end, she could not tell if she had moved the judges: each one sat impassively, then cast his vote. These now lay stacked before the empty throne awaiting the arrival of Caiaphas.

He entered the chamber from behind a screen, once more dressed in full ceremonial regalia. In his hand he carried the rolled scroll which summarized the evidence. He unfurled and placed the parchment before him on the bench and turned to the stack of votes; each consisting of a small square of parchment containing a verdict.

Caiaphas picked up a square and placed it on the Bench to the right. Acquittal. He picked up a second slip and put it down on his left. Guilty. He picked up a third piece of parchment...

In moments he had completed the ritual. The stack on his left contained many more votes. He stared dispassionately at Hannah. She tried to hold his gaze, but failed.

Whispering had started in the public area. Caiaphas silenced it with one look.

Next he addressed Hannah in words which had remained unchanged since the Court had first sat in the Temple. 'Hannah of Hebron. This court has found you guilty. You will be taken from here to the appointed place and stoned until you are dead.'

A gasp from Hannah; Jonathan moving quickly to her side to bind her with the rope; the judges filing out behind Caiaphas, disappearing behind the screen; the crowd in the public area rushing out of the chamber eager to get a ringside seat at the execution: these were familiar images at the end of any major trial.

After bringing Lazarus back from the dead, Jesus and the disciples and Mary Magdalene had left Bethany. His mother had remained with Mary and Martha; the three women had arranged to meet Jesus at the onset of Passover in Jerusalem.

The apostles were glad to be on the move again. They had seen the Temple agents hurrying to Jerusalem; they sensed that the raising of Lazarus would be bound to produce a hostile reaction from the Temple authorities. They would see it as the ultimate proof the Master possessed supernatural powers.

For Judas it was yet another signal that the time was fast approaching for the revolution to begin. If the Master could raise the dead, he could arouse a nation. In that buoyant mood, Judas picked his way over scree and through wadis towards a familiar landmark, the massive outcrop of Ha-Zoafim that dominated the landscape to the east of Jerusalem. The route had been deliberately chosen by Simon the Zealot because it would bring them close to the city walls where their enemies would not expect them to be. Simon had brought them past the place where King David's army had captured the city from pagan forces.

David had led his troops forward, the defenders had lined the wall ramparts with the city's pox-ridden prostitutes and beggars, screaming curses at the advancing Israelites. David had then advanced with a handful of officers through the city's water-supply tunnel and killed the wretches on the ramparts. Shortly afterwards he led his troops into the city.

Approaching Ha-Zoafim, Jesus led them past the tomb of another Jewish King, Manasseh, who, losing his faith, had reintroduced heathen cults into Israel and had ordered that Jewish children should be sacrificed to appease the pagan god, Moloch. Manasseh's ultimate sin was to introduce images into the Temple. The outraged prophets had thundered that 'the Lord will wipe Jerusalem as one wipes a dish, wiping it and turning it upside down.'

Judas, for one, believed Jesus had come to do no less, as they drew closer to the walls of Jerusalem.

From the window openings of the fortress counting room, Pontius Pilate had a clear view of the stoning pit. It was positioned outside the city walls in a slight hollow, beside the main road which led from the port of Jappa. Along it thousands of pilgrims, singing their repetitive psalmodic choruses, made their way towards the city.

Many had stopped to join the crowd gathering at the pit. The atmosphere was a mixture of commerce and religious piety; pedlars sold refreshments; people sorted out stones and took up positions around the rim of the pit.

The crowd fell silent as Jonathan led Hannah out of a city gate. With him was Shem, Caiaphas' scribe, who held a white cloth in one hand.

Protocol dictated what followed. Jonathan unbound Hannah and positioned her in the centre of the pit. Perhaps, like so many, at this moment she was beyond terror, staring at the crowd wondering from where the first blow would come. Jonathan took the cloth from Shem and told Hannah she was entitled to have it draped over her head, partly to hide her fear. The onlookers were silent and watchful. Those at the rim lifted their stones.

Suddenly, from the back of the crowd came a commotion. A voice was demanding people should make way. People turned to see what was happening. Shem stood on tip-toe for a better view. Jonathan and Hannah watched the crowd continuing to part.

Jesus walked to the edge of the pit.

Behind him stood Mary Magdalene.

For a long moment Hannah's eyes remained locked on his face. The sudden tension in the crowd was a palpable, living thing. People had begun to recognize Jesus and a man called out: 'Master, this woman was caught in the act of adultery.'

Was the man trying to be helpful in explaining the gravity of Hannah's crime? Or was he another of those whom Jesus had preached against: scandalmongers, the character assassins, all those who enjoyed nothing better than to condemn others? A hint of that was there in the man's obsequious use of 'Master' in the words he now spoke.

'In the Law, Moses laid down such women are to be stoned. What do you say about it?'

The man was more than a muckraker. He was using Hannah to once more try and entrap Jesus. In these past three years Jesus had frequently preached about the sanctity of marriage. What position would he take over a clear-cut case of adultery? But there was also another trap in the question. As part of the Imperial legal code the Romans had assumed the decision for the death sentence upon *any* Jew. But the Law of Moses was older. If Jesus challenged that Law, he would be challenging the Mosaic code, bringing him into conflict with the Temple. Yet if he upheld the Mosaic code, he would be provoking a breach of Roman law.

Sensing the dilemma, the crowd began to whisper, 'you have called yourself merciful. Show us! you have eaten with sinners. Show us what you will do with one!'

They had pointed to Mary Magdalene. 'This woman you have kept in your company without condemning her. Show us what you will do with a woman judged by the Law of Moses!'

Their mocking tones grew in confidence as they threw back

words Jesus had often spoken these past three years. 'The Son of Man has come to seek and save what it lost.' And: 'Do not suppose that I have come to abolish the law and the prophets; I did not come to abolish but to complete.'

Mary Magdalene must have sensed how close the trap was to being sprung. Many people now believed he was God: therefore the Law of Moses was his creation. Yet to deny that Law in the case of Hannah would be to deny his own divinity.

For the first time Jesus turned to Jonathan and Shem, as if by his very silence he would dominate them. His words were like a clarion call. 'Free this woman.'

The startled cries from the crowd; the incredulous look on Shem's face; Jonathan's demand: 'Who are you?', followed by the response, 'I am the one you call the Nazarene': all have remained as vividly clear as the next thing Jesus did.

He crouched and brushed aside the pebbles to expose a large piece of smooth stone. Then, the first time anyone had seen him do so in public, Jesus wrote with his finger on the stone. As the onlookers bent to see what the words were, he quickly brushed them away, leaving the stone as smooth as before.

The significance of the gesture was lost on the astonished crowd, but not on Shem. Over a thousand years before, Moses had received the two tablets containing the Ten Commandments and 'They were the handiwork of God, and the writing was God's writing, engraved on the tablets.'

The Nazarene was not only reminding them of where those Laws came from but, in the very gesture of writing on the stone, he was once more saying he *was* God!

The crowd had begun to show anger, to them writing on stone was an act of sorcery. And, sensing they were about to be denied their sport, the air was filled with shouts. 'Adultress!' 'Sinner!' 'Kill her!'

Mary Magdalene saw that Jesus was allowing their anger to grow, as if he expected no less from these people. He stood up and looked at the faces. When he spoke, his voice was calm. 'If anyone of you is without sin, let him throw the first stone.'

It was not only a challenge but an invitation to look into their own hearts. He was reminding them again that only those who had been redeemed could judge in the name of God. Implicit in that judgment would be mercy; without that, justice was sterile.

For Mary Magdalene the words were a reminder of what he had preached in the Sermon on the Mount which Matthew had later copied down: 'Pass no judgment and you will not be judged. For as you judge others, so you will yourselves be judged, and whatever measure you deal out to others will be dealt back to you. Why do you look at the speck of sawdust in your brother's eye with never a thought for the great plank in your own? Or how can you say to your brother, "Let me take the speck out of your eye, when all the time there is that plank in your own?" You hypocrite! First take the plank out of your own eye, then you will see clearly to take the speck out of your brother's eye.'

Once more Jesus glanced around, saying nothing, his very look conveying the contempt he felt for them. It was a look which challenged the very core of their sanctimonious attitude. In his silence he was asking them: were they satisfied they each had a stone big enough to inflict the maximum damage? Would they know which point to aim at to cause the greatest pain? Perhaps they should select a bigger stone – or make sure their neighbours had one?

That man with the smug, self-satisfied look of the righteous: had he never been tempted to adultery himself? The man standing close by, weighing his stone: was the look on his face rooted in avarice, or perhaps it was permanently engraved through a life-time of bullying? And his companion's face: how well it fitted Jesus' searing condemnation of all those who were 'like whitened sepulchres, outside clean, inside full of dead men's bones'.

Jesus was demanding of them: what right did they have to judge Hannah or any other sinner? Had they ever stepped back and, even for a moment, judged themselves? Had they dared to ask: what gives me the right to say or do this?

He looked into each face as if he wanted to remember them: recall their greed, their empty pride, their bogus respectability. He was not condemning them – only trying to prepare them for what lay ahead. When their day came to be judged, would each one of them be able to answer the one question he had put?

Would that old man, stooped with ague, who had the look of a moneylender, be able to truthfully answer he had lived a blameless life? Or that young man, so eager to mete out his justice to Hannah that he held a stone in each hand: could he say he was without sin? Or any one of them?

In the silence the echo of Jesus' words hung in the air: 'If anyone of you is without sin, let him cast the first stone.'

He was reminding them that, as they had cited the Law of Moses to try and entrap him, they had better understand well what had happened after Moses had received the commandments. The prophet had shattered the tablets after discovering his people were worshipping the graven image of a golden calf. God had written a second set of tablets which Moses had installed in the Ark of the Covenant, where it had remained as evidence of the Lord's readiness to forgive.

With that soul-searching look, Jesus was asking each one of those who had been preparing to stone Hannah: where was their forgiveness?

Once more the images have survived: the old man dropping his stone and walking away; the younger man on the other side of the pit doing the same; then another and another. The only sound was of stones being thrown down and feet shuffling away. No whispering, no second thoughts – nothing but that silent surrender to Jesus' implacable stare.

A dozen men left, then a score, each silent and defeated, shamed by what they had seen in themselves. They had come to kill, but their consciences had stayed their hands.

Jonathan's face remained a mask. Shem's mouth worked, but no words came. Hannah was too dazed to react to what was happening. Having steeled herself to die, she could not bring herself to believe she might yet live.

A new person entered the drama. Claudia Procula drove into sight, urging on her stallion. The chariot skeetering over the ground, Miriam clinging to the guard rail as the horses responded to every twitch of the reins, parting the crowds, heading towards the stoning pit: these images, too, have survived.

Close to the pit, Claudia Procula reined in her team and stood, like everyone else, silent and watchful.

Jesus gave no sign he was aware of her presence. Or of Jonathan's. Or Shem's. Of anyone. His entire attention was on Hannah standing in the centre of the pit, the ground around it littered with discarded stones.

Once more Jesus put a question that went to the heart of the situation. 'Who are they who condemn you, woman?'

The Temple required the witness to a crime to be present when sentence was carried out. But neither Hannah's husband or their neighbour were there. This oversight was no doubt the result of the rush to judgment.

But Mary Magdalene had not missed the underlying significance of the way Jesus had addressed Hannah as 'woman'. With it the Master had drawn her into the circle of women around him: his mother, Mary and Martha and Mary Magdalene herself. Jesus was telling Hannah that, like them, she could become a worthy representative for all women who wished to be forgiven and redeemed.

He stepped into the pit, took Hannah by the hand and led her out. No one moved to stop them – not even Jonathan and Shem. They, too, were accepting that all their earthly power could not change what was happening.

Mary Magdalene put an arm protectively around Hannah's shoulder and led her away in the footsteps of Jesus.

From her vantage point on the chariot, Claudia Procula continued to watch in silence. Jesus and the two women walked away from Jerusalem.

When news of the resurrection of Lazarus reached the Temple, a number of senior Sadducee priests and scribes, including Disham, met with Caiaphas in his salon.

They told the High Priest they did not doubt a dead man had come back to life: it had been witnessed by several Temple agents as well as a large number of villagers. Neither was there any possibility that the event would be kept secret; already it was being spoken about in the streets of Jerusalem.

Disham had given voice to their fears: 'This man is performing many signs. If we leave him alone, the whole population will believe in him. Then the Romans will sweep away our Temple and our nation.'

Disham was accepting that if Jesus was allowed to perform further miracles, it would arouse the people to rebellion and the Roman retribution would include the destruction of the Temple. The scribes demanded to know what action Caiaphas was going to take.

Caiaphas had sat impassively behind his desk. The coldness in his voice was there in the words recorded by Shem.

'You know nothing whatever; you do not use your judgment.'

For the moment the High Priest would not share with them his own plan of how he intended to use Jesus. Instead he ordered his visitors to take no action against him.

Pilate's private office reflected the best of the empire: its walls were hung with paintings of the gods and goddesses of Rome. A bust of the Emperor stood in one corner. Rugs covered the floor. One wall was lined with shelves of scrolls.

Here had come the news of what had happened in Bethany and the stoning pit, brought by Quirius. The garrison commander told Pilate neither event posed a threat to the administration. Personally, he doubted if the resurrection had taken place: in the run-up to Passover the Jews were always claiming their God could perform impossible feats; not even the gods of Rome could bring back life. What had happened at the stoning pit was a further sign of the hopeless discord within the Jewish religious community: the woman had been sentenced by the Temple but a rabbi from Galilee had objected and taken her away in some sort of protest.

Pilate's curiosity was sparked. How had he managed to do so without anyone interfering?

Quirius shrugged off the matter. 'The Nazarene has a following. Rather than provoke matters and so involve us, the Temple let him do as he wished.'

The exchanges which followed survive as a precursor to the truth that where a stone had been rolled back from a grave and Jesus gave back life to Lazarus, so the seeds had been sown to ensure a stone would be positioned before his own tomb.

'The Nazarene,' Pilate had prompted. 'Tell me about him.'

'What is there to tell, my Lord Procurator? He is the son of a carpenter who now walks the hills of Galilee preaching nonsense.'

'What kind of nonsense?'

'Promising a better life for those who listen to him. He's the latest in a long line. They come and go. If we think they are a problem we nail them up.'

'I want no trouble during Passover, Quirius.'

Those were the words of a self-serving man who had another matter on his mind. This surfaced during Pilate's daily visit from the fortress astrologer.

Dressed in a white robe, the symbol of his office draped around his neck – a necklace from which hung effigies of the gods of Rome – the seer had spent his usual morning consulting astrological tables, searching for signs of unrest among the population or any indication of unexpected weather. Both were of abiding concern to Pilate during his visits to Jerusalem. A sudden sandstorm could entrap the carts carrying the tribute back to Caesarea.

Reassurance given that he had seen nothing alarming in the tables, the astrologer discussed the continued failure of Claudia Procula to produce a child.

Pilate had one question: why didn't Juno, the goddess of fertility, help his wife?

The astrologer's words would echo down through the centuries:

'The Lady Procula must ask personally for intercession, my lord. She must believe in the power of Juno, of all the gods and goddesses. She was born to believe. That she does not do so is evident by her barrenness. Not to believe is a danger to both herself and to you.'

In Caiaphas' salon, Annas prowled the room, in marked contrast to the High Priest who sat with a cat's still eyes behind his desk. The two matters under discussion were the resurrection of Lazarus and the freeing of the condemned Hannah.

Annas had separated the incidents. What had happened at

Bethany was tantamount to sorcery – or possibly fraud. They now knew that Lazarus and his sisters were close friends of the Nazarene. Lazarus had feigned death; food and water could have been secretly placed in his tomb so he could have survived all that time. The whole business could have been an elaborate hoax to show off the Nazarene's alleged powers. There was ample evidence in the agents' reports of the Nazarene's skills and trickery.

What had happened at the stoning pit was different. Lawful sentence had been passed after a properly conducted trial. But the Nazarene had overturned the verdict. No one on earth had the authority to do that. It was a challenge which went to the very core of all the Temple stood for.

Annas' argument had been smoothly persuasive, couched in the voice of a skilled prosecutor.

Caiaphas' interruption conveyed the first hint of what was in his mind. 'The Nazarene wants us to see he is worthy.'

The scene survives of Annas caught in mid-pace, mid-thought; Caiaphas saying no more for the moment; the older man regaining his train of reasoning. The issue was not of the Nazarene's worthiness; it was a matter of the authority of the Great Sanhedrin being debased. If the Nazarene had felt so strongly about the woman's innocence, he could have argued her case before the court. Instead he had delivered a crude challenge, the mark of an upstart, a troublemaker.

Caiaphas had once more intervened, his voice filled with portent. 'For ten years we have waited for someone we can use. The Nazarene is the one!'

The silence, the exchange of looks, one equally certain, the other still not convinced: who can deny the moment?

Annas suggested that Jonathan should bring Jesus to the Temple. They could then question him, perhaps even expose him to the interrogative skills of Disham and the other scribes. Then they could judge how best to make use of the Nazarene.

But Joseph Caiaphas would not be rushed. 'The Nazarene will return. Of that, be sure.'

✳   ✳   ✳

The rift between Pontius Pilate and Claudia Procula filled the procurator's private salon with tension. The cause covered familiar ground: her role in All-Judaea.

Pilate upbraided his wife for stopping at the stoning pit. 'They are sensitive about such matters.'

She replied that he was always telling her to take an interest in the Jewish way of life. More than once Pilate had said: 'To understand them is to control them. And to control them is to make our life easier.'

Control was best achieved through understanding, Claudia Procula had replied. And that included trying to understand why a condemned woman had been allowed to walk free. The Nazarene' authority over the crowd had been absolute. That was real control.

Pilate's sigh, a headshake even, a feeling that his wife was meddling in matters that were not Rome's concern; all were in his. rebuke that the High Priest knew how to control his own people.

Claudia Procula had not troubled to hide her contempt. 'That man will bargain the truth to serve his hour! He's like your astrologer!'

Their row had shifted to a more personal ground. He had asked if her failure to bear a child was because she no longer believed in her gods and goddesses.

Her flared response and his cold fury gave further potency to their words.

'Your only concern is that unless I have your child, you will never progress within the Imperial dynasty!'

'I want a child for us, Claudia! Would you at least speak to the astrologer? He says the gods and goddesses are certain the fault is not mine!'

'You know what my father was to say about his first wife? She was most barren when most used. He never understood his seed died in her because there was not enough love there.'

'Are you saying your love has died?'

'In a place like this anything can wither.'

'Claudia, listen to me. In a year I can apply for another posting, perhaps back to Rome. There, among our own people, you will see things differently. And the gods will welcome you back.'

They looked at each other. On his face was a willingness to wait, the belief that he would be proven right. On her face was the realization that the gulf between them was wider than before.

Fifteen

Nightfall on the sixth day before the onset of Passover came as swiftly as any other. One moment the encampments around Jerusalem were visible, a tented city, burnished by the setting sun, stretching as far as the eye could see, the next the camps were only marked by pinpricks of light from cooking fires. One burned out at the mouth of the cave which Jesus had chosen as a resting place for the night for Mary Magdalene, the disciples and himself.

As usual she had gathered wood and drawn water from a nearby spring and cooked the evening meal. The food had been bought by Judas earlier in the day from one of the vendors going around the camps.

The disciples had taken some of the fire's embers into the cave to take away the chill from the chamber and to light brush torches to search for spiders or rats. These were either killed or driven out. It was a nightly routine for all cave dwellers.

After leaving the stoning pit, Jesus had taken Hannah to Bethany, leaving her in the care of Mary and Martha. Lazarus was sufficiently strong to have gone to Jerusalem to meet cousins who had made the long journey from Spain for Passover.

That night, they had all dined at the home of a neighbour, Simon, whom Jesus had previously cured of leprosy.

Mary Magdalene as usual had helped to prepare the meal and serve it in the courtyard of Simon's home. Afterwards she had produced her jar of spikenard and used its remaining contents to anoint not only Jesus' feet, as she had done three years ago in the altogether grander courtyard of Simon the Pharisee. This time she shook drops of the precious ointment on Jesus' head, rubbing it into his scalp.

The gesture was the clearest evidence yet of not only how well she grasped all he had taught her, but also of how much she realized what shortly lay ahead for Jesus.

Jacob, the grandson of Abraham, was the first to pour sacred oil on to a slab of stone and dedicate it as an altar to God. In drizzling the spikenard on to the head of Jesus, Mary Magdalene was showing the others they were all in the presence of the Messiah – the word meant 'the anointed of God'.

Touched by her foresight, Jesus said: 'She is beforehand with anointing my body for burial.'

The Magi also had anticipated his death by offering him gifts of myrrh, the holy oil used in embalming. Now, a lifetime later, it had fallen to Mary Magdalene to anoint him in readiness for his earthly tomb. But she had no fear he would remain there long. Jesus had demonstrated the truth of that through the resurrection of Lazarus. Just as John had been the forerunner of his coming to earth, so Lazarus was the irrefutable evidence of eternal life beyond it.

Now, on the sixth night before Jesus' Passion would begin, seated around the fire in the mouth of the cave, Mary Magdalene at his side, he reminded them of the importance of what had happened in Simon's courtyard: 'What she has done will be held for all time in memory of her.'

On the sixth evening before Passover, Pilate's day had reached another regular fixed point: a meeting with Maximus, Rome's senior legal advisor in All-Judaea.

The lawyer had travelled with the procurator from Caesarea, making his first visit to Jerusalem. His presence was required in case there was a need to rule on any Roman point of law. Maximus did not expect to have to do so. However, he had other concerns: the number of pilgrims was greater than in previous years, and many of them were insisting what had happened at the stoning pit was a sign their God was coming.

Pilate had dismissed Maximus' concerns: that there were more pilgrims than usual was due to a determined attempt by the Temple to remind its faithful throughout the Diaspora of their obligations to attend Passover – and pay their Temple tax. A portion of each tithe went to Rome. As far as the souk gossip about a sign went: 'They say that every Passover. Then, when nothing happens, they go home and start dreaming of next year.'

The matter might have ended there had not Maximus asked Pilate if he could see one of the parchments on the wall of the procurator's private salon, the Scroll of Thrasyllus of Alexandra, an astrologer who was an outstanding Platonist and the author of a standard text on numerology.

Thrasyllus' scroll contained such remarkable predictions as the conquest of Gaul, Caesar's invasion of Britain, Rome threatened by famine, Carthage in revolt and half the Imperial fleet lost at sea in a storm. All had come to pass.

One other prediction interested Maximus: 'During the reign of the Emperor Augustus Tiberias, a great challenge will rise from the East.'

Pilate had asked Maximus if he thought the prediction was in any way linked to the Nazarene.

The lawyer took his time before replying. 'I know two matters. Geographically we are to the east of Rome. The Emperor will expect you to deal with any threat.'

Pilate's response contained his famed arrogance. 'I also know the danger of creating a threat.'

That evening Maximus followed his own post-dinner routine, strolling the walkways behind the ramparts of the Antonia Fortress with Quirius.

Pausing to look across at the now silent Temple, Maximus asked a question that intrigued him: did their God really live, invisible to all, in the building?

Quirius had given a soldier's reply. How could anyone worship someone he couldn't see? He wouldn't know if he were asking Mars to bring victory or Bacchus for a decent flagon of wine.

Looking out over the city, Maximus had a second question: despite Pilate's reassurances, could there be trouble this year?

Quirius had promised Maximus that 'though these people were born to make trouble,' if they did they would be dealt with.

Next morning, the fifth day before Passover, daylight bounced across the landscape beyond Jerusalem and the world was created anew. Looking out from the mouth of the cave, Mary Magdalene saw the rock and scree taking on their familiar shapes. From the back of the cave came stirrings. Figures rose and struggled into wakefulness. One detached itself and approached the cave mouth.

Standing beside Mary Magdalene, Jesus studied the countryside.

People were slowly making their way from all directions: women, children, strong-limbed men helping the aged and afflicted.

Jesus stepped out to meet them. When they had formed an ever-increasing circle around his vantage point, a rock, he raised his hands.

Once more Jesus began to preach.

'In truth, in very truth, I tell you: a speck of grain remains a solitary grain unless it falls into the ground and dies; but if it dies, it becomes a rich harvest.'

In the courtyard of the Antonia Fortress, the daily routine was underway: centurions practised hand-to-hand combat; spearmen hurled javelins at life-size targets; troopers assembled themselves into another tortoise while others tested the mechanics of a catapult, manoeuvred a siege tower, charged with a battering ram. The air was filled with the roars of the Drill Commander and the grunts of the centurions.

Near the courtyard gate a groom waited with a pair of Arabian stallions. On the far side of the square Pilate watched the drills in the company of Quirius. It was another part of his daily routine.

From the fortress entrance Claudia Procula and Miriam, her maid, emerged. Both were dressed in servants' garb, making Claudia Procula almost unrecognizable.

They had walked some way across the courtyard between the drilling centurions before Pilate realized who she was.

Trailed by Miriam, the couple continued across the square, oblivious to the drilling men. Pilate's angry demands and her cool responses survive in the exchanges.

'Where are you going?'

'Am I obliged to ask you permission to ride?'

'You are still curious about that Nazarene!'

'He interests me, certainly.'

'If you want to know more about their religion, I will arrange for one of the Temple priests to speak to you.'

'It would not be the same.'

'So what interests you in this preacher?'

'You have long forgotten what interests me, Pontius!'

'Very well. I will give you an escort!'

'There's no need to. Dressed like this I will pass for a Jew.'

'You will embarrass the Emperor, Rome and me! In the name of the gods, why do this? What drives you? What is the Nazarene to you?'

'He had the courage of his own convictions. That's what interests me. It's not what drives me. It's what drives Him!'

Claudia Procula walked past Pilate to the stallions, followed by Miriam. Together they rode out of the courtyard.

That morning, the fifth day before Passover, Jesus had chosen a natural open-air amphitheatre to preach once more. The crowd sat in their hundreds on the ground before where he stood on a rocky outcrop.

Mary Magdalene and the disciples stood on the edge of the throng, watchful stewards on the lookout for the first sign of reaction from the group of horseback riders close by. The moment they had ridden into sight, Barabbas and his Zealot guerrillas had been recognized.

Their presence had caused no alarm. For many of the crowd Barabbas symbolized courageous defiance of the Romans. For their part, Barabbas and his men accepted with rough grace their role as architects of the Jewish resistance.

Silent and commanding like a prophetic figure, Jesus looked out over them all. Then his voice rang out.

'The hour has come for the Son of Man to be glorified.'

The words would have sent a frisson of excitement and pain through Mary Magdalene. For these past three years, she had seen how Jesus, despite being surrounded by enemies, had repeatedly assured her and the disciples that his time to die had not yet come. Now he was telling them it was very close; that while he would die in an earthly sense, in enduring all he must he would triumph over death and be glorified.

In that moment who can doubt that Mary Magdalene wondered if there was some way her beloved Master could avoid what lay ahead.

Then, as if sensing her concerns, Jesus had repeated the analogy of the seed he had used on the previous day, reminding her, all of them, that 'the Word is seed'. The speck of grain having decomposed would, through the wonder of Nature, start to grow into a new plant. So it would be with him. At his moment of earthly death would be born a new and everlasting life for everyone. The grain of his existence on earth would become an eternal harvest.

Once more he reminded them what they must do to be part of it: 'The man who loves himself is lost, but he who hates himself in this world will be kept safe for eternal life. The day of the Lord is drawing close.'

From the midst of the crowd came the strident voice of a Temple agent demanding to know when that day would come.

Jesus' reply underscored the great physical trial shortly befalling him: 'Only my Father knows the hour.'

The agent seized upon the words. 'Your father has been dead for years. Are you saying you can speak to him? That is sorcery!'

Jesus stared at the heckler; he would not be diverted from what must be said. 'Now is the hour of judgment for this world.'

The agent shouted: 'Have you come to judge us? Only God can do that!'

Suddenly Barabbas rode into the crowd and effortlessly lifted the agent across the pommel of his saddle and guided his horse out of their midst. The crowd laughed and cheered. Followed by the other Zealots, Barabbas rode towards a nearby stream into which he tossed the hapless agent.

The incident had been witnessed by Claudia Procula and Miriam, standing with their horses on a nearby hillock.

Jesus continued to impinge on the thoughts of Pontius Pilate and Joseph Caiaphas.

In his salon the High Priest had spent his day reviewing the scrolls which Shem brought. Having delivered his every prayer from the roof of the Temple, Caiaphas had returned to the task.

A stone's throw away, separated by no more than the Temple outer walls and the ramparts of the fortress, Pontius Pilate remained alone in his private salon, reading the scroll of Thrasyllus on predictions.

Near a pilgrim camp Claudia Procula and Miriam sat together, their horses tethered nearby and barely visible in the darkness. From the camp came the sounds of people settling down for the night, but still preoccupied by the same excited talk the two women heard when they had passed other camps.

'They also believe the Expected One is here,' Miriam said.

'How could they be so sure?' Claudia Procula asked.

·Miriam spoke for many: 'As a people we are good at believing what we cannot prove.'

They had curled up on the ground to sleep.

Throughout the day, Jesus had led the others through several encampments preaching familiar themes, each one describing a new covenant between God and his people in which there would be 'one flock and one shepherd'.

At the end of the day, he had chosen a shepherd's hut as their resting place. It was a poignant reminder that the Cross had been there from the moment of his birth and that like the stable at Bethlehem, Salvation could be found in any place, however humble.

The slumber of the pilgrims close to where Claudia Procula and Miriam slept was broken by a rush of feet as cudgel-wielding tax collectors rampaged through the camp.

The two women watched in helpless horror as the collectors began to savagely bludgeon the pilgrims.

Then, out of the darkness came Barabbas and his Zealots on their horses. They fell upon the collectors with merciless ferocity, despatching them in a flurry of rising and falling swords and daggers.

Suddenly a larger force of horsemen arrived and attacked the Zealots. They were soon overcome and Barabbas found himself cornered. Those of his men who had survived fled into the darkness. Barabbas was trussed and bound and slung across the saddle of a horseman.

In the flickering camp-fire, Miriam recognized him. It was Molath, the commander of Herod Antipas' troops.

Inside the stable the disciples slept, except Judas. He sat alone guarding the entrance, looking out at the distant walls of Jerusalem.

Jesus emerged from within the stable, followed by Mary Magdalene. The portent of the conversation between Jesus and the treasurer has survived:

'You could not sleep, Judas?'

'I was thinking, Master, how impregnable the city looks.'

'There will be no walls in the new Jerusalem.'

Then, in the same certain tone, Jesus told Judas that in the morning he should go to a nearby encampment. There he would find a donkey which had never been ridden before. Judas was to untie it and bring it to Jesus. If challenged he should only say: 'Our Master needs it.'

The significance of the words were not lost on the treasurer. To him they were the first order for the coming battle. In his silence we can hear the thought coursing through Judas' mind: 'Your people are waiting for you to bring them victory, Master.'

His expectations remained as tragically misplaced as ever. He had forgotten so much: how in the beginning Jesus had needed a fisherman's boat from which to preach to the crowd gathered on the shore of the Lake Galilee; how he had needed barley loaves and fishes to feed the multitude; how he had needed water to turn into wine; how he had needed the death of Lazarus to show there was life eternal. Jesus was going to need the donkey to remind people he was always ready to be needed by them – once they accepted him into their lives.

In telling Judas exactly what to say – 'Our Master needs it' – if he was challenged over taking away the donkey, Jesus was also expressing the ultimate paradox. The ass would be his earthly symbol of messianic authority while Jesus' use of the word 'need' was to reflect his humility at the terrible fate he had accepted for himself to become the ransom for the sins of everyone.

Herod Antipas' palace was situated to the east of the Temple. Late though the hour, the tetrarch was entertaining his courtiers when Molath arrived and dumped Barabbas on the floor of the banqueting hall. A drunken silence fell as the guests peered at the inert figure of the most feared outlaw in All-Judaea. No one was more curious than Herodius and Salome.

Upon hearing that Barabbas had killed Roman tax collectors, Herod Antipas once more displayed his unpredictability: anything which would annoy Pilate would please the tetrarch. Herod Antipas turned to Salome and put the question she had once asked him: 'Would you like his head?'

The slightly uneasy laughter of the onlookers; Salome's further glance at Barabbas; his befuddled glare; Salome's headshake: all would be remembered long afterwards.

Just as Herod Antipas had toyed with John the Baptist, he now proceeded to do so with Barabbas. He posed a question: what should he do with the Zealot? Incarcerate him in the palace dungeons – or send him to the Antonia Fortress?

Herod Antipas called for a show of hands. His guests voted to hand over Barabbas to the Romans.

Sixteen

Sunrise came, swift and magnificent, and in its customary glory on the fourth morning before Passover in the month of Nisan, the month the Book of Exodus ordained was the time to choose the Passover Lamb for sacrifice.

As the light bathed the walls of Jerusalem with a golden hue, the piercing blasts of Rome's trumpeter and the defiant mournful tone of the Temple horn player sounded. Their competing calls drifted above the city walls and out across the hills to the pilgrims. Each morning they had looked towards Jerusalem hoping this would be the day the horn would triumph. It did not.

Then, as the trumpeter blew a final riff to signal another victory, slowly at first, then in increasing numbers, people turned and stared towards the distant hillbrow of the Mount of Olives. From it a track led straight as an arrow to the Eastern Gate in Jerusalem. Already people were starting to line each side of the path, drawn to do so as if by some unspoken signal.

Against the fiercely-bright morning sun, coming into ever-sharper focus, was Jesus on a donkey.

Behind him walked the disciples and Mary Magdalene. On her face was shining hope and acceptance.

Like a bush telegraph came the repeated whispers from the crowd:

'... On the back of an ass!...

... His saddle is made from cloaks!...

... And held by girdle belts!...

... Just like the prophets said!...

... He has to be the Expected One!...'

To them Jesus riding an ass was fulfilling not an act of ordinary militarism, a conquering king, battle-hardened, with a string of victories behind him: he was more.

The devout among the crowd remembered the prophecy of Zechariah who, six hundred years before, had predicted the coming of the Messianic Age in which the enemies of Israel would be subdued. The Jews would live in peace in their land, and Jerusalem would be called the faithful city, the capital of a restored and purified Jewish Kingdom. In Zechariah's promise that could come after 'your King comes to you in gentleness, riding on an ass'.

The prophecy had been made after Zechariah had returned from exile in Babylon. There he had spent years surrounded by murals and motifs depicting pagan kings in mighty chariots pulled by the most powerful horses in their world; rulers riding pell-mell over the bodies of their slain enemies and, in their every gesture, proclaiming their power over all.

But Zechariah had chosen a very different animal to remind his people of what they should expect when their king came. His power would shine through the simplicity and humility of the lowly donkey.

Jesus stared down the ever-deepening avenue lining the track; all eyes were on him. His eyes were on Jerusalem. Once more he spoke the very same words he had before leaving Capernaum:

'O Jerusalem, Jerusalem, thou that killed the prophets and stoned them which are sent unto thee; how often would I have gathered thy children together even as a hen gathered her children under her wings, and you would not!'

It may well have been Judas who broke the all-enveloping silence with his shout 'Hosanna'.

The word – in Hebrew – *Hosha-na* – means 'save, please', and had its own liturgical meaning, a cry for God's power to allow Israel's rulers and fighters to defend the nation against its enemies.

Yet, there could be no gentler or less threatening image than Jesus on an ass. For Judas it may well have been further evidence that through sheer charisma, Jesus had attracted such a huge crowd: there was no need for military methods. He would achieve victory on the back of a donkey. The triumphalism was once more in the treasurer's voice:

'Hosanna!'

Money pouch flapping at his side, Judas began to run down the track urging everyone to join him in shouting:

'Hosanna!'

The cry was taken up. Finally there was only a sustained roar: 'Hosanna! Hosanna!'

People did what their ancestors had done when acclaiming David and Simon Maccabeus and all the other great Jewish leaders who had come to celebrate their victories in Jerusalem. They removed their jerkins and waistcoats and their protective scarves against the wind, and these they scattered in the path of the donkey. Others climbed to the trunks of palm trees and cut off branches or snipped them from the groves which gave the Mount of Olives its name.

'Hosanna!'

The repetitive cry held a reminder for Mary Magdalene of a Galilean river in full flood. Like rushing water, the great wall of sound hemmed her in on either side. Ahead of her, Jesus controlled the donkey by the merest touch of his heel on a flank. Beyond, Judas led the mighty chorus:

'Hosanna!'

Now the sound was boosted by the words of Hillel, whose own name meant 'Praise', and who had been Israel's chief judge for eight years over a millennium before. The crowd roared:

'Blessings on him who comes as King in the name of the Lord.'

In that moment they had no doubt who Jesus was. In saluting him they were echoing the salutation the Magi had bestowed on him in the Bethlehem stable: 'King in the name of the Lord.'

Jesus continued to ride resolutely ahead between two great walls of sound.

In Caiaphas' salon, the still distant sound of the unifying cry, 'Hosanna!', made the High Priest pause in his paperwork and stride to the window. Annas joined him. Both saw the crowd merging behind Jesus to form a great mass. The impression of a leader advancing with an army was a powerful one.

An unbroken layer of fronds and clothing stretched ahead of Jesus. The crowd had taken up new chants to intersperse with their Hosannas.

'Welcome to the son of David!'

'We see you, O King of Israel!'

'Hosanna to the heavens!'

With every hoofbeat Jesus continued to raise political hopes which he would not satisfy.

Who cannot sense the tears in the eyes of Mary Magdalene that people still had no understanding of the true purpose of his procession? How many times had her beloved Master tried to make people see reality? But still they could not do so. Like Judas they clung to the misbelief that he would physically vanquish their enemies. Only then would the acclaim they shouted be completely fulfilled.

Instead all they saw was a man who stared fixedly ahead and who, by his very silence, had come to save them in an earthly manner, the only one they understood.

Only once did Jesus break his own silence, when a group of Pharisees forced their way to the front of the crowd and demanded:

'Reprimand your disciples!'

By now the apostles had joined Judas in shouting: 'Hosanna!'

The Pharisees' intervention brought a momentary silence; suddenly all was tense and expectant. How would Jesus deal with the matter? Was it to end with still a considerable distance to go to the Eastern Gate of Jerusalem?

Jesus reined in the donkey and turned to the black-robed Pharisees. 'I tell you, if my disciples keep silence, the stones will shout aloud.'

Nervous laughter; puzzlement over the words; realization followed by anger in the eyes of the Pharisees; relief on the faces of the crowd that Jesus was not abandoning his advance on Jerusalem: they have all survived.

Jesus was telling them all that it was now too late for silence and even those with hearts of stone – the Pharisees – must recognize who he was. He turned and looked towards Jerusalem and through his next words came the first hint of the pain awaiting him. 'If only you had known, on this great day, the way that leads to peace. But no; it is hidden from your sight.'

Once more Jesus guided the donkey forward.

* * *

Inside his private salon, Pilate and Claudia Procula faced each other. She still wore her servants' garb. He was dressed in his magnificent uniform which somehow emphasized the unbridgeable emotional gap between them. Here, in a room adorned with the emblems of paganism, would be set the ground for the anguished Gospel appeal of a wife to her husband. 'Do not harm this man!'

Those words would be spoken by Claudia Procula later in the week when Pilate faced the truth about himself.

But now, in the confines of his salon, surrounded by the props which had sustained him, the procurator could only express incredulity at what his wife had told him.

'You really want me to believe the Nazarene is greater than all our gods?'

'Yes.'

'Then may the gods forgive you!'

'I don't need their forgiveness.'

'I could have him arrested! Sent to Rome in chains! Paraded as the man who tried to suborn the Emperor's daughter! my wife!'

'Do that and you only humiliate yourself. Christus has done nothing.'

'Christus?'

'Yes. That is what his people now call him. The Messiah. The One True God.'

'And you believe that?'

'Yes.'

'Then Christus has cast a spell on you!'

In the silence the repetitive chanting from the Mount of Olives finally reached them. They both stared out of the salon window as, in the distance, Jesus on his donkey moved slowly forward through joyful acclamation.

His eyes were fixed on the city walls drawing ever closer.

Mary Magdalene may well have been the only one to sense that beyond them lay his rejection – to be as great as the praise which now engulfed him. On all sides he was being hailed as a king. But only she understood that Jesus' true coronation would be in his death.

On the Temple ramparts, Nicodemus and Gamaliel were joined by more judges emerging from their offices behind the Great Sanhedrin, together with their scribes and other Temple staff. All were transfixed by the approach of a huge, unstoppable force led by a man on a donkey, stepping numbly over a multi-coloured quilt. Both Jesus and the ass were oblivious to the garments showering in their path.

High above them, Caiaphas and Annas watched the scene from the window of the High Priest's salon.

Hidden in shadow, their reaction would escape record. But who can doubt their expectation? Out on the Mount of Olives was striking proof that the Nazarene had the power and authority they had hoped for. He was their man!

From his own vantage point in his palace, Herod Antipas could only have been amused by the spectacle. How could he take seriously a man being proclaimed a king seated on the back of an animal which, for the tetrarch, symbolized the lowliest in his Kingdom?

Following behind Jesus, on they came, spread out across the broad width of the Mount of Olives. Men, women and children with not a visible weapon between them, their chanting interspersed with one word: 'Hosanna'.

In the courtyard of the Antonia Fortress, centurions had manoeuvred a siege tower closer to the wall. Standing on the tower's storming bridge were Pilate, Quirius and Lentinus. Below, waiting inside the fortress gate, were a force of legionnaires, their officers' eyes fixed on the storming bridge.

Quirius said his men were ready to push out and arrest Jesus.

Pilate may well have fulfilled the legend by glancing towards the window of his salon where Claudia Procula still stood, before saying that 'This Christus is no threat to us.' his commanders would certainly have looked at the procurator in surprise: it would have been the first time they had heard the name. The image of them glancing towards the window and then at each other, making the connection between Claudia Procula and what was now happening, would also become part of the legend.

At the Eastern Gate, Jesus dismounted and turned to face the crowd and its thunderous, joyous, repetitive 'Hosannas'. He waited a moment for the cry to once more reach its peak. Then, with one swift commanding gesture, he stilled those nearest to him. As they fell silent, so did those behind, and those still further back... all the way back to the brow of the hill over which he had first appeared. Finally, like a dying breath, came one last Hosanna.

And still Jesus waited, displaying total mastery over the great throng. Suddenly, his voice carried far and wide. 'People of Israel. Go about your work.'

Jesus turned and walked under the archway of the gate into the city.

Judas emerged from the crowd as if to follow only to stop, confusion and uncertainty on his face, the look of a man whose expectation of how the revolution he had expected would be launched had been denied.

At the Nicanor Gate, Jonathan had assembled the Temple Guards, ready to repel any attempt by anyone to enter the sacrosanct Inner Temple. In the Outer Temple area, everyone had withdrawn into the cloisters. Suddenly all eyes swivelled to a gate.

Jesus stood there. He strode to the centre of the courtyard and looked around; a long raking look at the moneychangers' booths, the caged sacrifices, the materialism on all sides.

He turned and strode back out of the gateway, gone as swiftly as he had appeared. No one moved. Then, like a wind rustling before it gained strength, came the questions. 'Why did he come? What did he want? Why did he leave with no word?'

The sound of feet sloshing through water was followed by the light of a reed torch casting shadows on the stonework, sending rats squeaking and scurrying back down the tunnel. Ithamar appeared holding the torch, followed by Caiaphas and Annas. The echo of their words have come down through the centuries, the wonder in Annas' voice as clear now as when he spoke.

'First the Nazarene has half the country cheering him on. Then he tells them to disperse and everyone obeys.'

And Caiaphas' response: 'Think what the Nazarene will do when we tell him to go against the Romans.'

After leaving the Temple Jesus had joined Mary Magdalene and the disciples outside the Eastern Gate. They looked expectantly at him. But all he said was that they would return to Bethany and spend the night at the home of Mary and Martha.

There would be no donkey to carry Jesus there; he had asked one of the crowd to return the beast to its rightful owner.

Having fulfilled the prophecy of Zechariah, Jesus wished to end the idea that he had come to claim an earthly kingdom. His bid for power was of a very different kind. He wanted to be no more or less than a spiritual King, a monarch who ruled through power over their souls.

Recovering from his disappointment, Judas began to tell the dispersing crowd to be patient: that soon they would have what they had waited for so long; their earthly freedom.

Judas was not saying they were wrong in their expectations. Far from it. He was insisting that the apocalyptic hopes which had begun when Jesus first appeared over the brow of the Mount of Olives would yet be realized.

That Jesus did nothing to correct this tragic misapprehension was understandable to Mary Magdalene. Alone of them all, she understood the reason. Her Master was drawing ever closer to his own redemptive suffering from which would come the joy of spiritual freedom for them all.

How many times she had heard him refer to this moment as 'the hour'. At first, when she had thought he would be arrested for his outspoken defiance of the present Law, he had assured her that 'the hour' had not yet come. Later, after meeting with Elijah and Moses he had said 'the hour' was coming for him to be glorified. Now, the journey to Bethany brought it closer, the cries of Judas acting as a counterpoint to reality.

'You saw,' Judas shouted, 'neither the Temple nor the Romans raised a hand against the Son of David for fear of retribution.'

Then, one more time, he urged the crowd to join in his exultant shout.

'Hosanna.'

But this time few did so.

Caiaphas and Annas stood before Herod Antipas, seated on a throne in his palace audience chamber. Both priests showed visible signs of their journey through the passageways. If the tetrarch expressed surprise they had used the subterranean route linking the Temple and the Palace, the need to do so soon became clear.

Caiaphas explained they had come to discuss how the Nazarene could help them all to overcome the Romans.

Annas had reminded the tetrarch of the words of the psalmist: 'Our enemies fall by the sword when we are united.'

Herod Antipas convulsed with sudden, unnerving near-maniacal laughter – and Caiaphas' and Annas' swift glances of alarm – have provided the backdrop for the exchanges which followed between the tetrarch and the High Priest.

'We wish you to put your forces alongside the Nazarene's.'

'Place my men under the donkey man? Never!'

'We all saw how well the Nazarene can command. But the people need weapons and your officers and men to guide them. Then we will have a victory greater even than David's over Goliath!'

But Herod Antipas rejected the idea with another laugh of the not quite sane.

*   *   *

On the third night before the onset of Passover, from the flat roof of Mary and Martha's house in Bethany, the glow from thousands of encampments were like fireflies against which shadowy figures could be seen. Likely it was those which had prompted Judas to review his call for action. Soon he was in full flow, excited and voluble, his words accompanied by restless little gestures: touching his money purse, rubbing his tunic, scratching his face: there was about him a tireless energy and a nagging aggression. So it would be recorded to accompany his demands that Jesus should mobilize the pilgrims.

Their sheer numbers would enforce the all-important element of surprise. They would strike where least expected, against the Antonia Fortress. The fortress would provide the weapons needed to attack Herod's palace and other fortifications, Roman and the tetrarch's, across the country.

The former Zealots acknowledging these were sound tactics; the other listening; Mary Magdalene, Martha and Mary, his mother, standing to one side: Jesus remaining silent and apart: all are images that centuries of retelling have burnished.

Encouraged, Judas had continued. Judas Maccabeus, Samson, Joshua and Gideon had all fought and won against apparently hopeless odds. Would not the Master, openly acclaimed as the Son of David, put the Romans to flight? Had he not shown he possessed the prophetic power of Solomon and was able to work greater miracles than even Moses and Elijah? Had he not in this very village raised the dead? Had he not proved he was greater than all the prophets of old?

For a moment longer Judas' fantasies sounded promising. Then Jesus had intervened. There would be no violence.

The women sighing, perhaps in relief, realizing it was going to be ever so; Judas still looking around him challengingly, others finding his intensity too painful to confront; Iscariot turning to Jesus: each fleeting moment had its own immutable poignancy.

For a moment Jesus and Judas' eyes met: despair in Jesus' eyes and inability to accept in the treasurer's. In the continuing silence, Judas left the rooftop.

✳   ✳   ✳

Later that night pilgrims were to recall, they were visited by Judas urging them to go to Bethany and tell Jesus they were ready to fight for their freedom. The treasurer found no one prepared to do so.

In the courtyard of Mary and Martha's house, Jesus and all but one of the disciples were curled in their robes on the ground, deep asleep. Simon, who was standing guard at the courtyard door, opened it to admit the cowled and caped figure of Judge Nicodemus.

What brought him to Bethany may have begun as curiosity to know how Jesus had exercised authority over the crowd on the Mount of Olives. Perhaps Nicodemus was more interested to learn what had brought Jesus to the Temple.

He had shown no threatening behaviour. Indeed, his very silence negated the claims of the crowd that he was the Messiah. Instead he had appeared overcome by his surroundings. While he had clearly been an inspiring figure to the crowd, he had done nothing to impress the Temple authorities.

Nicodemus had chosen to make his visit under cover of darkness, revealing something about his own motives. It was a sign that he, as a member of the Establishment, also feared to be openly acknowledging Jesus.

Yet, as Nicodemus had made his way out of Jerusalem and along the twisting path to Bethany, he had begun to experience his own conversion. Possibly he had overheard the talk in the pilgrim camps he passed; people may not have been ready to do battle for Jesus, but they did acknowledge he was a man like no other: a performer of miracles, a teacher 'sent by God'. By the time Nicodemus had been admitted to the courtyard, he was prepared to say to Jesus: 'No one could perform these signs of yours unless God were with him.'

Yet, behind the words was still an intellectual arrogance which Jesus dealt with swiftly and sharply.

'In truth, in very truth I tell you, unless a man has been born over again, he cannot see the Kingdom of God.'

This may well have been the moment when Mary Magdalene, always a light sleeper, awoke, heard the voices in the courtyard and came out of the house to investigate. To avoid disturbing the others, Jesus had led Nicodemus up the stairs out on to the roof. She followed, sitting at the top of the stairs, listening to the ebb and flow between the Master and the judge.

Nicodemus had asked Jesus to explain the meaning of being born again and Jesus, with the patience he always showed to the genuinely interested, had begun to do so.

Physical life came from an earthly coupling, but spiritual life could only be achieved through the realization of what was meant by spirituality. There was no other way for anyone to experience the Kingdom of God.

The judge in Nicodemus took over. He homed in on what he saw as the nub of the matter.

'But how is it possible for a man to be born when he is old?'

It was the question of a man who had spent his years untangling the obfuscations of the accused and witnesses. The law had taught him the importance of clarity: he was a literalist, used to putting a precise meaning upon each word. A man's earthly guilt or innocence depended on no more or less. How indeed was it possible for a man to be born when he was already old?

But Jesus, with his hours on earth moving inexorably to their close, was only concerned with making a man who patently had good in his soul grasp a new reality.

'In truth I tell you, no one can enter the Kingdom of God without being born from water and spirit. Flesh can give birth only to flesh; it is spirit that gives birth to spirit. You ought not to be astonished when I tell you that you must be born over again.'

For a long moment they sat in silence, Jesus to allow time for the new truth he had introduced to be understood by the older man. There was no question of Nicodemus miraculously being returned to his mother's womb to be born once more in a physical sense. But it was possible for him to shake off his entire life, since he had been delivered into the world in preparation for a new life in a new world.

Still sensing the reluctance of Nicodemus to grasp this simple truth, Jesus offered the judge another way to free himself from the intellectual bonds which constrained his thinking: 'The wind blows when it wills; you hear the sound of it, but you do not know where it comes from, or where it is going. So it is with everyone who is born from the Spirit.'

Like the wind, the Spirit of God was free and its movements could not be confined or controlled by any human mechanism. No one could foretell the moment when the Spirit would speak to the human heart, or what the response would be.

Still unable to let go of the sophisticated thinking which had governed his entire adult life, Nicodemus struggled to hold onto old values and understanding. Nevertheless, there was an acceptance in his voice in the choice of the word rabbi, Master, to prefix his next question to Jesus:

'Rabbi, how is this possible?'

Jesus told Nicodemus to be patient, adding: 'No one went up into heaven except the one who came down from heaven, the Son of Man whose home is in heaven.'

In those words, Jesus finally began to win over Nicodemus to a greater understanding.

In the hours they spent together, Jesus confided in Nicodemus what lay ahead for him. 'God so loved the world that he gave his only Son, that everyone who has faith in him will not die but have eternal life.'

The words were Jesus' earthly biography, encompassing a life which had begun long before Bethlehem, before time itself had started to be understood by humanity.

Now part of that timeless time was coming to an end for Jesus. Yet, only through his impending death, Jesus had said to Nicodemus, would people begin to understand. 'When you have lifted up the Son of Man, you will know I am what I am.'

Only then would the world grasp the truth he had spoken; his death would represent the glorious climax of his mission to earth.

When the judge finally left Bethany at daybreak, he well understood that he had not only been with a great teacher, but also his Redeemer.

✳   ✳   ✳

In the darkness, Judas Iscariot made his lonely way towards Jerusalem. He was a man driven by his own pressure of thought, trying to cope with the thoughts coursing through his head. From time to time he stopped as if listening, as if some voice only he could hear was telling him what to do. The only outward sign of the mental changes he was undergoing was that people shrank away as he passed them. That night he may well have slept, as legend claims, in a cave close to the appointed place of crucifixion, Golgotha.

In the Temple on the third day before Passover, the noon hour was fast approaching when the Shema would be recited by Joseph Caiaphas: meantime business continued at its usual frenetic pace, and nowhere more so than in the cloisters where the moneychangers had their booths.

Suddenly, 'with uplifted scourge and flaming eyes', Jesus entered the Outer Temple. Where he had obtained the whip would remain a small mystery; what he intended to do with it was not long in doubt.

There were some who would claim that Mary Magdalene bought it; that after Judas' disappearance she had taken over control of the group's finances. Those same people would place her standing in the gateway of the courtyard watching what was happening.

More certain, in the time it took people to recognize him, Jesus had begun to send booths toppling, wielding the whip against anyone who tried to intervene. His repeated cry rose above the tumult, and then became a small roar in the stunned silence: 'Out! you must not turn my Father's house into a market!'

And: 'My house shall be called a house of prayer! You have made it into a robber's cave!'

For the moment nobody realized that in those words, 'My Father's house' and 'My house', Jesus had once again reiterated his personal relationship with God. Everybody was too shocked at what was happening.

The scene took on its own choreography: Caiaphas at the Nicanor Gate standing frozen-faced, his eyes following every destructive act of Jesus, his ears straining to hear every word;

moneychangers scrabbling for coins; Temple guards forming a protective ring under Jonathan's command at the Nicanor Gate; pilgrims beginning to pocket the money from the upturned booths; Jesus rampaging on, toppling more stalls, opening more cages, the whip cracking through the air; traders fleeing in his path; all the time the thunderous words of denunciation pouring forth as, whip in one hand, he cleared a path with the other.

As Jesus swept on through the cloisters, the first counter-attack came. A moneychanger screamed:

'What authority have you for your actions?'

Barely breaking stride, Jesus shouted, 'Destroy this Temple and in three days I will raise it again!'

The words brought a new stunned silence. What was the Nazarene saying? That he could physically pull down the Temple and then restore it in an impossibly short time? The man was mad, said the look on a score, then a hundred and more, faces.

Moneychangers turned to Caiaphas; appealing to him to order Jonathan to have the guards arrest Jesus. But the only words which the dazed High Priest spoke were: 'It has taken forty-six years to build this Temple. How are you going to raise it again in three days?'

Jesus did not bother to answer, intent not only on removing the defilement of the place where God lived – but on providing a warning that the time for redemption was close. He wanted them to understand that the Temple was more than just a magnificent structure. It was a place of worship, a place where they could begin to take the first step to salvation by removing the profanity of commercialism.

But, just as had Judas and the other disciples, the crowd on the Mount of Olives, all those who had hailed Jesus as their earthly King, so now did Joseph Caiaphas join the legions of those who misunderstood. He did not grasp that the temple Jesus spoke of was also his own body. The High Priest did not see that Jesus was saying that in the coming three days the temple of his earthly body would go to its death only to rise again in all the glory of the resurrection.

Instead, all Joseph Caiaphas could hear was the growing crescendo of three words in his mind:

'Destroy... the Temple.'

But, even as the words emerged as a strangled cry, Jesus had tossed aside his whip and left the courtyard with Mary Magdalene.

Seventeen

Deepest night had settled over Jerusalem. Preparations for Passover were all but finished. Sacrificial lambs for the celebration meal had been bought in their thousands and ritually slaughtered and left to hang. Every household had purchased wine and the candles needed to mark the passing of another year of the covenant in which God had made Israel a nation after the avenging angel had passed through Egypt on a deadly mission, killing each Egyptian first-born to force the Pharaoh Ramase to let the Israelites leave.

Now, seventeen hundred years later, the streets of Jerusalem were filled with the redolent stench of hyssop dipped in lamb's blood and tied to door mantles as a reminder of what their ancestors had done to show the angel they were God's people.

Those who had no homes slept in the streets, huddled together for warmth, oblivious to the tramping of sentries on the ramparts of the Antonia Fortress. Its massive gates were closed and barred and behind them nothing disturbed the silence of the citadel. The last of the tribute had been counted and was now on its way to Caesarea under heavy escort. In their quarters, Pilate and Claudia Procula slept, their disagreements for the moment silenced.

Sentries stood watch at the closed Temple gates, only the stamp of their feet against the chill night air marking their presence. Only a faint glow from the furnace lit the Courtyard of the Altar. Beyond, silent and brooding, rose the massive structure of the Temple, the gold filigree around its rooftop a dull gleam in the starlight.

Pinpricks of light from oil lamps marked the salon of Joseph Caiaphas. Inside, the High Priest was gripped by a torment which, at this hour, only Ithamar witnessed.

Time would not dim the image of the ravaged face of Caiaphas pacing the salon, his voice rising and falling as he ranged through the spectrum of emotions. The essence of his words would survive beyond the confines of the salon and would mark the High Priest's entry into infamy.

'First the Nazarene mocks our Court. Then he abrogates the Law and takes to himself the power to forgive sins. Yet there is no greater sin than in challenging me. Where does he get the authority to destroy the Temple? To mislead our people! To lead them to destruction! Everything I have done has been for their good. I bargained with Rome to keep our faith free of its idols, to keep the Temple as pure as our faith. Without the Temple there would be nothing. The Temple is the people's only hope. But the Nazarene wants to destroy it. Those were his words – destroy it!'

The sudden silence in the salon; the exchanged looks of two men with one thought; then the High Priest resuming his soliloquy: they provided a punctuation point before the High Priest resumed.

'How could I have been so blind? The Nazarene has well understood the deep longing we all have for freedom and he has used it to cruelly deceive our people. He has tried to turn them not against our enemy, Rome, but the very home of our faith, the Temple. We must now allow our people to die for Him! This nation must not perish for one Man! The Temple must not be destroyed! Only God has the power to do that. And the Nazarene is not God.'

They were the words of a man immured in his own blindness.

On the morning before the start of Passover, Jesus said his first farewell. In a house in the Lower City, he met his mother and Mary Magdalene. The two women had been invited to stay there by friends of Mary and Martha, who planned to join them later when the four women would then share the Passover meal.

Mary Magdalene had returned from market with the last of the food needed for the meal when, early though the hour, Jesus had arrived.

'Jesus knew that his hour had come and he must leave this world and go to the Father.'

His first ministry had begun in the synagogue in Jerusalem to those who had 'received him not'. Now that it was all but over, he wanted to assure those to whom he had grown close that they would be cherished 'unto the end'.

His mood and manner would go unremarked, Mary Magdalene confining herself to the observation that Jesus sat with them for a while on the floor while they served him fruits, honey and unleavened bread. To drink he may have had water drawn from one of Jerusalem's underground springs. Who can doubt that his manner would have been tender and affectionate? Jesus was going on a journey like no other. And he wanted to leave no sadness.

Every exchanged look, every word which passed between them, could only have conveyed a portent of what was to come. Yet, nothing of what ultimately lay ahead must, in their final moments together, lessen the deep and abiding love Jesus felt for the two women whom, more than any of their sex, he loved the most.

One had given him the opportunity to be born to die; the other epitomized the true meaning of salvation. He could pay them no greater tribute than to spend this time alone with them before others would claim his body, to do as they would with it.

In the peace and privacy of that room, Jesus reminded Mary Magdalene and his mother that, no matter what would happen to him on earth, they must go on believing in the glory beyond. Then he asked them to pray with him – 'and we did so'.

For a brief moment longer they remained together. Then Jesus walked from the room and did not look back.

They would not meet again until his earthly life was drawing to a close.

Throughout the day before Passover, Jerusalem went about its normal business, the Roman presence heard but not seen, only the sounds of drilling carrying from the fortress courtyard into the streets beyond. From there news spread that Barabbas was being held in the Antonia's dungeons and that Pilate planned to have the Zealot crucified shortly before the onset of Passover.

The report had created tension among Zealot sympathizers. But they knew there was little they could do. Many also felt deflated after seeing their expectations of Jesus dashed. Those who saw him leaving the house in the Lower City jeered and mocked: he was no longer their acclaimed king but another rabbi who had promised so much, then failed to deliver.

Ignoring them, Jesus hurried on his way to join the disciples in another house in the Lower City where they would all celebrate Passover.

Shortly after reciting the noon prayer, Joseph Caiaphas convened a meeting of the Great Sanhedrin in its chamber to discuss what to do about Jesus. The High Priest told the assembled judges he wished them to consider several possible indictments.

A charge of blasphemy would be based upon Jesus' claims to be directly carrying out God's orders. A charge of sorcery would be rooted in the many claims the Nazarene had made to cure the incurable and even raise the dead. A charge of incitement against the authorities would be based on the way Jesus had ridden into Jerusalem. A charge of desecration of the Temple would be founded in his attack on the moneychangers and other vendors. All were offences which, if proven, carried the death penalty.

Given that Passover was almost upon them, Caiaphas wanted an immediate trial: for him the main charge should be incitement, against not only the Temple but also the Roman authorities. Such an accusation, once proven, would mean that Jesus would be handed over to Pilate for sentence to be carried out. That would deflect from the Temple an anger the Nazarene's supporters would display over the execution. He would become another victim of Roman oppression.

Among those who were present was Nicodemus, who immediately demanded to be heard. While his precise words would be lost to record, the gist of what he said was: where was the hard evidence to support any of the charges?

The reports he had seen from the Temple agents would not survive serious cross-examination. Many appeared to be based on rumours, gossip, tavern talk, not evidence. While it was perfectly true the Nazarene had ridden into the city in procession on a donkey, by itself that was not a crime. It could be argued that men rode in on donkeys every day. The crime would have been if the Nazarene had acknowledged the crowd and proclaimed himself. Manifestly he had not. Indeed, he had ordered them to disperse.

Nicodemus turned to Jesus' behaviour in the Temple. On his first visit he had done nothing except to observe what many visitors found offensive: the level of commercialism; older pilgrims could remember when the sellers of sacrifices had not been allowed to encroach into the Temple but, over the years they had been allowed to do so on the grounds they were blocking the surrounding streets.

On his second visit, when Jesus had attacked the moneychangers, he could mount a respectable defence that he was acting in the public interest. While it was perfectly acceptable that every pilgrim to the Temple must pay half a shekel – a sizeable sum often equal to a day's pay for a man – and that no foreign currency should be accepted in lieu, over the years this had led to excessive profiteering. This abuse had created a thriving market in which the moneychangers charged as much as they could squeeze from pilgrims. The Nazarene had been right to call their cloister a 'den of thieves'. And, in support of what he had done, the Nazarene could cite the Talmud which clearly stated no one must defile the Temple.

The only crime the Nazarene had committed was one of common assault against the moneylenders and, if the Great Sanhedrin was to start trying those cases, half of Jerusalem would be likely brought before it. If the vendors believed they had a case, they should take it before the Lower Courts; at best they could only mount a civil action for loss of earnings. But not one trader had instituted such proceedings.

Nicodemus' measured, unemotional delivery; Caiaphas stony-faced; the other judges silent and attentive: the image has persisted down the centuries.

Nicodemus turned to the proposed charge of incitement. Again there was no evidence to support it. The Nazarene's words: 'Destroy the Temple and in three days I will raise it again,' was really no more than typical Galilean rhetoric. He could be laughed at and dismissed as a fool, but never sentenced to death! As far as inciting the people against the Romans went, there was no evidence to support that which had come from the Nazarene's mouth. What people chose to interpret was a matter for them. But no man could be condemned on the interpretation of another!

Realising his case was slipping from his grasp, the High Priest demanded to know upon what personal evidence did Nicodemus insist that Jesus was innocent of all the proposed charges.

As Nicodemus began to describe his visit to Bethany, the atmosphere in the court became electrifying. Judges who had spent a lifetime interpreting the law from the security of their salons could not recall a precedent for what Nicodemus had done – gone in search of the truth himself.

Evidence! That, Nicodemus insisted, was what had sent him out into the night. And he had found that the Nazarene was a man of peace, whose sole mission was to rekindle faith and bring everyone closer to God. He tried to do so by teaching in a way no one had heard before. But all he said was rooted in Scripture. In the time they had spent together not once had the Nazarene attacked the Word of God. Quite the opposite. While much of what he said was indeed hard to follow and the Nazarene refused to make it easy, there was nothing blasphemous in anything he said. He was a good man.

The sudden silence was broken by Caiaphas demanding to know whether Nicodemus, using the criteria of a judge, expected them to believe all he had heard the Nazarene say.

Without hesitation Nicodemus said he did, attaching for the first time the words 'the Master' to Jesus when the judge said he would vote against putting him on trial.

All around Nicodemus, other judges were nodding support.

Caiaphas' hope of gaining the full support of the Great Sanhedrin had gone.

Shortly before nightfall, none of the people leaving the Temple would have paid any attention to Judas talking to one of the guards preparing to close the Nicanor Gate. Shortly afterwards Jonathan joined them.

It was not uncommon for a pilgrim to enquire about life within the Inner Temple and a guard would satisfy such curiosity in return for a small fee. Among the more cynical of the Temple staff there was a saying that the more money which changed hands, the more colourful the tale.

Judas was there for a very different purpose. Where he had spent the time since leaving Bethany was another of the mysteries he would attract. He must have been presentable enough and momentarily in control of his feelings for, first the guard, and then Jonathan to take him seriously enough to lead him beyond the Nicanor Gate.

Visitors were rarely permitted to enter the Inner Temple courtyard, let alone the building itself. Anyone doing so had to take a ritual bath in a room adjoining the one reserved for the High Priest's purification. Afterwards a visitor must put on a priest's robe before being admitted into the Temple.

Cleansed and dressed, Judas was brought to Shem's office through a passageway used only by visitors and junior Temple staff who had business with the Chief Scribe.

Judas repeated to Shem what he had told Jonathan. The Chief Scribe had then entered the High Priest's sanctum. Some time later, Judas was brought before Caiaphas.

Shem was the note-taker for the interrogation.

'Your Master's intention is to create a new Kingdom, Iscariot of Kerioth?'

'Yes, my Lord High Priest.'

'On whose authority does he claim that?'

'The Lord above all others, my Lord High Priest.'

'He identifies himself with God?'

'Yes, my Lord High Priest.'

The formality of the questions, with the use of Judas' surname and place of birth, and the treasurer's own exalted way of addressing Caiaphas, probably on Shem's instructions, gave the interrogation added menace. This was no mere interview by a Temple agent or a scribe, but was being conducted under the full authority of the highest ranking member of the Jewish judiciary.

'And you have heard your Master say he will create his new Kingdom shortly?'

'Yes, my Lord High Priest.'

'And he will do so by claiming he is acting on God's instructions?'

'Yes, my Lord High Priest.'

'And your Master knows by doing this he would raise insurrection?'

'Yes, my Lord High Priest.'

'Knowing such insurrection would involve the Imperial authorities?'

'Yes, my Lord High Priest.'

That may well have been the moment when the dividing line between sanity and mania finally blurred in Judas. An intrinsic disturbance of thinking began to underpin his words.

'My Master keeps changing his mind, my Lord High Priest. One moment he says his Kingdom is about to happen. Then he does nothing! It has been like that for months. He starts something, then stops. Now he says the hour is close. That must be why he wants us all to join him on Gethsemane after our *seder*.'

The news that Jesus would be going after the Passover meal to one of the loneliest places in the vicinity of Jerusalem could only have set Caiaphas' mind racing.

'I would like to speak to your Master. To hear for myself of his plans, Iscariot.'

'I could bring him here, my Lord High Priest.'

'No. I will send the Temple guard to escort him from Gethsemane. But how will they recognize your Master in the dark?'

'I will kiss him on the cheek, my Lord High Priest.'

In offering to perform this act, Judas would become the most vilified figure in history, the very epitome of betrayal. But had that always been his intention?

Certainly his fellow disciples had no doubt that from the time Judas had joined them, he had calumny on his mind. Later, with the benefit of hindsight, they would claim:

'Jesus knew all along who was without faith and who was to betray him.' And: The Master said, 'you are clean, though not every one of you'. And: 'A man will find his enemies under his own roof.'

Yet there was no evidence to support that Judas had plotted and schemed from the beginning. His only tangible sin was an obsessive thriftiness. He had most notably displayed it to Mary Magdalene when he had tried to make her sell her precious ointment. But that can hardly justify the particular attack that would later be directed at Judas.

'Judas Iscariot was a thief; he used to pilfer the money put into the common purse and was his charge.' And 'Satan had entered him.'

There is no evidence offered to support accusations of theft, let alone that Jesus upbraided the treasurer for any such act.

Was it simply then that Judas' act of betrayal was so unexpected that it needed to be rooted in a background of sin?

So what had driven Judas to betray Jesus? Was it some form of mental breakdown brought on by disillusionment that all his expectations of a successful earthly revolution had come to naught?

Or did Judas still cling to the hope that even at that late hour he could somehow still force Jesus to launch it? Did Iscariot believe that indeed so great were Jesus' powers that, no matter what forces were arrayed against him, he would still emerge victorious in the only way Judas understood – a worldly victory? Had Judas deliberately gone to the Temple to cast himself in the role of the trigger factor? Did he see himself still as the outsider among the disciples who would prove himself greater than all of them by finally forcing their Master to act in the only way Iscariot thought appropriate?

Did Judas believe that launching insurrection was the only way to show the Temple, everyone, that Jesus was the one unifying person capable of mobilizing the nation and bringing about its freedom?

These questions would dog the footsteps of Judas Iscariot as he left the High Priest's salon to join the other disciples at the Passover meal.

*   *   *

Some time during the evening, news reached the Antonia Fortress that the High Priest was preparing for a trial to be held, not in the Great Sanhedrin, but in the palace of Annas. In the past, its great hall had been occasionally used for purely religious trials. Pilate was informed that the charge was blasphemy under Jewish law. The accused was Jesus.

The procurator showed little interest.

On the flat roof of the house in the Lower City, Passover continued along its precise way for Mary Magdalene and the other three women. Before the meal they recited psalms, then bowls of bitter herbs were passed around along with the platter of roast lamb and wine; all were ceremoniously served. It was the same all over the city, except at one meal.

On a roof top, Jesus sat with his disciples and, for the last time, used their coming together to explain why he had to die. First:

'He took bread, gave thanks and broke it, and gave it to them with the words "This is my body which is given to you."'

Then he offered them his cup of wine with the words:

'Drink from it, all of you. For this is my blood, the blood of the covenant, shed for the forgiveness of sins.'

His choice of bread and wine was deliberate, a reminder of all that had happened and what was to come. Wheat had to survive the harshness of winter and was then ground between the millstones and baked in the fire before becoming bread. Grapes had to have one life crushed from them before being transformed into wine.

From time immemorial, bread and wine had nourished humanity. Now, in symbolically transforming them into his flesh and blood, Jesus was saying he would provide spiritual nourishment through the final redemptive act he must shortly endure. In giving himself he was reminding them that no sacrifice was too great for him because of the glory that would assuredly follow.

In offering this special means of communion with him to his disciples, Jesus was guaranteeing them that they, too, would share in his glory. As would all those who 'will do this for me'.

It would remain part of her story that during the night Claudia Procula stood alone on the Antonia Fortress ramparts looking down on the pilgrims celebrating in the light of candles and oil lamps.

At some point she saw a figure moving from one celebration to another, proffering a cup and a platter.

Mary Magdalene would also be described as being on the flat roof of the house in the Lower City, her eyes dwelling on where the apostles sat in silent contemplation, and then moving on to the unmistakable figure of Claudia Procula standing on the ramparts.

For a moment it may well have seemed as if both women were staring at each other.

Then Claudia Procula was gone.

Some time later, Jonathan led a column of Temple guards out of the city towards Gethsemane.

Eighteen

From her rooftop vantage point, Mary Magdalene would have been among the first to see Jesus arrive in Jerusalem in very different circumstances to his triumphant entry. Then he had been fêted by a vast crowd as their King while he rode between them on a donkey. Now, despite showing no resistance, he had been manhandled from Gethsemane; his behaviour had fulfilled yet another prophecy, the prediction of Isaiah that people would recognize the Messiah because 'he will be led like a lamb to the slaughter'.

Later, Mary Magdalene would learn the circumstances of his arrest. Jesus had been praying in an olive grove when the Temple force arrived. 'Knowing all that was coming to him, he went to them.' Peter rushed to Jesus' aid with a flailing sword, managing to slice off the ear of one of the guards. Instantly Jesus healed the wound and rebuked Peter. 'Sheathe your sword. This is the cup my Father has given me, shall I not drink it?'

Even in that dire moment, Jesus wanted the apostles to remember one of his favourite analogues – the cup. He had used it repeatedly over the past three years to remind the disciples of the salvation contained in the cup of redemption he offered. Once more he had told them that, at the onset of his earthly torment, the context of the 'cup' would make it more bearable.

Judas stepped forward and planted his kiss. As the guards reached for Jesus, he stopped them:

'Do you suppose that I cannot appeal to my Father who would at once send to my aid more than twelve legions of angels?'

There was a grim irony in Jesus' choice of 'legion' – the epitome of Roman power. But twelve legions of angels would be more than a match for any army. Who can doubt the words sent a surge of excitement through Judas? Here, at last, was the action he longed to see – and it had come about by his own determination to bring the Master into confrontation with the authorities.

In the next breath, Jesus shattered all such hopes when he addressed Jonathan.

'Did you take me for a bandit, that you have come out with swords and cudgels to arrest me? This has all happened to fulfil what the prophets wrote.'

Then Jesus stepped forward, telling the disciples to leave – 'And they all deserted him.'

He had predicted no less.

But for Jonathan's military mind, Jesus' capture still left a problem. The disciples might have gone to fetch reinforcements. Soon a mob could arrive to free the prisoner. To take the direct route back to Jerusalem would be too risky.

Instead, Jonathan chose to travel as far as possible outside the city walls. The route took them past the Temple, on across the desolate Kidron Valley and along the upper slopes of the steep Valley of Hinnon, Jerusalem's natural defence in the south. Beyond, where the walls continued north towards Herod's palace, the arrest party entered the Lower City, through the gate through which sacrificial animals passed. From there the force swiftly made its way to Annas' palace.

Mary Magdalene's first reaction was to seek help from the most powerful figure she knew. The home of Nicodemus was nearby and she was quickly admitted to his presence. He immediately ordered his servants to make enquiries. They returned with the news that Jesus was about to face trial in Annas' palace which was ringed with Temple guards.

While holding a trial by night was unprecedented, there was no time to mount a successful legal challenge. The only ray of hope was that the Law did not allow for the death penalty to be carried out if a crime was also against Rome. Then the case had to be referred to Pilate for ratification.

Nicodemus was banking on the procurator dismissing any possible charge under the Imperial code as lacking in evidence. Again, Pilate would no doubt take into account the public attitude. Jesus was a charismatic figure; to kill him without the best possible reason would be to risk arousing the pilgrims: the pious could become a rampaging mob, the last thing Pilate would want.

Nicodemus told Mary Magdalene there was no more she could do; she should return to Bethany with his mother and Mary and Martha. Anyone who could be identified as a follower of Jesus could now be in danger of being arrested.

In the Great Hall of Annas' palace, staff put the final touches to a makeshift courtroom. Supervised by Shem, scribes arranged parchments and law books behind the Bench of Judgment where black-robed judges had already taken their place. All were Sadducees: Caiaphas had made sure that Nicodemus, Gamaliel and any other Pharisee judge would not be permitted to exercise dissenting votes.

The High Priest wore his magnificent outer robe, the ultimate symbol of his priestly authority. 'This was their moment, the hour when darkness reigns,' as Jesus had said on his arrest.

Caiaphas set about giving a spurious legality in a pre-trial speech to his fellow judges.

He stood before the bench, his eyes never leaving them, holding all in thrall.

'The Law is the one embodiment of everything that is good in our life. It has no fault or flaw. And we, my lords, embody the Law. We execute it in the name of our people and in the sacred trust given to us by God, through Moses, without the Law our people would have ruined the very earth God gave them. Without the Law, the justice or injustice of any cause would be impossible to judge.'

He continued to search their faces, challenging them to deny the truth of any of this.

'Tonight the Law and we face the greatest challenge. We have had impostors before. False prophets. Men who cruelly promised our people a way out of their bondage. But never this: a man who has threatened to destroy the Temple that is the very epitome of our Law. There has never been a greater challenge to all we represent as God's earthly judges. And yet, the Nazarene will have justice.'

The consummate orator, Caiaphas once more paused to allow the sub-text to be absorbed. The scribes silently gathered behind the judges must have sensed they were witnessing an authentic moment in their history. The High Priest resumed his slow, measured delivery, the beginning of an inner journey he had travelled all his life.

'When the pharaohs tried to force our ancestors to kneel before their gods, our people killed themselves rather than betray the True God – because that is the first Law: worship no others. They were still butchered in their thousands. It was the first pogrom on our people. But not the last.'

Heads began to nod: this was history being enunciated by one of its great students. Like the skilled trial lawyer he undoubtedly was, Caiaphas did not respond, only gathered himself.

'Moses led our people into exile and they endured plague and bondage because they tried to live their lives under the Covenant God gave Moses on Mount Sinai. For forty years the Commandments guided our people through the wilderness. They led them to this city God had chosen for them, for us. Jerusalem was already a thousand years old when Rome was still a village. To reach here God gave our people Joshua to overcome their enemies. And who cannot remember how he defeated the combined forces of five pagan kings? Later, God was there to lead our people through pestilence. To provide food when there was famine. To anoint Saul as the first King of our twelve tribes, to be our shield in those terrible wars against the Philistines and Midianites. To guide David's sling to kill Goliath when our people were all but lost. Each time those who survived knew they had done so because they must make sure the Holy Ark of the Covenant would one day rest here in Jerusalem, in the Temple.'

His listeners knew all this; but never had they been so powerfully reminded.

'The Holy Ark survived when the pagan, Nebuchadnezzar, destroyed the First Temple and exiled our people to Babylon. Two hundred thousand left here. Only five thousand returned.'

Caiaphas passed to allow the terrible figures to make their impact.

'We are all descended from those survivors. Strength of faith is all they had. But it enabled them to rebuild the Temple – to go on believing, to go on surviving. And that is why we are here tonight. To survive by full redress to the Law!'

Caiaphas roamed the inner depths of his own soul; his pain was that of his listeners and all those who had gone before them.

'King David promised our ancestors that from his dynasty would one day come our ultimate Deliverer. The Messiah. We have waited centuries for him to come. For that our people have continued to suffer more than any nation deserves. Hatred of our very name – Jew – provoked, and still does, a violence no other race has ever endured! And why? Because we want to, must, go on believing! Believing one day we will be free to worship in peace. That's all our people have ever wanted. To be allowed to offer thanks to the One True God. And for that they have been put to the sword. Crucified and beheaded. Slaughtered by every form of death imaginable. All because they refused to stop believing. Because they held true to the belief that one day the Expected One will come!'

Caiaphas falling silent, closing his eyes, lost in an inner reverie as if the memories he had unleashed were too painful, too terrible, to evoke; preceded his next words:

'Belief in God. All we have is founded on that. Our Second Temple, our Sanhedrin, were both raised in the name of belief. And from belief came the Law. And our own predecessors have judged by God's Law at no small cost to themselves. Three hundred years ago those who sat where you now do, at the Bench of Judgment, were put to death on the orders of Alexander because they refused to endorse his order that Greek should be the first language of our people. Our predecessors went to their deaths singing psalms in the language God gave them!'

Caiaphas stopped again, watching their faces, almost as if out of their mouths would come those laments. Instead there was only a silent working of lips. The High Priest resuming his patrolling, his silence for a moment longer dominating them before he continued.

'Remember what happened when the Syrians came? Never was there such brutality. In one week in this very city, a hundred women were raped because their husbands insisted on coming to the Temple to pray. And still the men came. That is faith in its true meaning. And even when the Syrians murdered our ancestors' very children in their cradles, the men continued to come to pray. Because that is who they were and we are! A God-fearing people who want no more than the right to live in the fear of God! Sixty-three years ago this very Passover, Pompey came with his legions. A pagan in his belief and in his cruelty. For sport he had one of our priests crucified. For his amusement Pompey sat in our Holy of Holies and dared God to show himself. Yet our people survived such terrible mockery because they had faith that one day they would be delivered. That one day the Messiah would come. I was a boy when Caesar came here. Many of you will remember what was said then: Caesar was the only good Roman. He respected our ways. He left us to worship in peace. And his reward? His own people assassinated him.'

Caiaphas paused for the impact of the words to be driven home.

'After Caesar the persecution resumed. I expect like me you can all remember as young priests having to confront those who had lost loved ones to the cross. I told them what I have always believed. That deliverance would come. And that God would tell us when.'

The image survives of Caiaphas standing before the judges, preparing them for what must be done.

'The Nazarene has given no sign deliverance is at hand. Instead he is that most dangerous of all: a Jew who seduces his own people by guile and false promises. That is why we must not hesitate to do our duty. We must not allow an impostor to deceive us, or cruelly betray our people.'

The High Priest took his place on the Bench of Judgment while Shem ordered Jonathan to bring in Jesus.

Near Bethany a small army had assembled. Having fled from Gethsemane, the disciples had spread the news that Jesus had been arrested. John and Peter had just returned from Jerusalem, having managed to talk their way past the Temple guards at the gate to his prison. Inside, Peter had been challenged three times as being a follower of Jesus. On each occasion he had vehemently denied the charge.

Now, surrounded by a driving force, his courage had returned. He supported Simon's plans to launch a rescue. In the midst of avid discussion on how it should be carried out, Mary Magdalene arrived.

'There was about her a great strength,' Philip would recall.

Her words left them in no doubt. 'Have you forgotten what the Master always told you? "Go in peace." That is what he wants from you. Peace. Not violence.'

The throng melted into the darkness. If Mary Magdalene did not smile at the other disciples, she would at least be glad they finally understood what now had to happen to Jesus.

From the outset of his trial, the sole intention was to extract from Jesus the admission that would lead to one result: death. 'It would be to their interest if one man died for the whole people.'

The idea was reflected in the formal indictment. Jesus of Nazareth was charged that:

'On divers dates you did attempt to alter, subvert and overthrow the appointed constitution of the Temple and its servants; and by your actions and statements you did attempt to incite rebellion against the Lord Tetrarch and that by all your actions you did imperil the nation's safety by attempting to bring it into direct conflict with the Imperial authority of Rome. And that in sight of this most holy city you did attempt all this by falsely proclaiming to be the Expected One.'

It was a catch-all set of charges, each of which carried the death penalty, but one that could only be carried out by the Roman authority.

Jesus refused to plead or speak in his defence except to say to the Court:

'I have spoken openly to all the world: I have always taught in synagogue, where all Jews congregate. I have said nothing in secret. Why question me? Ask my hearers what I told them. They know what I said.'

Jonathan, standing nearby, slapped Jesus across the face saying: 'Is that the way to answer the High Priest?'

The tone had been set.

* * *

During the night, Claudia Procula had awoken Pontius Pilate to say that in a dream she had seen 'great harm' coming to Jesus. She had asked her husband to intervene with Caiaphas to protect him. Pilate had refused. She had warned him, 'to let no harm befall this good man.'

Twice more, just as Peter had denied Jesus, so over the coming hours would Claudia Procula repeat the warning to her husband.

After cutting short any rescue attempt, Mary Magdalene and Jesus' mother had returned to Jerusalem, arriving in the city some time before dawn. They had made their way to Annas' palace but had been refused admission. They had gone to the home of Nicodemus. The judge had just returned from fruitless attempts to gain entrance to the palace. But all was not lost, he told the women; news trickling out of the Great Hall suggested: 'the Chief Priest and the whole Council had failed to find some allegation against Jesus on which a death sentence could be based, though many had come forward with false evidence.'

In the Great Hall, the sorry procession of perjurers had continued until daybreak. Their evidence had been contradictory and none of it in any way supported the indictment that Jesus had brought the Temple into direct conflict with the Roman administration.

Now, as the first sounds of the Imperial trumpeter, swiftly followed by the Temple horn players, drifted over the city, Jesus stood in the witness position. The rapid-fire questions of the High Priest filled the Great Hall.

How long had he plotted revolution? Planned to overthrow the Temple? Remove the Lord Tetrarch? Drive out the Imperial Procurator? And his forces?

To each question Jesus gave no answer. On Jesus' face was renewed strength, as if sensing Caiaphas was staking all on a final question. He framed it with all the authority of the High Priest's office:

'By the living God, I charge you to tell us: Are you the Messiah, the Son of God?'

Caiaphas had put Jesus under the supreme oath to tell the truth: there could be no prevarication; no lying as the other witnesses had done; no evading. There could be nothing but to tell the truth, the whole truth and so help him God.

The silence stretched. Everyone in the Great Hall knew that all else would flow from the answer.

'If I tell you, you will not believe me.'

'You are saying you are the Son of God?'

Jesus did not hesitate. 'I am.'

The simple dignity of the two words rang out around the Great Hall. The collective gasp from the court was stayed in his next declaration.

'I tell you this: from now on, you will see the Son of Man seated at the right hand of God and coming on the clouds of Heaven.'

Not only had Jesus once more confirmed his divinity, but he had chosen to do so by using the personal pronoun 'I'. He wanted everyone to understand his humanity in earthly terms, as well as his divinity in spiritual terms.

'Blasphemy!' The word escaped from Caiaphas' lips and, a moment later, from the mouths of the other judges.

There was one further act to be performed before the passing of sentence. Caiaphas ripped his robe, not along the seam, but the cloth itself so that the damage was beyond repair. The other judges followed him. This expression of public pain and grief dated from the day Jacob had rent his robe upon hearing of the death of his son, Joseph, and later David had torn his clothes after being told that Saul was dead.

Caiaphas addressed the other judges:

'Need we call further witnesses? You have heard the blasphemy. What is your opinion?'

The judgment was unanimous: guilty.

Caiaphas addressed Jesus. 'The crime of blasphemy is only punishable by death. But you have also committed capital offences against the law of Rome. You shall now be brought before the Lord Procurator.'

With those words the High Priest had achieved all he had intended. Jesus had been convicted of the greatest sin possible under the Law, but at the same time the witnesses had perjured themselves sufficiently for Pilate now to exercise his authority to have Jesus crucified.

Not for a moment did the High Priest stop to consider that the prophecy of Isaiah that the true Messiah would be delivered into the hands of the pagans was now to be fulfilled.

At daybreak in the temple, the business of sacrificing was once more underway in the courtyard of the Great Altar when suddenly a shower of coins fell on the priests and sacrificers. Judas, his money pouch empty, ran out of the Temple.

Shortly before, he had been brought into the presence of Caiaphas who had thrust thirty pieces of silver into the Treasurer's hand for his assistance in the arrest of Jesus.

Judas threw the money on the floor 'seized with remorse, shouting "I have sinned: I have brought an innocent man to his death."'

He had run from the floor. Shem had gathered up the money, telling Caiaphas 'This cannot be put into the Temple funds; it is blood money.' The Chief Scribe then suggested that the money could be used to buy a field outside the city walls that could become a burial place for foreigners.

Among those who saw Judas run out of the city was Mary Magdalene. She had been heading for the Temple Courtyard of the Women hoping to learn news. Judas ignored her shout and ran on, the madness in his eyes now a living thing.

His was the behaviour of someone who, though hating what he had done, had not sought repentance. Judas hoped that throwing back the money would absolve him, as would the admission he had sent an innocent man to his death. The realization that his actions were not enough were the final factor in carrying him over the border of sanity.

Outside the city walls, Judas stumbled towards a rocky

outcrop on which a tree grew. He removed the girdle around his waist and fashioned it into a noose. He climbed into the tree, tied one end of the girdle to a branch and placed the noose around his neck and jumped. Witnesses would claim he 'swung in the throes before the rope snapped, sending him on to the rocks below.'

The tragedy of Judas is what might have been. That Iscariot believed in Jesus was all too evident. Judas was, in one sense, a man possessed of a terrible blindness; right until the very moment of Jesus' arrest, Judas had failed to see the truth and encouraged others to share his misbegotten hope of Jesus bringing about an earth-bound victory.

To the end Judas was the outsider: he had lived on sufferance among the other disciples those past three years; he had annoyed, even angered, them in so many ways. Only Mary Magdalene had come close to understanding him. She saw Judas as a sad, lonely figure.

So why had Jesus chosen Judas? For the same reason that he had selected Peter. In both there was an inherent weakness. Peter had boasted that even though others would deny the Master, he never would. Yet three times, following Judas' kiss, Peter had done so, driven by the same fear that had gripped Judas: that Jesus would not do what he had promised.

One became the founder of the greatest faith on earth, the other was destined to become the world's most infamous betrayer. Yet the gap between St Peter and the man who might have become St Judas was only as wide as their understanding of the meaning of redemption – something that Mary Magdalene understood better than either of them.

By the time the sun had burnished the gold filigree around the Temple roof, a silent crowd lined the short route from the Outer Temple gate to the Antonia Fortress. Among them was Mary Magdalene.

Her description would form an everlasting memory: 'Through the Temple portal advanced a formation of guards, forcing all out of the way. Behind them followed Caiaphas and Annas. Then came the Master, bound like a common criminal. At the sight of him, traders and priests started to jeer.'

In their behaviour was an echo of what had happened after the verdict had been returned: 'Then they spat in his face and struck him with their fists and others covered his eyes before they beat him and said: "Now, Messiah, if you are a prophet, tell us who hit You!"'

In the Great Hall, his tormentors had covered Jesus' eyes so they need not see the truth in them, or fear that in the reflection of his gaze, they would themselves see they were blinded.

Now certain of their victory, the priests and vendors mocked at the sorry figure, bruised and swollen from his beatings. But, as Jesus drew level with Mary Magdalene, she saw in his eyes 'still a great certainty'.

In minutes the procession had reached the gateway to the fortress.

Anticipating its arrival, three thrones had been placed before the portal. Through the arch Pilate could be seen striding across the courtyard. With him was his ranking officer Lentinus, and Maximus. When they reached the thrones, each official sat on either side of Pilate.

Caiaphas and Annas stood together. Behind them Jonathan held Jesus. The Temple guards formed a protective circle around the group.

Both sides stared at each other, allowing the silence to stretch.

Both High Priest and procurator understood this was not confrontation. This was *realpolitik*, realization that it was indeed better one man should die than that Joseph Caiaphas and Pontius Pilate, Israel and Rome, should be brought into conflict.

Still, there were formalities to be observed.

Pilate demanded: 'What charge do you bring against this man?'

In the tense silence, Mary Magdalene could sense Caiaphas weighing how best to answer. To say Jesus had been convicted of blasphemy would be pointless: in the pagan lexicon of Rome, the word had no meaning.

Caiaphas overcame the problem. 'If he were not a criminal, we should not have brought him before you.'

There was an oily flattery in Caiaphas' words, an invitation for the procurator not to trouble himself with details, merely to endorse the Temple verdict and have Rome carry out the sentence.

Mary Magdalene watched Caiaphas and Annas hold a whispered consultation. Then once more the High Priest's voice rang out:

'We found this man subverting our nation, opposing the payment of taxes to Caesar and claiming to be the Messiah, our king.'

Now it was the turn of Maximus to confer with Pilate. Subversion was sedition. That was an offence against Rome. Subverting lawfully due tax payments was a similar offence. Claiming kingship in those circumstances was a threat against the Emperor. This was a case now within Rome's jurisdiction.

Lie had been compounded by lie. No evidence had been offered in support of the charge of sedition because none existed. At no time or place had Jesus issued a call to arms. To accuse him of telling the people not to pay their taxes was a fabrication. On the one memorable occasion an attempt had been made to entrap Jesus over tax payments, he had said that people must give to Caesar what was due to Caesar. As to the charge that he had claimed kingship in an earthly sense, Jesus had tirelessly opposed such a claim on his behalf.

Nevertheless, Pilate needed to reassure himself. The man before him, bloodied but unbowed, was clearly no immediate threat to the Emperor or to any Imperial authority. Yet there was something about the prisoner that needed further investigation.

The procurator rose from his throne and ordered Jesus to be brought to his salon in the fortress.

Pilate's interrogation which followed was sharp, short and swift.

'Did you usurp the Emperor's divinity?'

'I have said or done nothing against Rome.'

'What were you hoping to achieve on that donkey?'

'It is written.'

'My patience is not endless.'

'And you also have little time.'

'To sign your death warrant? I can do that now.'

'You have spoken truth there.'

'Are you not afraid of death?'

'There is nothing to fear.'

'Who taught you this?'

'It is the word of the Lord God.'

'Where is this God of yours?'

Jesus was silent. Pilate glanced at the wall murals of Rome's gods.

'Does your God rule where the gods of Rome rule?'

'God is beyond their power.'

'Be careful how you respond.'

'It will make no difference.'

In the renewed silence, they stared at one another.

'You know I could free you?'

'It would still make no difference.'

'I could give you an escort. All the way to Syria or Egypt. You could never return, of course.'

'It is too late for that.'

'Would you rather die than leave?'

'The question does not arise.'

'It does! I can save your life.'

'You can do nothing for me unless you believe. Then you will know the truth.'

'What is truth?'

The question hung in the air.

At the gateway to the fortress the crowd surged forward as Pilate led Jesus, flanked by Lentinus and Maximus, back to the entrance. In a loud voice, Pilate proclaimed: 'I find no fault with your prisoner.'

Until then, by his standard, the procurator had behaved correctly. He had asked all the questions he felt appropriate; the answers had come in a forthright manner, though some of the responses were beyond comprehension for someone who believed truth was not objective but subjective.

Pilate may well have been about to say he was going to release Jesus when the voice of Caiaphas rose above the roar of the mob. Caiaphas screamed:

'His teaching is causing dissatisfaction among the people all through Judaea. It started in Galilee and has spread as far as this city.'

That one word – Galilee – explained Pilate's next decision.

The daily jurisdiction of Galilee was in the hands of Herod Antipas. He would let the tetrarch ratify the Temple sentence. Doing so would absolve Rome from further interest in the matter. At the same time it would show the Temple that the Imperial power had not been seduced by the prisoner. And last but not least, by stepping aside he could placate Claudia Procula.

Pilate's command assuaged the mob's mounting fury.

'Take your Christus to Herod!'

Nineteen

Jesus' journey across Jerusalem was accompanied by the relentless jeering of a crowd orchestrated by the Temple priests. The same pilgrims who had acclaimed Jesus only a few days before now cruelly taunted him and threw rotting fruit and vegetables at him, in the way any convicted criminal was abused. Soon his face was smeared with pulp and juice. Yet, not once did Jesus flinch, staring steadfastly ahead, sustained by an inner certainty that nothing and no one could change the course of the drama in which he had the central role. He had not chosen it for Himself, only for humanity.

Mary Magdalene had managed to remain relatively close to her beloved Master as he was frog-marched through the narrow streets. She, too, was unflinching and resolute, a woman who knew there could be no other way for her to behave. What was happening to Jesus was a salutary reminder of what he had once told her: those who chose to follow him must expect the odium of the masses. She was herself pelted with the vegetables hurled at Jesus; almost certainly she was not a deliberate target, for 'no one knew me, so blinded were they with fury at the Master.'

Reaching Herod Antipas' palace, Mary Magdalene was swept through its gateway before the tetrarch's troops stopped the crowd from entering.

Short though the notice had been, Herod Antipas had nevertheless made preparations to receive Jesus. In the fortress courtyard a throne had been positioned. Surrounding it were courtiers and Molath's troops. A space had been left for the Temple party.

Mary Magdalene found herself squeezed among the spectators who had gained admission. Cowed by the presence of the tetrarch's guards, they were silent.

Caiaphas and Annas stood to one side of the throne. They were tense and nervous, the memory of their last encounter with Herod very possibly on their minds.

Jesus was flanked by Jonathan and Molath.

Herod emerged from the palace, the crown on his head slightly skewed like his smile. A regal robe was draped over his shoulders. Many of those who saw him assumed the tetrarch had been drinking.

This was the man, Mary Magdalene would reflect, who had murdered 'the foreteller of the Messiah'. To the epitaphs more commonly associated with the tetrarch's name – sensual and lascivious, carnal and boorish – Herod Antipas now added two more: unpredictable and superstitious.

Since ordering the murder of John the Baptist, the tetrarch had become obsessed with the fear that the preacher had returned to haunt him. From his earliest years, his father had encouraged Herod Antipas to link religion with magic, and that included the ability only few men understood to return from the dead by trickery. The tetrarch had decided John the Baptist possessed such skills.

Time and again prisoners had been brought before Herod Antipas and questioned to see if they were the reincarnation of John. Despite there being no evidence to support such a possibility, the tetrarch had treated them with unprecedented politeness, before ordering them to be set free.

This may explain the reaction of Herod Antipas that eye-witnesses later told the gospel-writer Luke.

'When Herod saw Jesus he was greatly pleased. He had long been waiting to see him and he had been hoping to see some miracle performed.'

Perhaps a miracle would have finally convinced the tetrarch that here indeed was the reincarnation of the Baptist and someone to be set free. But Jesus had never performed a miracle for his own benefit. Since those days in the wilderness, when Satan had challenged him to perform tricks to prove who he was, Jesus had firmly refused to indulge in cheap theatrics. He would not do so now.

Once more Herod demanded that Jesus should reveal his power by some feat.

Jesus remained silent.

For Mary Magdalene the sight of him standing there, erect

and proud, might well have served as a reminder of those words he had spoken during the Sermon on the Mount: 'Do not give dogs what is holy; do not throw your pearls to the pigs; they will only trample on them and tear you to pieces.'

Herod Antipas chose the laughter of the not-quite-sane to mount his attack.

'One trick! That's all. One little trick and I will set you free.'

The promise was taken up by his courtiers. 'A little trick and he's free! A little trick and he's free!'

Jesus remained still and silent. Early in his ministry he had predicted: 'When they call upon me, I will not answer them – because they hate knowledge and have not chosen to fear the Lord!'

Herod Antipas ordered a servant to fetch a pitcher of water. When the man returned, the tetrarch promised Jesus: 'Turn the water into wine and you will walk free.'

Once more the mocking chant came from the crowd: 'Wine for water sets you free!'

Jesus silently handed the pitcher back to the tetrarch. He looked at Jesus dumbfounded. Then he hurled the pitcher at a courtier, causing a nasty head wound. The tetrarch roared at Jesus: 'Heal him!'

The crowd changed their chant: 'Heal him sets you free! Heal him sets you free!'

Herod Antipas rose from his throne and stood before Jesus; he removed his robe and draped it about Jesus' shoulders.

The tetrarch's crazed laugh; Caiaphas and Annas looking despairingly at each other, the High Priest's nod to Jonathan; the captain of the Temple Guard, gripping Jesus firmly by the arm and leading him out of the courtyard: the memories would remain with Mary Magdalene for the rest of her life.

Shortly afterwards she was hemmed in by the clamouring mob who had returned from the tetrarch's palace and were back at the Antonia Fortress gateway.

From a window in her private quarters, Claudia Procula watched her husband once more striding to the gateway. With him was Maximus, carrying a scroll.

Claudia Procula's mood can be judged from the anguished messages she had sent to Pilate in his salon while he awaited the decision of Herod Antipas. She had told her husband 'no man ever spoke as the Nazarene spoke' and she had begged Pilate to free Jesus.

She could do no more than make an anguished appeal. As a woman, however exalted, she had no right to interfere in the due process of law. She could only approach Pilate as his wife.

He had not responded to her messages. Like a man trapped by his own weaknesses, Pilate had chosen the easy way of not replying, hoping Herod Antipas would solve the matter. Shortly after news reached him that the Temple authorities had returned with Jesus to the fortress gate, Claudia Procula had sent a further message.

'Have nothing to do with that innocent man. I was much troubled on his account in my dreams last night.'

Her final, desperate plea bore witness to the way Jesus had entered her heart, stirred her soul, turned her from paganism into a believer. She became his first follower from Roman womanhood, a woman of the highest rank who had risked everything to save the life of a man she clearly saw as her Saviour.

Pilate may well have thrust her note inside his uniform, fearful of anyone discovering it, before he made his way back to the fortress gate.

Ignoring the throne, Pilate stood directly in front of Caiaphas. Annas remained a pace behind the High Priest.

Jesus stood to one side, held in the grip of Jonathan. The Temple guard and priests formed a semi-circle around them.

Walking the distance between the fortress building and the courtyard gateway, Pontius Pilate had undergone his own transformation, which for the moment no one could sense: neither Maximus, the High Priest, Annas, Jonathan, the Temple Guard and priests, not even Mary Magdalene.

Whatever had happened in Pilate's mind, his face was a mask. He was already 'a man sorely tried' by those he once more faced. The High Priest had all but outwitted him, made a mockery of his Imperial authority, broken the tacit arrangement they had of a common accommodation to maintain peace. Instead, Caiaphas had generated a mob's anger to show his own power. Very well: he would show the High Priest who had the ultimate authority.

Pilate addressed only Caiaphas. He reminded the High Priest he had already examined Jesus and had found nothing to support the charges upon which the Temple had convicted him. Then, his voice rising, the procurator added that Herod Antipas had found a similar lack of evidence. 'Clearly the prisoner has done nothing to deserve death. He should be set free.'

Mary Magdalene would recall the stunned look on Caiaphas' face; Annas whispering in his ear; Pilate already half-turning to walk back into the fortress; Maximum uncertain.

Then, loud and clear, came the voice of Caiaphas.

'My Lord Procurator: at Passover, Rome allows punishment to be administered for an offence against the Temple. I now make such a request for the prisoner to be punished by you.'

Now it was Pilate who was astonished and Maximus who explained that the *Lex Julia*, the Imperial law that gave the Jews certain special privileges, allowed for such a punishment to be administered.

What passed between the procurator and his legal adviser would never be known. But after a few moments, Pilate turned to Caiaphas.

'We have a prisoner, the Jew, Barabbas, a leader of the resistance, awaiting death for killing our tax collectors. He can be punished under the Lex Julia.'

At this point the procurator may well have paused; Caiaphas may well have whispered to Annas who, in turn, had whispered to the Temple priests; who, for their part had passed the word on through the crowd.

Slowly, gathering strength with every repetition came the mob's demand:

'You must punish Jesus of Nazareth.'

Caiaphas watched remorselessly as Pilate struggled in his own mind to find a new way out of the impasse.

'Very well, High Priest. I will chastise the prisoner, then release him.'

Mary Magdalene would remember Pilate turning to summon legionnaires to take Jesus from Temple custody as the crowd began to bray:

'Punish the Nazarene!'

Caiaphas asked the procurator. 'You will scourge him?'

Scourging was automatically inflicted by the Romans as part of punishment for any major crime. But the choice of instrument was left in the hands of the official responsible for sentencing. Pilate could order a light cane to be used which, while capable of drawing blood, would not slice to the bone. Only a heavy, brine-soaked whip did that – and was only used preceding crucifixion.

Pilate's intention may well have been to order a flogging with the lighter whip, a punishment he hoped would satisfy the crowd's blood lust. It would leave Jesus cruelly marked, but still alive.

As if sensing what could happen, the mob began to shout: 'Crucify him!'

Caiaphas had to shout to make himself heard. 'My Lord Procurator, your law allows for any form of scourging to be followed by crucifixion. We demand that for the prisoner.'

The cry from the mob was louder and more insistent. 'Crucify him!'

Pilate's anger erupted. 'Take him and crucify him yourselves!'

He had plainly had enough of what had become an unedifying spectacle. The Imperial authority had been reduced to bargaining virtually on the street for the life of a man whom Pilate had already judged to be innocent. It made a mockery of everything Pilate stood for: firmness, decisiveness. Enough was enough.

'Take him! Be gone!'

It was the procurator's final attempt to absolve himself from further responsibility.

Sensing victory was close the mob, encouraged by the priests, roared: 'If you let this man go, you are no friend of Caesar.'

The words could only have alarmed Pilate. If he released the prisoner, he could indeed face censure from the Emperor; he might even be accused of conspiring against Rome. The punishment for that could be his own death.

Mary Magdalene watched the procurator beckon to a centurion waiting inside the fortress gateway. The soldier stepped forward and handed a long stick to Pilate.

In one swift move, the procurator broke the stick across his knee and threw the pieces at the feet of Jesus. The gesture signified a Roman sentence of death.

Pontius Pilate now continued to intone in Latin the words that accompanied it.

'*Ibis ad crucem!*' 'Thou shalt suffer the cross!'

The procurator turned to the centurions. '*Expedi crucem!*' 'Prepare the cross!'

The crowd began a new chant: 'Free Barabbas!'

Caiaphas turned to Jesus and spoke one last time to him: 'By next Passover no one will remember you.'

Jonathan released Jesus from his grip and thrust him forward into the hands of a centurion.

Mary Magdalene continued to watch as Barabbas was led out of the gateway, passing Jesus as he entered the fortress. For a moment the Zealot and the Messiah exchanged glances, united in that moment by the terribly physical suffering they had already endured. Then Barabbas lowered his head in a gesture of submission as if saying: 'It is you, not I, who should be set free.'

Caiaphas was intent on what was happening in the courtyard. Around the scourging post, the scourger swiftly shackled Jesus to the post, then ripped the robe from his upper body. Next he stepped back, flicked his whip and measured the distance.

In the sudden silence, each lash carried to the crowd around the gate. Mary Magdalene forced her eyes to remain open, tears running down her cheeks.

His work finished, the scourger sloshed a bucket of water over the body of Jesus as he staggered to his feet.

Suddenly Jesus became the plaything of the soldiers standing around the post. One placed a makeshift crown of thorns on his head. Mocked and reviled by the Romans, bleeding and cut to the bone, Jesus still managed to stand proud and erect. He looked towards the gateway at Mary Magdalene.

She looked back at Jesus. In his eyes there was still all he had promised: the promise of a better future.

It took a short while for the execution squad to form up. They were led by a trumpeter playing the same imperious calls that signalled the start of a new day from the ramparts of the Antonia

Fortress – and now announced the beginning of the earthly end of Jesus' time on earth.

Soldiers placed the beam of the cross on his shoulders. Despite the weight and the fearful punishment which had been meted out; Jesus remained unbowed by his burden.

Slowly, steadily, he walked towards the gateway. The crowd was suddenly hushed.

Passing Mary Magdalene standing close to Caiaphas, Jesus nodded reassuringly.

The place of the skull – in Hebrew, *Golgotha* – was a raised hillock to the north of Jerusalem, and offered the crucified a last view of the city. Secured to his cross, Jesus saw the sky darken over the Temple and the Antonia Fortress.

At the foot of Golgotha, a ring of bored soldiers kept back the weeping crowd, predominantly women. On his way there, Jesus had asked them not to weep for him. For once, in their grief, they had refused to obey him.

Mary Magdalene and his mother had been given special permission to remain close by the foot of the Cross. They had watched the darkness of night settle over the land at noon, as if God himself wished to hide the inhumanity being committed on this barren ground, reputed to be the burial place of Adam.

His executioners had stripped away his blood-stained garments, ready for their own ritual of shaking dice to see who would win them.

The women had listened as Jesus offered them forgiveness, 'They do not know what they are doing.' They had heard him say – 'I thirst'. For Mary Magdalene it could only have been a bitter-sweet memory of that other afternoon when Jesus had spoken to the harlot of Samaria at the well: 'He who drinks the water I give him will not know thirst any more.'

They had watched a soldier soak a rag with wine, fix it to the point of his spear and hold it up to Jesus' lips. And finally they heard him utter the immortal prayer: 'Father, into Thy hands I commend my Spirit.'

At that moment, from the Outer Court of the Temple came the bleating of thousands of lambs awaiting slaughter.

But for Mary Magdalene, 'the lamb of God was already slain and all the prophecies foretold are now fulfilled on earth'.

That night she was among a small band that included his mother, Judge Nicodemus and Joseph of Arimathea who lowered Jesus from the cross.

The two women took turns to hold his ruined body. For his mother it was the loving embrace of a mother for a son; for Mary Magdalene it was the act of a woman who had loved Jesus in her own very special way.

The two women helped Nicodemus and Joseph to embalm his body with 'a hundred pounds of myrrh and spices and then wound him in pure linen'.

Jesus was then placed in the tomb Joseph had purchased for his own family vault. A stone was placed in the sepulchre's entrance – just as there had been one at the tomb of Lazarus.

Afterwards there was a short discussion among the groups as to who should return after the Jewish Sabbath – Christianity's Holy Saturday – with spices to sprinkle inside the tomb. They were all exhausted and no one objected when Mary Magdalene volunteered for the task.

For the next thirty-six hours, the mourners rested in the house of Joseph. What they spoke about escapes record. Mary Magdalene confined herself to observing, 'It was a time of the greatest sadness.'

Undoubtedly the downcast mood was compounded by the absence of the disciples. They had sought shelter and safety in the hills outside the city, understandably fearful that the death of Jesus would be the prelude to a general round-up of all his followers.

Early on the Sunday that would become known as the first Easter, Mary Magdalene made her lonely way back to the tomb. The sun was shining, forcing her to shade her eyes. Consequently she was close to the tomb before she saw the protective boulder had been removed from the entrance.

For a moment she stood transfixed, uncertain what to do. Yet, though she should have been, she was not frightened. She had seen this once before, at Lazarus' tomb in Bethany. She looked around her. There was no one to be seen.

Then, as the co-mingling of Roman trumpeter and Temple horn player, the signal for a new day, a fresh start, she became aware she was, after all, not alone.

Jesus said to her. 'Mary!'

He stood there, free of the winding sheet, the marks of the crucifixion on his living body.

'Master!' she said.

That one word established her right to be forever remembered as the woman who saw the beginning of the New Kingdom. Jesus had chosen her because she represented the epitome of all he had proclaimed about the power of true redemption. She was the first to bear witness, to see fulfilled the promise he had made: 'Be assured, I am with you always, to the end of time.'

Standing outside the tomb which, like death, had no meaning, Jesus had shown her that his promise had no limitation. He would remain a constant presence until 'the consummation of the world'. He would be there until the end of time itself.

All Jesus had ever asked in return was the same repentance from others that Mary Magdalene's salvation epitomized.

No woman – or man – could have a worthier reason to be remembered for all time.

Just as Jesus had taken on a new body, so had Mary Magdalene assumed a new identity. She was truly 'the woman who loved Jesus'.

Beyond the Cross

Twenty

Mary Magdalene disappears from the immediate narrative following her central role in the supreme drama on that Sunday dawn when she encountered the risen Christ. In all the Gospel accounts describing the events leading to the Ascension, she is excluded. That this has been deliberate cannot be in doubt. Once they had recovered their faith, the Apostles take over the narrative; the story of Jesus became *their* self-serving story. It is their new-found joy that dominates the Gospel accounts and those which accompany them.

The reason for Mary Magdalene's exclusion is not that she had less faith than the disciples: she had more. Unlike Thomas, she had not asked for proof that Christ had risen from the dead. Thomas, the doubter, had said: 'Unless I see the mark of the nails on his hands, unless I put my finger into the place where the nails were and my hands into his side, I will not believe it.'

Mary Magdalene required no such evidence, simply because she had never stopped believing in Jesus. But, having recovered and accepted it was indeed he who stood before them in the Upper Room eight days after he had walked out of the tomb to meet Mary Magdalene, the disciples claimed him for their own. Consequently, they no longer needed her to show them the meaning of faith.

And that may well have been the moment when the total reality of who Mary Magdalene was faded, and in its place came a blend of fact and fiction. Down the centuries this may have done nothing to enhance her role in Christianity – or made it any easier for women to find their own place in the church.

Removing the essential truth of her identity was a deliberate decision by the early Fathers of the Church. For them to admit she was the equal of any of the apostles, that she could even stand comparison with the Virgin, Jesus' mother, was impossible for them to countenance. The feminist author Marina Warner would observe that instead the Magdalene we have come to know like Eve, was brought into existence by the powerful undertow of misogyny in Christianity which associates women with the dangers and degradation of the flesh.

To substantiate that image, the first witness of the resurrection became the subject of folklore the like of which has been ascribed to few women. In the medieval *Golden Legend*, the historian Jacopus de Varagine claims that Mary Magdalene actually *owned* Magdala, while 'her brother Lazarus owned a large part of Jerusalem, and her sister, Martha, the town of Bethany'. Having created a genealogy for which no historical evidence exists – as well as confusing Mary Magdalene with Mary of Bethany, Martha's sister – de Varagine then tells us 'and for so much as she shone in beauty greatly, and in riches, so much the more she submitted her body to delight.' At best the words are only an elegant way to remind us she was once a whore; at worst they mock the truth about her.

De Varagine was largely responsible for the mystery plays of the Middle Ages which portrayed the resurrection through Mary Magdalene: their simple plot was the penitent whore who was granted forgiveness by Jesus. Those dramas, in turn, gave Mary Magdalene cult status, particularly in the south of France, where her body was allegedly discovered in the crypt of St Maximin's Church in Aix-en-Provence in 1265. Local legend has it that she was one of several women of the Gospel story – among them Mary and Martha of Bethany and Mary Salome – who, with Lazarus, were washed ashore on the French coast 'in a rudderless boat after they fled persecution in the Holy Land. They brought with them the head of James the Less.' There is nothing to substantiate this, but the stuff of legend is often more powerful than the simple facts.

In the French version, the other women remained on the coast and their relics were unearthed in the fifteenth century and led to a small town being named after them. Every year the bones are taken in procession through Les Saintes Maries de la Mer.

The story goes that Mary Magdalene travelled inland to a great forest. There she preached the Gospel to the locals while living the life of a hermit. Again there is no evidence to support this, or no way of establishing if the bones held in St Maximin's are actually hers. More likely Mary Magdalene died in the Holy Land, but when and where remains so far beyond record.

In the eighth century she had become the subject of a full-length biography, *The Life of Mary Magdalene*, by Archbishop Raban Maar (AD 776-856). In the fifteenth century a copy of the manuscript reached Oxford University and 'inspired the founding' of Magdalen College in 1448.

By then Mary Magdalene had acquired a style of dress as distinctive as that of the Virgin. The woman of Magdala was invariably portrayed in a red cloak over a green dress, the green representing fertility.

The genealogist Lawrence Gardner has observed that

the concept of a red-caped women of religious rank – the red was intended to equate her with a cardinal's roles – infuriated the Vatican. In 1659 it issued a decree that all images of Jesus' mother should depict her wearing blue and white only to separate her from Magdalene.

By then Mary Magdalene had attracted the claim that she experienced visions and insights that went far beyond anything the disciples possessed. In the apocrypha Gospel of Philip she is described as the one follower whom Jesus loved above all others. According to Philip 'the rest of the disciples were offended by this and they complained to him, "why do you love her more than all of us?" The Saviour answered and said to us, "why do you not love me as she loves me?"'

Another Gnostic document, the Dialogue of the Saviour, has no doubt of her supremacy: she was 'a women who knew the All.' Running through these writings is the common thread that Mary Magdalene had received her spiritual authority directly from Christ. There was even the claim that the first pope was not Peter but Mary Magdalene! She was known as the Papess, the female Pope.

Such a claim enraged the early Christian Church, not least because of its clear-cut attempt to place Mary Magdalene in equal standing with the apostles.

Her supporters countered that her authority dated from that moment when she used her cloak to wipe Jesus' face when he was on his way to Calvary. They claimed that later she had found his image miraculously imprinted on the fabric. There is no independent evidence to support that the incident happened. But it survived down the centuries and had gained widespread respectability by the time Mary Magdalene's body was supposed to have been discovered.

With the story grew another, based on a document called *Pistis Sophia*, whose author is not known. The core of the document is an account of Peter repeatedly complaining that during her time with the Apostles, Mary Magdalene 'dominated the conversation with Jesus and displaced the rightful priority of Peter and the other male apostles.' The document claimed that, when Peter asked Jesus to 'silence her', he was 'severely rebuked'. There is some canonical Gospel support for this but none for the claim that 'she confided in Our Lord that she hardly dare speak to Peter because he makes me hesitate. I am afraid of Peter because he hates the female race.'

Nevertheless, such claims deeply offended the early church, not least when one of its branches, the Celtic Church, which had spread Christianity across Britain, believed that women had an equal right to the priesthood, and maintained that position until the Synod of Whitby in AD 625. From then on the church focused on Mary Magdalene as the harlot who was forgiven. Such a person therefore could not possibly be the equal of Peter, let alone the first Papess.

Yet that particular legend would not die. So the Vatican in the Middle Ages introduced a check to ensure such a possibility could never happen again. All cardinals who became *papabile* – candidates for the throne of Peter –

are required to sit naked beneath their robe, on a specially-constructed seat that is elevated and open like a toilet seat, where their genitals can be inspected by their peers from below. Then a verdict will be returned – *testiculos habet, et bene pendente* – he had testicles and they hang well.

History is indebted to this insight into the papal election process to G.L. Simons and his commendable *Sex and Superstition*. Alas, he does not say when, or indeed if, the process was discontinued – and the Vatican, perhaps not surprisingly, refuses to discuss the matter.

But the clear and visible threat Mary Magdalene presented to the early Church needed even more robust action than a Vatican edict. One of the founders of the early church, Quintus Tertullian, had felt compelled to warn directly:

It is not permitted for a woman to speak in church, nor is it permitted for her to baptize, nor to offer the Eucharist, nor to claim for herself a share in any masculine function – least of all in priestly office.

Such authoritative comments were designed to stop the cult status which continued to grow around Mary Magdalene. This reached its peak with the claim that Jesus had enjoyed physical intimacy with her. The author of the Gospel of Philip, writes Marina Warner, 'sees the union of man and woman as a symbol of healing and peace.' This, of course, is still a long way from the claim advanced by William Phipps in his book, *Was Jesus Married?* Phipps, a scholar of sorts, argues that Mary Magdalene may have been Jesus' wife. More certain, the author did not suffer the fate of a film, *The Loves of Jesus Christ*, made with the financial support of the Danish government, which led to that country's embassy in Rome being firebombed. Public fury was understandable, given that the producer Jens Jürgen Thorsen, guaranteed that his film would portray Jesus 'as a warlord, love apostle, erotomaniac, drunkard, idealist and revolutionary', and he would include a 'direct and explicit portrayal of Jesus' relations with women mentioned in the Bible in group sex scenes'.

Such exploitive blasphemy has done nothing to achieve the very cause Mary Magdalene so eagerly wished to express – that of women in the Bible. It is high time the gross damage done to that laudable aim by men should now be undone.

✳   ✳   ✳

To begin the essential readjustment of her life and times, we need to turn to what the Bible says about women. All else can flow from accepting that Mary Magdalene *was* the first to see the risen Christ, and so is the *first* apostle of the resurrection. Yet in the Bible, the Old and New Testaments take a divergent position on the role of women. In the Old, the feminine voices are strong, and Wisdom herself is feminine, as is Israel. But when Christians speak about 'what the Bible says' with regard to women, they base their position on what is in the New Testament. So let us look at four key passages:

As in all the church of the saints, the women should keep silence in the churches. For they are not permitted to speak, but should be subordinate, as even the law says. If there is anything they desire to know, let them ask their husbands at home. For it is shameful for a women to speak in church (1 Corinthians 14:34–35).

Let a woman learn in silence with all submissiveness. I permit no woman to teach or to have authority over men; she is to keep silent (1 Timothy 2:11–12).

For as many of you as were baptized into Christ have put on Christ. There is neither Jew nor Greek, there is neither slave nor free, there is neither male nor female; for you are all one in Christ Jesus. And if you are Christ's, then you are Abraham's offspring, heirs according to promise (Galatians 3:27–29).

Mary Magdalene went and said to the disciples, 'I have seen the Lord', and she told them that he had said these things to her (John 20:18).

Those examples clearly illustrate the tensions that still dominate a male-oriented Christianity. While Mary's encounter with the risen Christ is reluctantly given its place in the resurrection, the exchanges between her and Jesus are virtually dismissed as 'she told them that he had said these things to her'. To have elaborated what did happen in further detail would have been to give the woman from Magdala a status the early fathers of the Church did not wish. It is to the credit of the gospel of John that she is included at all!

It can safely be claimed that much of the most creative Biblical scholarship in the past twenty-five years has come from women theologians. One has only to read Mary Daly's *The Church and the Second Sex*, or Sarah Bentley's powerful plea for women's liberation in the church – *The New Demand for Freedom in the Life of the Christian Church* – to realize that truth. I can also recommend Hazel Foster's outstanding thesis on Paul's attitude towards women. These women, and others, have launched an all-out assault on how we should see the role of women in Christianity. Mary Daly has written with insight and truth:

> This frightens people – the very notion of a feminist initiative in the interpretation of scripture. Many have been, and will be, put off by the sense of an aggressive set of special interests that are brought to the interpretation of scripture with destabilizing consequences to the authority of the scripture, the order of the church, and the structure of society and of civilization itself. In their fight for the Bible and the right both to take it and themselves seriously, feminist interpreters of scripture have much to teach us, and we ignore these lessons to the peril of scripture and of the church.

It has become a habit for many evangelicals and religious conservatives to dismiss the mountain of female scholarship on the Bible. For them, female theologians are all too often seen as pagans who advocate the worship of goddesses. Any challenge to the language of patriarchy or the thousand years of male interpretation is viewed as part of a 'liberal', 'feminist', or 'radical' conspiracy to subvert the faith once delivered to the saints. As in politics, there is clearly a paranoid attitude to much of the responses to women's scholarship on the Bible. When feminist scholarship concludes that it is no longer appropriate to pray to 'Our Father', and such masculine titles as

'Lord' and 'King' are excluded both from the text and from worship, the instinctual masculine reaction of those who feel deprived of the familiar and useful language of piety, is to reject the possibility that any helpful insights can be provided from such scholarship.

But there is more than language at stake. There is a rearguard action being forged at every level by Christian males. Nothing is too small for them to desperately cling to. As Daly says:

> The popular piety of most Christians, particularly Protestants, has been expressed in the hymns people sing in church. The late New Testament scholar and poet, Amos Niven Wilder, once said that what incense is to the Catholic, hymns are to the Protestant: 'an indescribable, primal association of the personal and the holy'. One learns the hymns of faith in childhood. Worship depends upon the hymns. The sermon may be good or bad, the liturgy indifferent, but the effect of the service depends upon whether or not the people know and like the hymns. And most people like the hymns they know, and on that basis know what they like. Thus to tamper with the hymns is to get perilously close to the emotional centre of the worshipper.

Just as for men, women have always recognized that hymnic images are part of the core of faith, Dianne Bergant, an American feminist theologian, argues persuasively that, for women, the language of worship is as important as the act itself:

> Women would ask, where am I? When at funerals we sang Isaac Watt's great paraphrase, Time, like an ever-rolling stream, bears all its sons away. Even in so basic an act of Christian praise as the Doxology which affirms, Praise Him all creatures here below, and closes with the Trinitarian formula of, Father, Son and Holy Ghost, women increasingly asked where they were in these classical formulations. When the congregation is asked to sing Rise Up, O Men of God are the women to remain seated, or are they to think of themselves as

Queen Elizabeth the First did, as a man trapped in the body of a woman?'

Bergant defines herself as a reformist and argues that, in every generation, 'successive communities of faith' have struggled with the relationship between the received tradition and the demands of their own unique experience.

Bergant's method demonstrates that the best of feminist scholarship is both accessible and constructive, taking both scripture and its interpretation as seriously today as ever it was taken in the great historical days of male biblical interpretation. She calls her method 'recontextualizing'; it involves

* looking carefully at the received tradition: how has this text come down to us in the history of interpretation?

* operating out of a feminist sensitivity to the contemporary context; how is the text received now?

* pointing out how 'the dynamics within the text' can achieve a significance within the community that now reads and hears it.

Bergant concludes: 'The result of such an approach is a reading that is both faithful and challenging. It is faithful because as "word of God", it is challenging'.

Part of that challenge lies in understanding the life of Mary Magdalene. She provides every woman a chance to liberate herself from the constraints men continue to impose on women's role in Christian worship. The woman of Magdala could have asked for no more, and wished for no less.

That powerful voice of English feminism, Eva Figes, has said that Christianity is a religion created by men for men, and that, while that position remains, it will continue to undervalue that great contribution women can make, and want to make.

Certainly many women feel that their rejection can be traced all the way back to Eve, who is made to take the blame for the fall of all humanity. Added to that is understandable female anger that Eve is someone tacked-on to the Genesis story, created as she was from Adam's rib to ensure that he did not feel lonely; in other words Eve is there on sufferance, an inferior female only in existence to satisfy the needs of Adam.

This theme of women's failure, of not being allowed to stand on equal terms with men, found a ready echo in the early Christian church. Ambrose, an early Christian misogynist, wrote that 'Adam was deceived by Eve, not Eve by Adam. It is right that he whom that woman induced to sin should assume the role of guide lest he fall again through feminine instability.' Justin and Jerome shared that view, and even Augustine who, by his own account, had a close, loving and spiritual relationship with his own mother, dismissed women as 'unreliable'. Thomas Aquinas called women: 'defective and accidental... a male gone awry... the result of some weakness in the father's generation power.'

It is men like these, in their monastic asceticism, who shaped the attitude of the Church towards women. Kate Millet, another feminist theologian has written that there was a tendency among these celibate men to see women as 'unclean and sinful'.

Such claims were part of the early church's decision to distance itself from the ways of the Roman Empire which had become sufficiently degenerate for Christianity to have a powerful appeal in the discipline it offered, and the Puritanism which came with it. Men decided that women could not be trusted to obey the (literally) man-made rules which went with those qualities.

Mary Kenny in her excellent *Why Christianity Works* wrote:

The Fathers of the early church were expressing ideas which still exist in the unconscious of the male... there is also in man a primitive fear of woman. Man is frightened of woman for several reasons: he fears her anger as part of his memory of his own childhood when he was within his mother's power, and when his mother had the means to make or break him either through providing or withdrawing love and nourishment; man also fears woman's 'irrational' 'primitive' nature because the logic of woman is considered to be intuitive, and thus she cannot be relied upon to make a judgement based upon the consistent grid of male logic.

There could be no place for Mary Magdalene in that framework within the idiom of its time. Nobody saw that she could, and should, be used by Christianity as the epitome of tenderness, compassion and the perfect example of redemption. That would only come later when she was finally given her feast day. But many women feel that is poor reward for what she really was. She is a crucial part of their quest to become more important within the Church so that they can add to its development.

Patriarchy does not have God on its side. The New Testament, which is the source of the revelation of God, does not extol the masculine – as men like to believe. It promulgates salvation through love and redemption. Those are the two qualities which single out Mary, the Virgin, and Mary Magdalene. In that respect they stand equal. The day may yet come when they will be so treated as such in all respects.

Like women theologians I, too, do not understand a need to cling to the pattern of male dominance reflected in the Bible, as being an expression of the will of God. If anything, it is a mark of fear among the descendants of those other men who feared Mary Magdalene, and continue to misunderstand the importance of her place in the Christianity of the new Millennium.

Bibliography

Aaron, R., *Jesus of Nazareth, the Hidden Years* (translated by F. Frenhaye), Hamish Hamilton, London, 1962.

Albright, W.F., *The Archaeology of Palestine*, Penguin Books, Harmondsworth, revised edition, 1956.

Allegro, J.M., *The Dead Sea Scrolls*, Penguin, Harmondsworth, 1964.

Ambrose, G. and Newbold, G., *A Handbook of Medical Hypnosis*, Bailliere Tindall & Cassell, London, 1968.

Anderson H., *Jesus and Christian Origins*, Oxford University Press, 1964.

Baigent, M., Leigh, R. and Lincoln, H., *The Dead Sea Scrolls Deception*, Jonathan Cape, London 1991.

Baigent, M., Leigh, R. and Lincoln, H., *The Holy Blood and the Holy Grail*, Jonathan Cape, London, 1982.

Barclay, J., *The Mind of Jesus*, Harper & Row, New York, 1960.

Bell, H.I. and Skeat, T.C., *Fragments of an Unknown Gospel*, British Museum, London, 1935.

Black, M., *The Scrolls and Christian Origins*, Thomas Nelson, London, 1961.

Brandon, S.G.F., *The Fall of Jerusalem and the Christian Church*, SPCK, London, 1951.

Brandon S.G.F., *Jesus and the Zealots*, Charles Scribner's Sons, New York, 1967.

Brooke, G., *Temple Scroll Studies*, Sheffield Academic Press, 1989.

Carmichael, J., *The Death of Jesus*, Victor Gollancz, London, 1963.

Catchpole, D.R., *The Trial of Jesus*, E.J. Brill, Leiden, 1971.

Chase, M.E., *Life and Language in the Old Testament*, Collins, London, 1956.

Cranfield, C.E.B., *The Gospel According to St Mark*, Cambridge University Press, 1959.

Clark, D., Parkinson, J. and Stephenson, R., 'An Astronomical Reappraisal of the Star of Bethlehem. A Nova in 5 BC', in *Quarterly Journal of the Royal Astronomical Society*, 18, 1977, p. 443.

Cupitt, D. and Armstrong, P., *Who was Jesus?* BBC, London, 1977.

Cupitt, D., *The Debate about Christ*, SCM, London, 1979.

Danielou, J., *The Dead Sea Scrolls and Primitive Christianity* (translated by S. Attansio), New American Library, New York, 1962.

Dart, J., *The Laughing Saviour*, Harper & Row, New York, 1976.

Dodd, C.H., *Historical Tradition in the Fourth Gospel*, Cambridge University Press, 1963.

Doresse, J., *The Secret Books of the Egyptian Gnostics* (translated by P. Mairet), Hollis & Carter, London, 1960.

Dupont-Sommer, A., *The Essene Writings from Qumran* (translated by G. Vermes), Basil Blackwell, Oxford, 1961.

Dupont-Sommer, A., *The Jewish Sect of Qumran and the Essenes*, Vallentine Mitchell, London, 1954.

Eusebius of Caesarea, *The History of the Church from Christ to Constantine* (translated G.A. Williamson), Penguin Books, Harmondsworth, 1965.

Farmer, W.R., *The Synoptic Problem*, Macmillan, London and New York, 1964.

Farrar, F.W., *The Life of Christ as Represented in Art*, A. & C. Black, London, 1901.

Filliette, E., *Saint Mary Magdalene, Her Life and Times*, Society of St Mary Magdalene, Newton Lower Falls, Massachusetts, 1983.

Finkel, A., *The Pharisees and the Teacher of Nazareth*, E.J. Brill, Leiden, 1964.

Fleetwood, Rev. J., *The Life of Our Lord and Saviour Jesus Christ*, William Mackenzie, Glasgow, c.1900.

Gaster, T.H., *Samaritan Eschatology – Oral Law and Ancient Traditions*, Search, London, 1932.

Grant, M., *The Jews in the Roman World*, Weidenfeld & Nicolson, London, 1973.

Grant, M., *Herod The Great*, Weidenfeld & Nicolson, London, 1971.

Gilson, E., *The Mystical Theology of Saint Bernard* (translated by A.H.C. Downes), Sheed & Ward, London, 1940.

Gimbutas, M., *The Gods and Goddesses of Old Europe*, Thames & Hudson, London, 1974.

Godwin, J., *Mystery Religions in the Ancient World*, Thames & Hudson, London, 1981.

Hick, J. (ed.) *The Myth of God Incarnate*, SCM, London, 1977.

Jaubert, A., *The Date of the Last Supper* (translated from the French), Alba House, New York, 1965.

Jeremias, J., 'The Rediscovery of Bethesda' in *New Testament Archaeology Monographs*, I, Southern Baptist Theological Seminary, Louisville, Kentucky, 1966.

Jones, A.H.M., *The Herods of Judea*, Oxford University Press, 1938.

Josephus, *The Jewish War* (translated by G.A. Williamson, Rev. E. Mary Smallwood), Penguin, Harmondsworth, 1981.

Kee, A., *Constantine versus Christ*, SCM, London, 1982.

Kenyon, K., *Jerusalem, Excavating 3,000 Years of History*, Thames & Hudson, London, 1967.

Khan, M.F., *Deliverance from the Cross*, The London Mosque, London, 1978.

Klausner, J., *Jesus of Nazareth*, Allen & Unwin, London, 1925.

Kopp, C., *The Holy Places of the Gospels* (translated from the German by Ronald Walls), Nelson, London, 1963.

Kummel, W.G., *Introduction to the New Testament* (translated by A.J. Mattill), London, 1970.

Maccoby, H., *Revolution in Judaea, Jesus and the Jewish Resistance*, Ocean Books, London, 1973.

Maccoby, H., *The Sacred Executioner, Human Sacrifice and the Legacy of Guilt*, Thames & Hudson, London, 1982.

Mackey, J.P., *Jesus, the Man and the Myth*, SCM, London, 1979.

Margouliouth, D.S., *Mohammed and the Rise of Islam*, Putnam, London, 1931.

Marsden, J., *The Illustrated Colmcille*, Macmillan, London, 1991.

Martin, M., *The Decline and Fall of the Roman Church*, Secker & Warburg, London, 1982.

Moule, C.F.D., *The Birth of the New Testament*, A. & C. Black, London, 1962.

Neill, S., *The Interpretation of the New Testament 1861–1961*, Oxford University Press, 1964.

Neil-Smith, C., *The Exorcist and the Possessed*, James Pike, St Ives, 1974.

Nickell, J., *Inquest on the Shroud of Turin*, Prometheus, New York, 1983.

Oesterreich, T.K., *Possession, Demoniacal and Other*, Kegan Paul, London, 1930.

Olmstead, A.T., *Jesus in the Light of History*, Scribner, New York, 1942.

Pagels, E., *The Gnostic Gospels*, Weidenfeld & Nicolson, London, 1980.

Pines, S., *An Arabic Version of the Testimonium Flavianum and its Implications*, The Israel Academy of Science and Humanities, Jerusalem, 1971.

Pope, M.H., *Song of Songs*, Garden City/Doubleday, New York, 1977.

Qualls-Corbett, N., *The Sacred Prostitute*, Inner City Books, Toronto, Canada, 1988.

Rees, Rev. R., *An Essay on the Welsh Saints*, Longman, London, 1836.

Rees, Revd W.J., *Lives of the Cambro-British Saints*, Welsh MSS Society/Longman, London, 1853.

Roberts, C.H., *An Unpublished Fragment of the Fourth Gospel*, Manchester University Press, 1935.

Robinson, J.A.T., *Honest to God*, SCM, London, 1963.

Robinson, J.A.T., *The Human Face of God*, SCM, London, 1972.

Robinson, J.A.T., *Redating the New Testament*, SCM, London, 1976.

Robinson, J.A.T., *Can We Trust the New Testament?* Mowbray, London, 1977.

Robinson, J.M. (ed.), *The Nag Hammadi Library*, Harpers & Row, New York, 1977.

Sargant, W., *Battle for the Mind*, Heinemann, London, 1957.

Scholem, G., *Major Trends in Jewish Mysticism*, Schocken Books, New York, 1941.

Scholem, G., *The Messianic Idea in Judaism*, Schocken Books, New York, 1971.

Sherwin-White, A.N., *Roman Society and Roman Law in the New Testament*, Clarendon Press, Oxford, 1963.

Sizemore, C. & Pittillo, E.S., *Eve*, Victor Gollancz, London, 1978.

Smith, J.H., *Constantine the Great*, Hamish Hamilton, London, 1971.

Smith, M., *Clement of Alexandria and a Secret Gospel of Mark*, Harvard University Press, 1973.

Smith, M., *The Secret Gospel*, Victor Gollancz, London, 1974.

Smith, M., *Jesus the Magician*, Victor Gollancz, London, 1978.

Strauss, D.F., *The Life of Jesus Critically Examined* (translated by George Eliot), Chapman, London, 1846.

Streeter, B.H., *The Four Gospels: A Study of Origins*, Macmillan, London, 1927.

Suetonius, *The Twelve Caesars* (translated by Robert Graves), Penguin Books, Harmondsworth, 1957.

Tacitus, *The Annals of Imperial Rome* (translated by M. Grant), Penguin Books, Harmondsworth, 1956.

Taylor, G., *Our Neglected Heritage*, Covenant Books, London, 1969–1974.

Taylor, J.W., *The Coming of the Saints*, Covenant Books, London, 1969.

Throckmorton, B.H. (Jr), *Gospel Parallels, A Synopsis of the First Three Gospels*, Thomas Nelson Inc., New York, 1971.

Toynbee, A. (ed.), *The Crucible of Christianity*, Thames & Hudson, London, 1969.

Tzaferis, V., 'Jewish Tombs at and near Giv'at ha-Mivtar', in *Israel Exploration Journal*, 20, 1970, pp18-32.

Vermes, G., *The Dead Sea Scrolls in English*, Penguin Books, Harmondsworth, 1962.

Vermes, G., 'Quest for the Historical Jesus' in *Jewish Chronicle Literary Supplement*, 12 December 1969.

Vermes, G., *Jesus the Jew, A Historian's Reading of the Gospels*, Collins, 1973, Fontana 1976: quotations from Fontana edition.

Vincent, L.H., 'Le lithostrotos evangelique' in *Revue Biblique*, 59, Paris, 1952, pp. 513–30.

Walsh, J., *The Bones of St Peter*, Victor Gollancz, London, 1983.

Warner, M., *Alone of All Her Sex, The Myth and Cult of the Virgin Mary*, Weidenfeld & Nicolson, London, 1976.

Wells, G.A., *The Jesus of the Early Christians*, Pemberton, London, 1971.

Wells, G.A., *Did Jesus Exist?* Elek/Pemberton, London, 1975.

Wells, G.A., *The Historical Evidence for Jesus*, Prometheus, New York, 1982.

Wilson, C., *Mysteries*, Hodder & Stoughton, London, 1978.

Wilson, I., *The Turin Shroud*, Victor Gollancz, London, 1978.

Winter, P., *On the Trial of Jesus*, de Guyter, Berlin, 1961.

Yadin, Y., *Bar-Kokhba*, Weidenfeld & Nicolson, London, 1971.

Yadin, Y., 'Epigraphy and Crucifixion', *Israel Exploration Journal*, 23, 1973, pp. 18–20.

Yadin, Y. (ed.), *Jerusalem Revealed: Archaeology in the Holy City, 1968–74*, Yale University Press and Israel Exploration Society, 1976.

Zugibe, F., *The Cross and the Shroud*, Angelus Books, New York, 1982.